Family Formation Among Youth in Europe: Coping with Socio-Economic Disadvantages

A Volume in:
Perspectives on Human Development

Series Editors:
Isabelle Albert
Jaan Valsiner
Koji Komatsu

Perspectives on Human Development

Series Editors:
Isabelle Albert
University of Luxembourg

Jaan Valsiner
Aalborg University

Koji Komatsu
Osaka Kyoiku University

Language Editor:
Aida Spahić

Books in This Series

Families and Family Values in Society and Culture (2021)
Isabelle Albert, Mirza Emirhafizovic, Carmit-Noa Shpigelman, & Ursula Trummer

Children and Money:
Cultural Developmental Psychology of Pocket Money (2020)
Takahashi Noboru & Yamamoto Toshiya

Vygotsky's Pedology of the School Age (2020)
René van der Veer

Trans-Generational Family Relations:
Investigating Ambivalences (2018)
Isabelle Albert, Emily Abbey, & Jaan Valsiner

Particulars and Universals in Clinical and Developmental Psychology:
Critical Reflections—A Book Honoring Roger Bibace (2015)
Meike Watzlawik, Alina Kriebel, & Jaan Valsiner

Family Formation Among Youth in Europe: Coping with Socio-Economic Disadvantages

Mirza Emirhafizovic
Tali Heiman
Marton Medgyesi
Catarina Pinheiro Mota
Smiljka Tomanovic
Sue Vella

INFORMATION AGE PUBLISHING, INC.
Charlotte, NC • www.infoagepub.com

Library of Congress Cataloging-In-Publication Data

The CIP data for this book can be found on the Library of Congress website (loc.gov).

Paperback: 978-1-64802-903-5
Hardcover: 978-1-64802-904-2
E-Book: 978-1-64802-905-9

Copyright © 2022 Information Age Publishing Inc.

All rights reserved. No part of this publication may be reproduced, stored in a retrieval system, or transmitted, in any form or by any means, electronic, mechanical, photocopying, microfilming, recording or otherwise, without written permission from the publisher.

Printed in the United States of America

CONTENTS

Series Editors' Preface: Family Formation in Europe in Light of Societal and Individual Challenges ix
Isabelle Albert, Jaan Valsiner, and Koji Komatsu

Introduction to the Volume: Disadvantages in Starting a Family Across Europe xi
Mirza Emirhafizovic, Tali Heiman, Marton Medgyesi,
Catarina Pinheiro Mota, Smiljka Tomanovic, and Sue Vella

1. **Socio-Economic Challenges to Family Formation in Bosnia and Herzegovina: Major Issues** 1
   Mirza Emirhafizović and Andrea Puhalić

2. **Family Formation in Changing Economic and Societal Conditions in the Czech Republic** 17
   Vera Kucharova

3. **Disadvantages in Family Formation National Report: Germany** 39
   Dirk Hofäcker

4. **Disadvantages in Starting a Family in Hungary** 55
   Márton Medgyesi

5. **Families in Israel: Coping and Adjustment** 67
   Tali Heiman, Dorit Olenik-Shemesh, and Merav Regev-Nevo

vi • CONTENTS

6. Trends and Challenges in Family Formation in Italy: An Overview 83

Rosy Musumeci

7. Social and Economic Challenges and Opportunities in Family Formation in Latvia 105

Līva Griņeviča, Dina Bite, and Anna Broka

8. Changes in Family Formation: The Case of Lithuania 123

Edita Štuopytė

9. Young People and Family Formation in Malta 139

Sue Vella and Joanne Cassar

10. Challenges and Changes in Family(ies) Formation in Portugal Since the Transition to Democracy 159

Catarina Pinheiro Mota, Helena Carvalho and Paula Mena Matos

11. Family Formation in Serbia Between Normative Legacy, Structural Constraints, and Desired Prospects 175

Smiljka Tomanović and Dragan Stanojević

Contributors 191

ENDORSEMENTS

Gathering rich and novel information from 11 European countries that have been so far neglected in family formation studies this volume is an enlightening reading for policy makers, social policy students and young people themselves.

—Anu Toots
Distinguished Professor of Social Policy, Tallinn University, Estonia
Chair of the COST Action YOUNG-IN

This book brings together scholars from all over Europe to provide an updated account of demographic change and family formation in Europe. The book is quite impressive both in its scope and depth,and should be an essential read for those interested in the demographic challenges that our countries are facing.

—Johannes Bergh
Research Director
Head of the Norwegian National Election Studies (NNES)
Institute for Social Research
Oslo, Norway

This publication is based upon work from COST Action CA17114—Transdisciplinary solutions to cross sectoral disadvantage in youth, supported by COST (European Cooperation in Science and Technology).

COST (European Cooperation in Science and Technology) is a funding agency for research and innovation networks. Our Actions help connect research initiatives across Europe and enable scientists to grow their ideas by sharing them with their peers. This boosts their research, career and innovation.

www.cost.eu

SERIES EDITORS' PREFACE

FAMILY FORMATION IN EUROPE IN LIGHT OF SOCIETAL AND INDIVIDUAL CHALLENGES

Isabelle Albert, Jaan Valsiner, and Koji Komatsu

Starting a family is a lifelong endeavor—it is both an individual task as well as societally embedded, and key for a sustainable development. While overpopulation has been a concern with regard to limited resources for many years, the low fertility rates, particularly observed in some European countries, are related to population ageing and can entail difficulties with regard to the social security systems and standards of living.

Becoming a parent for the first time is typically associated with young adulthood, coinciding with other key developmental tasks such as entering the labor market, finding a partner, setting up an own household and gaining (economic) independence from own parents.

While in the past these developmental tasks were rather well-defined and followed a normative sequence, this is less so the case in many Western societies today, as an individualization of developmental trajectories has taken place. Parenthood is less bound to specific ages than in the past and is more and more postponed while fewer children are born. This comes as young adults remain longer in education and are confronted with difficulties when entering professional life,

---

Family Formation Among Youth in Europe: Coping With Socio-Economic Disadvantages,
pages ix–x.
Copyright © 2022 by Information Age Publishing
www.infoagepub.com
All rights of reproduction in any form reserved.

precarious employment has become more common and a stable professional position might not be achievable, leaving young adults for longer times dependent on their parental support where possible. The current global crises exacerbate the challenges young adults face at this particular and important stage of their lives.

To become a parent is by no means self-evident and automatic. Interdisciplinary and cross-cultural research on the Value of Children (VOC) has shed a light on the reasons why people want to have children or not, and how this is related to their intergenerational family relations, showing that emotional, social or economic reasons for having children are strongly linked to the context in which they are embedded (Trommsdorff & Nauck, 2010).

The individual challenges of starting a family are closely linked to societal challenges of sustainable development—an ageing society poses a number of problems as future generations are elementary for social security systems, at the same time society sets the context for individual live decisions.

This volume sheds light on the societal framework conditions and family formation in various European countries and Israel. By focusing on the specific contexts of selected countries—Bosnia and Herzegovina, Czech Republic, Germany, Hungary, Israel, Italy, Latvia, Lithuania, Malta, Portugal, and Serbia—it becomes clear that not only the objective framework conditions, but also the subjective experience of these—in harmony with values, social and personal expectations—play a central role in the decision-making processes with regard to starting a family.

Families are essential for the continuity of our societies but young people today are confronted with a number of difficulties related to family formation. It is the responsibility of society—which ultimately benefits from the offspring and whose continuity depends on future generations – to ensure that having children does not become a personal disadvantage for their parents. The contributions in this volume are an excellent basis to revise and renew current policies and to find good practice examples for future explorations into the grand mysteries of cultural organization of being a parent. Research on families in Europe would benefit from further international input from the Orient and South America where the topics are deeply investigated (Bastos et al, 2012). Such further widening of the scope of research would lead us to full understanding of the basic knowledge of humanity.

—Isabelle Albert Jaan Valsiner Koji Komatsu

REFERENCES

Bastos, A. C., Uriko, K., & Valsiner, J. (Eds.). (2012). *Cultural dynamics of women's lives*. Information Age Publishers.

Trommsdorff, G., & Nauck, B. (2010). Introduction to special section for *Journal of Cross-Cultural Psychology*: Value of Children: A concept for better understanding cross-cultural variations in fertility behavior and intergenerational relationships. *Journal of Cross-Cultural Psychology, 41*(5–6), 637–651. https://doi.org/10.1177/0022022110373335

INTRODUCTION TO THE VOLUME

DISADVANTAGES IN STARTING A FAMILY ACROSS EUROPE

Mirza Emirhafizovic

University of Sarajevo

Tali Heiman

The Open University of Israel

Marton Medgyesi

TARKI, Social Research Institute and the Centre for Social Sciences in Budapest

Catarina Pinheiro Mota

University of Trás-os-Montes and Alto Douro, Portugal

Smiljka Tomanovic

University of Belgrade

Sue Vella

University of Malta

(T)he demographic winter is really not about growing or shrinking populations. It is not about the economy. It is not even about the lifestyles of adults. But rather history will show that it is ultimately about the children—what children will yet be born.

It is they who will be consigned to wade through life's journey burdened by the consequences of the demographic winter.

—(Stout, 2008)[1]

---

[1] Documentary Demographic Winter: The Decline of the Human Family, 2008.

Family Formation Among Youth in Europe: Coping With Socio-Economic Disadvantages,
pages xi–xx.
Copyright © 2022 by Information Age Publishing
www.infoagepub.com
All rights of reproduction in any form reserved.

The global societal changes have been imposing a lot of pressure on today's young generations across major life domains. Transition to adulthood is usually accompanied by structural disadvantages that may have a negative spill-over effect. Extended education, entering the labor market, career, and becoming a parent are rather conflicting priorities nowadays, especially in the 20s.

Taking into consideration these issues, the COST (European Cooperation in Science and Technology) Action YOUNG-IN[2] is interested in sets of circumstances and factors that prevent young people from:

- Finding a decent job;
- Starting a family when they want;
- Making their voice heard in the policy process (COST, 2018, p. 3).

YOUNG-IN has brought together researchers from 32 countries and different fields of expertise in order not only to address common structural problems facing young people in the present time, but also to offer transdisciplinary solutions to cross sectoral disadvantage in youth. One deliverable of the COST Action is this volume, which synthetizes the main facts with regard to socio-economic challenges to family formation in the represented countries.

Quite often, almost on a daily basis, we can hear or read in the mass-media concerns about low fertility and socio-economic implications of a rapidly ageing population. Taking into consideration that Europe is the continent with the lowest fertility and the oldest population (by indicators), such narratives seem justifiable.

Total fertility varies from "the lowest low" (Kohler et al., 2002) (below 1.3 children per woman in Bosnia and Herzegovina, Italy, Spain, Malta, and Moldova) to "the highest low" (Andersson, 2008) (1.7 and above in France, Scandinavia, Romania, and Ireland). Those in-between the two extremes are the most numerous countries, albeit some of them are inclining to lower levels of fertility.

Both affluent European countries and those with a much lower GDP have been recording sub-replacement fertility which suggests very complex mechanisms lying behind the reproduction behavior of individuals. Lutz et al. (2006) formulated a hypothesis on the *low fertility trap* containing three independent mechanisms classified as demographic, sociological and economic.

The fact (or even the paradox) that the cluster (group of countries with some degree of socio-demographic similarity in broad or more narrow terms) consisting of the more liberal countries (Scandinavia) has substantially higher fertility rates than the more conservative South European cluster, characterized by strong family ties, might seem confusing for those who are not familiar with the contextual factors.

There is an impressive literature body dealing with the topics centered around family formation, fertility and so forth, including related policies both in national and cross-national perspectives, especially since the beginning of the new millen-

---

[2] More information about the COST Action YOUNG-IN on https://www.cost.eu/actions/CA17114/

nium. But research findings often remain untranslated into effective policy measures.

Hantrais (2006) outlined the main trends identified by demographers with respect to family formation and structure across Europe towards the end of the 20th century:

- The transition to parenthood is being postponed; an increase of the mean age of first-time mothers indicates that.
- Falling birthrates, even *below replacement fertility*, consequently resulted in reducing family size. Data on completed fertility are higher than those on period fertility rates as part of births occur at a later age.
- The permanent childlessness is rising, which also contributes to low fertility.
- National statistics on fertility are glossing over increasing polarization between families with children and the so-called "non-family sector" (Keilman, 2003) (childless couples and adult individuals).

Additionally, she summarized changes concerning the de-institutionalization of family life:

- Disconnection of marriage and parenting. In 2018, extramarital births outnumbered births inside marriages in eight EU Member States: France (60%), Bulgaria (59%), Slovenia (58%), Portugal (56%), Sweden (55%), Denmark and Estonia (both 54%), as well as the Netherlands (52%) (Eurostat, 2021).
- A strong linkage between marital instability and an upward trend in divorce rates.
- The proportion of single-parent households (children predominantly with their mother) continues to rise due to divorce, extramarital births, or less frequently, the death of the spouse/partner (Hantrais, 2006).

The rise of childlessness among persons in childbearing years in the last decades is one of the many shifts in demographic behavior but, unlike the other parallel trends, this phenomenon is usually seen through prism of ideology (Kreyenfeld & Konietzka, 2017).

Analyzing childlessness among women in the Netherlands, Coleman and Garssen (2002) noted that although being a minority, this group is rapidly increasing. Furthermore, in Germany and Austria, not having a child is perceived as preferable fertility option for around 4% of women, which is roughly twice as high compared to the average across the OECD countries (OECD, 2016). Discussing the social consequences of childlessness in old age, Kohli and Albertini (2009) hold a view that it is more important how someone ends up without children than not having a child *per se*.

In order to explain the societal/cultural dimension of fertility changes that have been taking place, scholars usually refer to theories incorporating a conceptional description of modernization as a historical process influencing the reproduction patterns. One of the theoretical views on the developments of fertility is certainly the Structure/Culture Paradigm (Hoffmann-Nowotny 1980, 1987, as cited in Hoffmann-Nowotny & Fux, 1991).

Postponement of childbearing (delayed transition into parenthood) became a common practice, although the reasons behind it may differ. On the other hand, fertility aspirations strongly depend on the circumstances at all levels and, for that reason, persons usually end their reproductive age with less children than wanted at younger age. Beaujouan and Berghammer (2019) studied the aggregate gap between the intended and actual fertility in 19 European countries and USA based on a cohort approach. In accordance with expectations, they found out that "in all countries, women eventually had, on average, fewer children than the earlier expectations in their birth cohort, and more often than intended, they remained childless" (Beaujouan & Berghammer, 2019, p. 507).

The study Value of Children (VOC) for Parents, that was conducted in different parts of the world in the mid-1970s, contributed to a better understanding of fertility behavior, as well as of family dynamics in the rapidly changing social context. The study has set the foundations for the later emerging Family Change and Self-Development Theory proposed by Kagitcibasi (Kagitcibasi & Ataca, 2015). Aries (1980) argues that the trend of the smaller family model in the West was not associated with the ambition of individuals to climb the social ladder, but rather with the benefits of a welfare system that removed the long persisting pressure of higher fertility for the sake of future (in parents' later life).

The European Value Study is also an important data source when examining family in a cross-cultural context. The World Cultural Map constructed by political scientists Ronald Inglehart and Christian Welzel is a useful reference when making comparisons between societies or clusters (Inglehart–Welzel Cultural Map, 2020[3]). In their research paper, Hunink and Kohli (2014) applied the life course approach as a methodological framework for the empirical analysis of fertility and family formation.

Differential fertility has been attracting researchers' attention: it is inherent to societies in which several ethnic groups coexist, including autochthonous minorities (e.g., Roma) or those with a migrant background stemming from countries with different fertility patterns and family values. Variations in fertility within the society are usually associated with socio-economic status, (sub)culture, religiosity, attachment to tradition, and so forth. Israel is representative in that sense.

Economic theories of fertility, well-known by their formulations such as "quality and quantity of children" (Becker, 1981) or "demand for children" (Easterlin, 1966), are bringing a materialistic value of children to the fore. However, psycho-

---

[3] https://www.worldvaluessurvey.org/WVSContents.jsp?CMSID=Findings

Disadvantages in Starting a Family Across Europe • **xv**

logical factors also have a great impact on fertility behavior (e.g., advantages of being a parent) (Yong Lee & Marwell, 2013).

The imaginary Hajnal line (drawn back in 1965), which once divided Europe into two main areas in a controversial way based on nuptiality and fertility levels, has almost faded, judging by today's comparative vital statistical data and findings from various studies. Apparently, the wave of the second demographic transition splashed Eastern and Southern Europe, bringing with it more liberal views on marriage behavior and parenthood. Even though socio-economic conditions for penetrating those values with respect to family are still suboptimal in many non-EU, and also poorer EU countries, such as the status of women (gender inequalities), lower living standards related to (un)employment and incomes and so forth, "Westernization" to some extent occurs in spite of it, especially among the more educated persons in the urban centers.

Transformation/diversification of family is at the core of the Second Demographic Transition (SDT) concept introduced by van de Kaa and Laesthege in the 1980s (Lesthaeghe, 2010). Following the SDT theoretical paradigm, Sobotka et al. (2001) provided a short historical overview of family values in the Czech Republic considering the changing societal context.

In their study, Thornton and Philipov (2007) analyze the dramatic family and demographic changes in Central and Eastern Europe in light of historical events in the late 1980s and early 1990s. To explain the interaction and influence (political, economic, cultural, etc.) of Western Europe and North America over the former socialist countries, they use the concept of developmental paradigm. In his earlier works, Arland Thornton introduced the well-known concept of developmental idealism as a cultural model constituted of a set of beliefs and values. His valuable discussion clarifies the convergence of family values and related behaviors across Europe (Thornton et al., 2015).

POLICY RESPONSES TO LOW FERTILITY

Although the benefits from employment, in terms of wealth and income, cannot be substituted by the welfare system (regardless of its type), the family-friendly state policy is an important source of support (Oinonen, 2008).

Structural disadvantages may be considered a set of severe obstacles to family formation or progression to a second child. One of the most dominant is certainly the conflict between employment and motherhood (Sobotka, 2004) or, put differently, incompatibility between a young mother's professional and family life.

What would be an ideal family policy? There are certain ambivalences in assessing its effects, especially if comparing different countries. Discussing the measurement of family policies in the industrialized countries, Gauthier accentuated constraints and challenges faced by researchers, especially the absence of a comprehensive database on state support for families and scarce knowledge of employer-provided policies in terms of their impact on fertility and further implications that could arise from it. Her well-known study sheds a light on the different natures of those policies, whose models are deeply rooted in the respective (political) cultures (Gauthier, 2007). Family-oriented policy objectives (defined either in explicit or implicit way) may vary, but their impact on fertility trends remains a pivotal point. Vaskovics (2001) underlines that those demographic goals are often pursued through family policy measures. Either explicitly or implicitly, or at times covertly. According to him, in an EU comparison, three goals of family policy could be recognized:

- Demographic goals (e.g., reproduction of the population);
- Gender-related goals (e.g., improvement of compatibility of family and work for mothers; social acknowledgment of upbringing, etc.);
- Child welfare (elimination of unequal socialization conditions for children, regardless of the parents' relationship, e.g., support for single parents and families with more children) (ibid.).

McDonald (2006) specified the following criteria for an effective family policy:

1. Horizontal equity between categories of parents;
2. Neutrality of child benefits with respect to the occupational situation of the parents;
3. Gender neutrality;
4. Existence of benefits in the work place;
5. Incorporation of measures to guarantee an optimal development and performance of the children;
6. A life cycle approach that does not abruptly withdraw the benefits of children after a certain age;
7. Simplicity and transparency;
8. Fiscal sustainability;
9. Efficacy;
10. Political acceptability; and
11. Durability: one-time measures that are not sustained over time are unlikely to have a lasting impact.

Some authors (Lutz et al., 2003; Lutz & Skirbekk, 2004) found policies aiming to a quantum of children less acceptable than those targeting the timing of childbearing (as cited in Sobotka, 2004).

Both models of family policy - French (pronatalist) and Nordic (pro-egalitarian) (cf. Gauthier, 1996)—deserve a special research interest for several reasons. State support for families that is being continuously adjusted to societal changes is reflected not only in the level of fertility, which is among the highest in Europe, but also in the gender dimension of parenthood (Letablier, 2003).

The Scandinavian model is famous for prioritizing gender equality over other objectives related to fertility. Family policies in these countries observed from outside share common features entailing egalitarian (Mahone, 2002), universal-

Disadvantages in Starting a Family Across Europe • **xvii**

ist (social democratic), (Esping-Andersen, 1989; Gauthier, 2002), or dual earner-dual caregiver welfare model (Gornick & Meyers, 2008 (as cited in Rostgard, 2014)). Symmetrical parenthood in Nordic countries means more involvement and participation of fathers in childcare. Father's quota is a part of policy enabled paternity leave—something that would be hardly implementable without resistance in more traditional societies with rigid gender roles in the family. The same applies to any other policy measures which work under specific societal conditions, and probably would not give similar outcome(s) in different ones.

It should be borne in mind that family-related policy measures are not always adequately targeting the most prominent issues faced by persons in childbearing years such as: gender inequalities, alleviation of costs for raising a child and opportunity cost for women, precarious work, housing, work-life balance, and services (e.g., availability and affordability of childcare), and so forth. All these reasons might be decisive for starting a family or having a second child by mid-30s.

ABOUT THIS BOOK

The above pages of the introductory chapter highlighted, drawing on various studies, the key issues concerning family formation. Sometimes, in a comparative, cross-national research, many country-specific circumstances are poorly contextualized due to overgeneralization. In an effort to get a first-hand overview of socio-economic challenges, as well as opportunities for family formation, the ideal chapter structure was envisaged by the call for authors. It entailed the following subsections: national context, demographic trends, normative and institutional framework (focusing on family policy), socio-economic conditions, and country-specific challenges to family formation. By doing so, the empirical evidence from each country included in the volume enables a comparison between them.

Thanks to the contribution from authors of different disciplines, we have collected eleven manuscripts, in form of national reports. These are (in alphabetical order): Bosnia and Herzegovina, Czech Republic, Germany, Hungary, Israel, Italy, Latvia, Lithuania, Malta, Portugal, and Serbia.

Potential contributors from other European countries have been contacted, however, unfortunately, their reports have not been submitted.

Rich bibliography/references (papers, studies, documents and other sources) are one of the assets of these reports, especially for those interested in further reading.

The present book was initiated by Working Group 2: Disadvantages in Starting a Family, whose intention was to identify adverse circumstances that might have an impact on family formation in terms of timing and the realization of fertility intentions. Accordingly, the focus has been directed at the most dominant contextual factors of different societies in a multidisciplinary perspective. Furthermore, the objective of WG2 was to analyze evidence and facilitate a debate on the vulnerable groups of childbearing age, as well as to identify gaps in research and potential new avenues of research.[4]

Certain contradictories/peculiarities stood out: familism and religiosity (typical for South Europe) do not coincide with large families—on the contrary. Many of the countries belonging to that cluster record the lowest low fertility (Bosnia and Herzegovina, Italy, Malta, Portugal, and Spain). On the other hand, economic prosperity and social welfare, for some reasons, do not necessarily mean optimal conditions for starting a family. In other words, low fertility occurs in contrasting socio-economic settings. For instance, unlike many countries, Germany provides a number of favorable socio-economic conditions for starting a family, such as high employment rates, generous public transfers, and other kinds of benefits. Contrary to assumptions, the total fertility rate in Germany is low in spite of the high living standard. Authors identified a series of common disadvantages in family formation: youth unemployment, precarious work (scarcity of stable jobs at a decent wage), the housing problem, family policies conditioned by individual's working status or inadequate policy measures (not in line with the actual needs) and so forth. Women's opportunity cost during the first pregnancy and after childbearing was recognized as one of the major issues that might affect progression to a second or third child.

One of the guiding ideas was that findings presented in this book may serve as a platform for improving/updating the existing policy measures with respect to young people striving to start a family at a younger age. We do hope that policy makers, as well as other stakeholders, will consult this volume as one of the relevant sources.

ACKNOWLEDGMENTS

This volume is a product of the COST Action YOUNG-IN on Transdisciplinary solutions to cross sectoral disadvantage in youth CA17114; https://young-in.eu, Action Chair Prof. Anu Toots, Tallinn University, Estonia; Action Vice-Chair Dr Johannes Bergh Institute for Social Research, Oslo, Norway. The book was an initiative of the members of WG 2: Disadvantages in Starting a Family; WG Leader Prof. Mirza Emirhafizović, University of Sarajevo, Bosnia and Herzegovina; Co-Leader Prof. Tali Heiman, Open University, Raanana, Israel.

REFERENCES

Andersson, G. (2008). A review of policies and practices related to the 'highest-low' fertility of Sweden. *Vienna Yearbook of Population Research, 2008*, 89–102. DOI: https://doi.org/10.1553/populationyearbook2008s89

Aries, P. (1980). Two successive motivations for the declining birth rate in the west. *Population and Development Review, 6*(4), 645. doi:10.2307/1972930

---

[4] https://young-in.eu/family-formation/

Beaujouan, E., & Berghammer, C. (2019). The gap between lifetime fertility intentions and completed fertility in Europe and the United States: A cohort approach. *Population Research and Policy Review, 384,* 507–535. https://doi.org/10.1007/s11113-019-09516-3

Becker, G. S. (1981). *A treatise on the family.* Harvard University Press.

Coleman, D. A., & Garssen, J. (2002). The Netherlands: Paradigm or exception in Western Europe's demography? *Demographic Research, 7*(12), 433–468. doi:10.4054/DemRes.2002.7.12

COST. (2018). Memorandum of understanding for the implementation of the COST Action "Transdisciplinary solutions to cross sectoral disadvantage in youth" (YOUNG-IN) CA17114. https://www.cost.eu/actions/CA17114/#tabs+Name:Description

Easterlin, R. A. (1966). On the Relation of Economic Factors to Recent and Projected Fertility Changes. Demography 3(1),131–153.

Eurostat. (2021). *Fertility statistics.* Retrieved July 19, 2021, from: https://ec.europa.eu/eurostat/statistics-explained/index.php?title=Fertility_statistics

Gauthier, A. H. (1996). *The state and the family: A comparative analysis of family policies in industrialized countries.* Clarendon Press.

Gauthier, A. H. (2007). The impact of family policies on fertility in industrialized countries: A review of the literature. *Population Research and Policy Review, 26*(3), 323–346.

Hantrais, L. (2006). Introduction: Living as a family in Europe. In L. Hantrais, D. Philipov, & F. C. Billari (Eds.), *Policy implications of changing family formation. Population studies No. 49.* Council of Europe Publishing.

Hoffmann-Nowotny, J., & Fux, B. (1991), Present demographic trends in Europe. In: *Council of Europe, Seminar on present demographic trends and lifestyles in Europe* (pp. 31–97). Council of Europe: Strasbourg.

Huinink, J., & Kohli, M. (2014). A life-course approach to fertility. *Demographic Research, 30*(45), 1293–1326.

Kagitcibasi, C., & Ataca, B. (2015). Value of children, family change, and implications for the care of the elderly. *Cross-Cultural Research, 49*(4), 374–392. https://doi.org/10.1177/1069397115598139

Keilman, N. (2003). *Demographic and social implications of low fertility for family structures in Europe. Population series N. 43.* Council of Europe Publishing.

Kohler, H.-P., Billari, F. C., & Ortega, J. A. (2002). The emergence of lowest-low fertility in Europe during the 1990s. *Population and Development Review, 28*(4), 641. https://link.gale.com/apps/doc/A96904137/AONE?u=googlescholar&sid=bookmark-AONE&xid=acbf6e33

Kohli, M., & Albertini, M. (2009). Childlessness and intergenerational transfers: What is at stake? *Ageing and Society, 29*(8), 1171–1183. doi:10.1017/S0144686X09990341

Kreyenfeld, M., & Konietzka, D. (2017). Analyzing childlessness. In M. Kreyenfeld, & D. Konietzka (Eds.), *Childlessness in Europe: Contexts, causes, and consequences* (pp. 3–15). Springer. https://doi.org/10.3917/popu.1801.0156

Lee, S. Y., & Marwell, G. (2013, August 25–31). *A general theory of gender preferences for children* [Paper presentation]. IUSSP. Busan, South Korea.

Lesthaeghe, R. (2010). The unfolding story of the second demographic transition. *Population and Development Review, 36,* 211–251. https://doi.org/10.1111/j.1728-4457.2010.00328.x

xx • EMIRHAFIZOVIC ET AL.

Letablier, M-T. (2003). *Fertility and family policies in France.* (Discussion paper 160). Center for Intergenerational Studies, Institute of Economic Research, Hitotsubashi University.

Lutz, W., Skirbekk, V., & Testa, M.R. (2006). The low fertility trap hypothesis: Forces that may lead to further postponement and fewer births in Europe. In: *Vienna yearbook of population research* (pp. 167–192). Verlag der Österreichischen Akademie der Wissenschaften. 10.1553/populationyearbook2006s167.

McDonald, P. (2006). An assessment of policies that support having children from the perspectives of equity, efficiency and efficacy. V*ienna Yearbook of Population Research, 4*(1), 213–234.

OECD. (2016). Family database, *Ideal and actual number of children,* OECD—Social Policy Division. https://www.oecd.org/els/family/SF_2_2-Ideal-actual-number-children.pdf

Oinonen, E. (2008). *Families in converging Europe: A comparison of forms, structures and ideals.* Palgrave Macmillan.

Rostgaard, T. (2014). *Family policies in Scandinavia.* Friedrich-Ebert-Stiftung.

Sobotka, T. (2004). *Postponement of childbearing and low fertility in Europe.* s.n

Sobotka, T., Zeman, K., & Kantorová, V. (2001, June 23–28). *Second demographic transition in the Czech Republic: Stages, specific features and underlying factors* [Paper presentation]. EURESCO Conference "The second demographic transition in Europe", Bad Herrenalb, Germany.

Stout, R. (2008). *Demographic winter.* [Video file] https://www.youtube.com/watch?v=lZeyYIsGdAA

Thornton, A., Dorius, S. F., & Swindle, J. (2015). Developmental idealism. *Sociology of Development, 1*(2), 277–320. doi:10.1525/sod.2015.1.2.277

Thornton, A., & Philipov, D. (2007). *Developmental idealism and family and demographic change in central and eastern Europe* (European Demographic Research Papers 3 / 2007). Vienna Institute of Demography.

Vaskovics, L. A. (2002). Familienpolitik und familienrelevante Politik als Kontextbedingungen für Familienentwicklung und Familienstrukturen [Family policy and family-related policy as context conditions for family development and family structures]. In J. Dorbritz, & J. Otto (Eds.), *Familienpolitik und Familienstrukturen* [Family policy and family structures]. Bundesinstitut für Bevölkerungsforschung.

World Values Survey Association. (2020). *Findings and insights.* https://www.worldvaluessurvey.org/WVSContents.jsp?CMSID=Findings

CHAPTER 1

SOCIO-ECONOMIC CHALLENGES TO FAMILY FORMATION IN BOSNIA AND HERZEGOVINA

Major Issues

Mirza Emirhafizović
University of Sarajevo

Andrea Puhalić
University of Banja Luka

NATIONAL CONTEXT

Bosnia and Herzegovina (BiH) is a multicultural, multi-ethnic, and multi-confessional country located in Southeast Europe. The specificity of the socio-historical context in which young people live in Bosnia and Herzegovina (BiH) is still determined by the consequences of the 1990s war in the country and beyond, with inter-entity disunity and decentralization of the state, and the never-ending transition of social, economic, political, and normative foundations. The Dayton Peace Agreement (or Accords),[1] reached in November 1995, brought not only peace in

---

[1] The official name of the agreement is *The General Framework Agreement for Peace in Bosnia and Herzegovina.*

Family Formation Among Youth in Europe: Coping With Socio-Economic Disadvantages,
pages 1–16.
Copyright © 2022 by Information Age Publishing
www.infoagepub.com
All rights of reproduction in any form reserved.

1

the country, but also a new constitution, which is still in force today, resulting in a very complex institutional set up.

The "Dayton" Bosnia and Herzegovina is divided into numerous levels of government and administration, from the state level, through the entity levels (Republika Srpska, Federation of Bosnia and Herzegovina and Brčko District), to the lower levels of individual cantons and local-self-government units (municipalities and cities). Both entities have their own governments, presidents and parliaments and, as such, have a high degree of autonomy. At the state level, there is a tripartite Presidency (representing three constituent peoples, namely Bosniaks, Croats and Serbs), a Council of Ministers and a Parliamentary Assembly. The Federation of Bosnia and Herzegovina (FBiH) is further divided into ten cantons that have their own governments and parliaments, also with a significant degree of autonomy. The specific responsibility for a number of state issues (such as social and child protection) has been transferred to the entity, cantonal and local self-government units.

According to the 2013 census, there are 773,850 young people aged 15 to 30 living in Bosnia and Herzegovina, or 21.91% of the population.

Bearing in mind the continuous out-migration, which mostly include young people in their 20s and 30s, and the smaller influx of younger generations due to low and declining birth rates in the last two decades, the share of this population is certainly decreasing every year.

The specifics of the BiH context are the distrust in institutions, high levels of corruption, high unemployment rates, and the general lack of elaborated and secure mechanisms for the protection of human rights. At the level of families and young people, this social atmosphere is primarily reflected in the departure of a large number of young people from the country. Regarding that, research shows that from the second half of the 1990s until 2015, tens of thousands of young people left the country; 80% of young people would leave BiH if they would be given the opportunity; and 90% believe that they have no influence on important decisions in the society to which they belong (Žiga et al., 2015).

Such data are worrying, because they indicate not only a pronounced tendency of young people to leave the country, but also a particularly pronounced and present (90%) experience of helplessness of a young person, in relation to decision-making in the society in which they live. This experience of personal helplessness can be viewed in close connection with the lack of more numerous and stronger initiatives of young people to create such social changes, which would enable the development of a safer and more just BiH society.

DEMOGRAPHIC TRENDS RELEVANT TO FAMILY FORMATION

The horrible war that took place in Bosnia and Herzegovina in the 1990s (1992–1995) has caused severe and longstanding demographic effects due to mass population displacement within and outside the state, as a result of forced and conflict-driven migration (around 1.2 million people refuged mainly to the European countries), as well as high mortality, including civilians of all age groups. Additionally, reduced fertility during the war and unsatisfactory return of former refugees (nowadays called the BiH diaspora) to the homeland, in other words, to their pre-war peacetime local communities, is reflected in the population pyramid. For all these reasons, according to the report prepared by scholars from the Vienna Institute for Demography of the Austrian Academy of Sciences (ÖAW) and the Wittgenstein Centre (ÖAW, IIASA, WU), Bosnia and Herzegovina has suffered the greatest population decline among the European countries over the period from 1990 to 2017, which is more than a fifth of the total population reported at the beginning of the 1990s (precisely, 22 percent) (Sobotka et al., 2018). As a result of the multiannual negative natural change alone (the number of deaths exceeds the number of live births), Bosnia and Herzegovina lost more than 61,000 inhabitants between 2007 and 2019 (Agency of Statistics of Bosnia and Herzegovina [BHAS], 2020). Observed by the entities, natural population decrease has emerged eleven years earlier in Republika Srpska (RS) (since 2002) and it is more intensive there than in the Federation of Bosnia and Herzegovina (Institute of Statistics of the Federation of BiH [FZS], 2014; Republic Institute of Statistics RS [RZS], 2006).

Based on the criteria of rurality (both by definitions and indicators), Bosnia and Herzegovina is one of the most rural countries in Europe (UNDP, 2013, p. 9). Convergence of the proportion of the urban and rural population to equal levels is associated with the permanent rural exodus generated by simultaneous industrialization and urbanization, as well as war consequences and socio-economic transition in the post conflict period. Its multiple demographic implications visible in depopulation and *dejuvenilization* of the countryside threaten to eradicate the rural way of life.

Bosnia and Herzegovina could be regarded as a family-centric society even though there are some signs of pluralization (diversification) of family structure. Accordingly, the most dominant type is a nuclear family household—married couples with children (around three quarters) followed by one-parent families (mainly single mothers with children) with almost 18 percent. Consensual couple with children is a very uncommon form of family representing less than two percent of all family households. There are some insignificant deviations from these percentages among the two entities (BHAS, 2017).

Calculations based on the 2013 Census data correspond to the Youth Study in BiH done in 2014: according to these two sources, between 79 (BHAS, 2017) and 81 percent of young people (more frequently males than females) (Flere, 2015) still co-reside with their parents. Judging by the stated percentage, one might get the impression that such residential status is a widely preferable living arrangement among youth in Bosnia and Herzegovina, which fits the overemphasized attachment to family or "overprotective" parenting, a style so common in Southern Europe. But this is not always the case, as one-quarter of respondents would like to move out of their parents' home and start living on their own if the financial situation permitted (Flere, 2015).

After a short "baby boom" period in the second half of the 1990s (in 1997, total fertility rate reached almost 1.7 children per woman), that occurred immediately after the war, there has been a continuous decline in the already low birth rates that started at the turn of the century. By looking at periodic fertility measures for a period of over 20 years, the previous statement gains its empirical foundation (Figure 1.1). "Translocation of baby booms and busts" (Frątczak, 2004) that has intensified during the 1990s is also one of the determinants of the reproduction capacity. In all cohorts under 30 years of age, the specific fertility rate has substantially dropped when comparing 1996 and 2018. Within the youngest cohort of 15–19, the indicator decreased for almost 70 percent (from 30.7 to 9.5 per 1,000 women in this age group), whilst for mothers aged 25–29, it more than halved (from 107.6 to 51.8‰) (BHAS, 2020).

In the last ten years, the average age of first-time mothers has increased by almost three years (from 24.9 in 2008 to 27.4 in 2018) (BHAS, 2020).

The very low fertility rate (TFR has been below 1.3 children per woman since 2002, except in 2009 and 2012) ranked Bosnia and Herzegovina among the first five world countries recording the "lowest-low fertility" in the five-year period 2010–2015 (United Nations [UN], 2015). A drastic fall in fertility rates is confirmed by the fact that the number of live births in 2018 fell by 44% compared to 1990 (two years before the war outbreak) (BHAS, 2020; Republic Institute of Statistics of SR Bosnia and Herzegovina [RZS SRBiH], 1991).

As a result of modernization processes that had determined the pace and intensity of the demographic transition, the prevalence of marriage and childbearing in adolescence belongs to the past. Since marriage among most of the population in Bosnia and Herzegovina is still a prerequisite for having a child, the increase in the average age of mother at first birth coincides with the increase in the average age of marriage, which in 2018 exceeded 27 years for women (BHAS, 2020).

Contrary to assumptions, the drop in the total number of marriages has not been so dramatic when comparing the absolute values in 1996 and 2018 (the

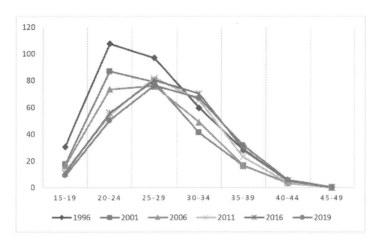

FIGURE 1.1.   Age-Specific Fertility Curves for Selected Years. Author's construction based on vital statistics data (BHAS, 2020)

Socio-Economic Challenges to Family Formation in Bosnia and Herzegovina • 5

difference is less than 1.200 marriages), and its distribution across age groups reveals a shift of patterns. Unlike the previous generations, in the present time, persons of legal age tend to postpone marriage until the late 20s or even older age: the number of brides aged 15–19 has decreased by 65% over 22 years (from 1996 to 2018), and almost by 23% within the next age group (20–24). Simultaneously, a reverse trend in all 30 plus age groups has been recorded. As men usually get married older than women, this phenomenon has been transferred in a linear manner to adjacent (older) age subgroups representing the groom.

The rate of out-of-wedlock births hardly exceeds ten percent and is still relatively low compared to many European countries. Even though the share of children born to adolescent mothers stood at only around five percent, it is indicative that the majority of them under 18 years of age who gave birth are unmarried, and mostly living together with their partners (BHAS, 2020). Although divorce rate is quite low, the number of divorced persons has been increasing across the country in the last two decades.

The results of the Household Budget Survey (HBS) conducted in 2015 confirmed the described norm with regard to age: more than 90 percent (93.1%) of persons aged 15–24 are unmarried, whilst only 6.5% of them are either married or live together with her/his partner (cohabitation). As expected, there is almost an equal percentage of the population within the age group 25–34 who are unmarried and those who are married or cohabiting (49.8% and 47.8%, respectively) (BHAS, 2018). Getting a divorce is (still) an extremely rare option among persons younger than 35 years of age, and hardly surpasses two percent (BHAS, 2020).

The marginalized Roma minority, being below the national average with respect to all dimensions of human development, deviates from the mainstream demographic indicators. In that sense, the Roma household size is larger by 1.35 persons than that of non-Roma counterparts, which is closely related to higher fertility (UNDP & World Bank, 2018).

Being a sending country with a long tradition, out-migration has a huge impact on the demographic profile of Bosnia and Herzegovina along with the (negative) natural change. According to different available sources of population data provided by the official statistics in host countries (census or population registries), the estimated number of persons born in Bosnia and Herzegovina in 52 countries worldwide, irrespective of their actual citizenship, was 1,807,602, of which around 60% reside in the EU-28, Norway and Switzerland (Ministry of Security of Bosnia and Herzegovina, 2020, p. 70). Over the ten-year period alone—2008–2018—first residence permits were issued to almost 250,000 citizens of Bosnia and Herzegovina within the EU-28, which indicates the extent of the still present emigration wave (Eurostat, 2019a).

When discussing population movements within the state borders, migration flows are primarily directed towards the capital (Sarajevo), as well as other important urban centers (Banja Luka, Bihać, Mostar, Tuzla, East Sarajevo, Trebinje, Bijeljina, and others) (FZS, 2019; RZS RS, 2020).

NORMATIVE FRAMEWORK

To understand the family aspect of a young person's life in BiH, it is important to point out that all the above social factors make the financial, spatial, and overall social independence very difficult and challenging. Therefore, the average age for marriage and starting a family is constantly increasing, although the prevailing view among young people is that marriage should take place while one is in his/her twenties. In the above-mentioned research study, for the majority of respondents, the most appropriate age for getting married was 25 for females and 27.1 for males (Flere, 2015). In a way, prolonged family life is compensated by young people through pronounced closeness with members of the family of origin, with whom they live in a joint household.

Taking into consideration some vital statistical indicators and cultural values, Bosnia and Herzegovina as a society belongs to the Mediterranean (Southern European) cluster, even though its 20th century historic legacy is mostly socialist due to the Yugoslav period 1918–1992. Generally, that cluster is characterized by rather traditional values in many respects: religiosity, unpopularity of unmarried cohabitation, low rate of out-of-wedlock births, relatively low divorce rate, perception of marriage as social status, strong family ties (familism before individualism), and the "latest late pattern of transition to adulthood" (living with parents even after completing secondary or tertiary education) (Billari & Liefbroer, 2010; Flere, 2015).

The findings of the 2019 European Values Study confirm that the inclination towards family traditionalism is associated with the educational degree of individuals. The percentage of respondents who "strongly agree" or "agree" with the statement that having children is a duty towards society drops as their educational level rises (Kolenović Đapo & Brkić Šmigoc, 2020).

However, behavior and attitudes toward marriage and family, including procreation, practiced or expressed among the more educated residents of major urban centers, may diverge from this paradigm (standardized biography), challenging the long-established social norms. From the life course perspective, such "heterogenization of biographies" is being typically equalized with de-standardization (Aboim & Vasconcelos, 2019). De-standardization is a concept that is used to describe intergenerational changes in the life trajectories whose dynamics became (more) individualized in relation to age and the normative framework (cf. Elzinga & Liefbroer, 2007). There is a lack of empirical evidence regarding the more pronounced impact of Westernization on family in Bosnia and Herzegovina in terms of the prevalence of various alternatives to marriage (cohabitation, living apart together and others), including the fluidity of living arrangements among younger cohorts and reasons for childlessness.

When it comes to fertility aspirations, the survey conducted in 2010 within the project *Strategy for Reduction of Negative Demographic Trends in the Sarajevo Canton,* which may serve as a point of reference, has shown that two children are the desire of most respondents. More than half of them (54.5%) have had such inclination, while 25.9% want to have three children. A lower percentage of the total number of respondents wanted four (4.6%) or more children (4.4%), while only 1% did not want to have children at all (Emirhafizović & Zolić, 2010).

If the family size preference exceeds the average, it is more likely that the desired number of children will not be achieved in later life. However, in Bosnia and Herzegovina, progression to the second child is often questionable. What might be controversial is that intentionally induced abortion[2] is often used as one of the methods of family planning. Although there are no reliable statistics thereon, as operations performed at private clinics remain unreported, rough estimates of the number of intentional abortions raise concerns regarding women's age, the reasons behind such a decision, and the possible side-effects of such a procedure (Emirhafizović, 2018).

Family is highly ranked in the life of individuals regardless of their demographics: age, sex, ethnicity, social status, the level of religiosity[3] and education. On the other hand, this primary social group was also severely affected by the crisis during the transition. Still, when the Household Budget Survey was implemented in 2015, as many as 98 percent of residents from different parts of the country responded that they are (very) satisfied with their family (BHAS, 2018).

SOCIO-ECONOMIC CONDITIONS

One of the important specificities of young people in the BiH society is their position on the labor market. All other features should be interpreted in relation to this one. The official website of the Ministry of Civil Affairs of BiH states that over 60% of young people in BiH are unemployed,[4] half of whom have been unemployed for over two years, and one fifth for five years or more (Ministry of Civil Affairs of Bosnia and Herzegovina, n.d.). These are official data of the state institution responsible for employment and labor.

Research shows (UNICEF, 2016: p. 98) that the process of finding a job for a young person is very long and uncertain. The search for a job lasts much longer than a year, which is why many agree to work outside of the profession for which they were educated. A relatively high percentage of the unemployed do not look for a job at all, which can be related to the previously established high level of helplessness of young people in relation to all social issues, including the labor market. Particularly worrying is the tendency of young people to, in a way, "give

---

[2] Abortion in Bosnia and Herzegovina is legal on request during the first ten weeks of pregnancy.

[3] In Bosnia and Herzegovina, all Abrahamic religions are represented (Christianity - Catholic and Orthodox Church, Islam, and Judaism). Taking into account that religion is a very important aspect of social life in Bosnia and Herzegovina, it does not come as a surprise that as many as 85.9% of respondents, who participated in the European Values Study (EVS), stated that they were religious (Kolenović Đapo & Brkić Šmigoc, 2020).

[4] This is the registered unemployment rate, and as such is **significantly higher** than the harmonized unemployment rate which corresponds to the ILO definition of unemployment used in the Labor Force Survey (LFS) (see more Khare, Ronnås & Shamchiyeva, 2010).

up" on the profession for which they were educated and accept any job outside the profession. Furthemore, approximately every fourth young adult in BiH is employed. Young people are rarely employed outside their municipality of residence or outside the country. Most young people believe that bribery in employment is not uncommon (ibid).

Structural unemployment (especially affecting young people) and social exclusion in Bosnia and Herzegovina have been generally perceived as huge problems and negative aspects of transition.

Youth unemployment rate is one of the highest in Europe, although its decline was registered consecutively for the last three years: 2017, 2018 and 2019. Referring to the Labor Force Survey (LFS), conducted in 2019, this indicator for the 15–24 age group was 33.8%. A drop in the unemployment rate was also notable for the older age group 24–49, which partly includes young people as well, and in the same year, it was lower than 18% (17.2%) (BHAS, 2019). Despite this positive trend, knowledge of the contextual features of the labor market (e.g., rising precariousness), *unsatisfying* business environment, and emigration trends of the work force at a younger age, do not leave much room for excessive optimism.

Focusing on differences in joblessness by gender, temporary or permanent absence from the labor market still affects women more than men (by about 6% within these two age groups in 2019). Education achievement also plays a significant role in positioning oneself on the labor market. In that light, there is an association between the education attained and unemployment: the lower the level of education, the higher the unemployment. Consistently, more than 80% of unemployed persons are those with (un)completed primary school or secondary school and specialization (BHAS, 2019).

Muris Čičić, the president of the Academy of Sciences and Arts of Bosnia and Herzegovina, deems that their unenviable status will hardly ever change: "(B)asically, they are unemployable, because they are a population structure that in this dynamic age has no pass for the labor market. These people will never get a job" (Đugum, 2019).

Bosnia and Herzegovina was one of two EU enlargement countries with the lowest rates of early leavers from education and training in 2018; the proportion was higher for young men than for young women (5.6% and 5.2%, respectively), as in the EU-27. Just under one quarter of the population aged 30–34 had completed a tertiary level of education, which, comparatively, is not only below the EU-27, but also the countries in the region (Eurostat, 2020).

With the Bologna Process introduced (in academic year 2005/06) and new universities and colleges being established (both public and private ones, on a commercial basis)[5] across the country from the 1990s onwards, the massification of higher education—in terms of the rising number of enrolled students—has been

---

[5] On the official website of Agency for Development of Higher Education and Quality Assurance there is list of 32 accredited higher education institutions in Bosnia and Herzegovina (see http://hea.gov.ba/akreditacija_vsu/Default.aspx)

contributing to the accelerated transformation of the educational composition. More accessible tertiary education, even in smaller urban municipalities, stimulated an increasing number of secondary school leavers to pursue a university or college degree.

Almost one-quarter (24.3%) of young people (aged 15–24) are identified as NEETs, neither in employment nor in education or training (World Bank & Vienna Institute for International Economic Studies, 2019, p. 31), which is substantially higher than in the EU-28. Bosnia and Herzegovina is an exception within the broader region (the non-EU Balkan states) as the NEET rate is rather gender-balanced (Eurostat, 2019b, p. 46).

Given the high unemployment rates and precariousness in terms of uncertain and underpaid work, quite often accompanied by job-education mismatch, it is very hard for young people in Bosnia and Herzegovina to solve the housing problem. Additionally, rent prices are rather high and home ownership in many cases is almost an unattainable goal.

Getting a place to live at a certain age is mostly related to private circumstances: taking a loan, inheritance, parents' financial support, an extension of the family house (when possible), and others. Sarajevo Canton, as the most financially potent region, is at the forefront with respect to all kinds of programs that are directly or indirectly intended for youth. Subsidies for first-time homebuyers aged 18–35 is a popular measure, although not consistent, as it strongly depends on the budget.

INSTITUTIONAL FRAMEWORK

Although BiH is one of the countries with the lowest total fertility rate in Europe (1.26 in 2018 (FRED, 2020)), population policy is predominantly focused on the financial support to families with children. In that way, the complexity of the causes that lead to a continuous decrease in the natural increase is oversimplified and reduced to poverty. Emigration, general insecurity, distrust in institutions, lifestyle and unequal social position of women are just some of the causes that are not recognized or regulated as an important aspect of population policies of the states and entities.

The state regulates its population policy through the relevant laws, whereby, in relation to the specificity of BiH, the jurisdiction is divided among the entities and cantons. Population policy of Republika Srpska is regulated by the RS Law Child Protection (2017). In the Federation of BiH, population policy is regulated by the relevant Federation-level and, more specifically, cantonal laws, that cover the entire field of child protection.

What are the benefits and state support that young couples/families with children can get in BiH? The laws distinguish and treat differently the two groups of such couples/families: 1) those who are employed; and 2) those who are unemployed and are social protection support users. These rights differ with respect to the entity in which the families live (RS or Federation of BiH).

The universal benefits for child protection, according to the Law on Child Protection of Republika Srpska, which are not related to the financial status of the family or the health of the child, are:

- One-time financial aid for newborn supplies (125 €);
- Salary compensation during maternity leave;
- Pronatal one-time financial support for a third-born (€ 300) and a fourth-born child (€ 225).

The same universal rights of financial support to a family with a newborn child are guaranteed in the Federation of BiH, with the only difference that the allowances vary, depending on legislation and economic powers of different cantons.

In addition to the general ones, the RS Law on Child Protection defines *special, additional rights* within the population policy, which are related to the unfavorable financial status of the family and endangered health of the child. These rights also refer to additional, unfortunately insufficient, financial support to poor families and families of children with disabilities. At this point, it is important to point out the degree of poverty in which the family needs to live in order to exercise these rights, as well as the average amount of financial support. One of the preconditions is that the parents are beneficiaries of the social security system. The amount of financial support for the child allowance ranges from 9% to 18% of the lowest salary in Republika Srpska, depending on the birth order of the child. The main problem of such financial support to families relates to the allowance amount, which cannot provide satisfaction for the minimum life needs of one family.

In a similar way, but unequally, special rights for the protection of children from socially endangered families or children with health problems are defined in the Federation of BiH. In this part of the regulation of children's rights, a special problem is the unequally regulated scope of rights and the amount of benefits that depends on the legislation and economic power of individual cantons.

For example, the Institution of the Ombudsmen of BiH (*Report to the UN Committee on Economic, Cultural and Social Rights,* 2019) indicates that in two cantons of the Federation of BiH, compensation during maternity leave is not regulated at all. At the session in early 2019, the House of Representatives of the Federation Parliament approved and proposed the Draft Law on Support to Families with Children, which aims to harmonize the rights in the Federation of Bosnia and Herzegovina (ibid.) with the goal of equalizing their scope and the benefits.

In addition to the mentioned allowance rights, there are also in-kind benefits to support family planning and having kids. These are also defined at the entity level in the RS by the RS Law on Social Protection (2012) and at the level of individual cantons in the Federation of BiH. In any case, the responsibility for the implementation of intangible support services is taken over by the centers for social work, as central institutions of social protection in local communities. These services primarily focus on counseling and psychosocial support for young couples.

In an attempt to make significant improvements within the population policy, there are formal boards being established at the entity and cantonal levels with a special focus on supporting families in planning their reproductive functions. One such example is the formation of the RS Council for Demographic Policy (2012), which monitors demographic trends, deals with the causes of demographic change and once a year submits the proposed measures in form of final reports.

An estimated 15% of couples will have difficulty conceiving (UCLA Health, n.d.). In both entities of Bosnia and Herzegovina; there are programs of assisted reproduction, although they are not available under equal terms in all cantons of FBiH. In order to qualify for assisted reproductive technology treatment program covered by the entity (RS Health Insurance Fund) and some cantonal health insurance institutes (FBiH), specific eligibility criteria need to be met (couples undergoing infertility treatment, documented diagnosis, including medical examinations, upper age limit of childless women, etc.) (cf. Prlić, 2016).

COUNTRY-SPECIFIC CHALLENGES TO FAMILY FORMATION

A whole range of macro-level structural determinants could be accounted not only for delaying entry into parenthood but also for the very low fertility in Bosnia and Herzegovina. The chronic socio-economic crisis, which followed in the post-conflict and transitional BiH society, undoubtedly had an extremely discouraging effect on family formation or, in other words, the realization of fertility aspirations.

The seemingly positive trend of decreasing the percentage of individuals falling below the poverty line over the period 2004–2015 (from 18.3 to 16.9) could be attributed to a decline in the total population rather than an increase in economic prosperity (Šabanović, 2018).

Extended education, the prevailing low-paid, short-term and insecure jobs on the labor market (usually as an alternative to being unemployed), and lack of or no institutional support for balancing professional and parental responsibilities could be identified as the main reasons that influence decisions with regard to childbearing. The burden of opportunity cost still falls onto women during pregnancy and after giving birth, which implies that gender asymmetry in parenting and family life in the contemporary BiH society almost goes without saying. Policy response to unfavorable socio-economic conditions for family formation is poor as pronatalist measures are unharmonized between the entities and cantons, in addition to being inconsistent and inadequate. It should be emphasized that women employed in the public sector are in a much better position when it comes to keeping their jobs in case of pregnancy and enjoying all the rights pertaining to maternity leave.

In addition to other macro factors, the postponement of marriage and, consequently, transition into parenthood could also be attributed to continued education after the completion of secondary school. Education statistics show that feminization of higher education is evident as females have been more dominant for years in the student population.[6]

Due to credential inflation and mismatch between the formally achieved education (often without any supplementary skills) and actual requirements of the contemporary labor market in terms of specific human capital, the social position of youth is not satisfactory in general (cf. Papić & Fetahagić, 2019). In other words, school-to-work transition is burdened by many problems: low education quality, in particular at some private universities and colleges, spread of precarious work, inefficient companies with no recruitment potential for upcoming job-seekers (Halilbašić et al., 2015), and absence of adequate policies targeting the key issues.

One of the problems related to structural unemployment is specifically identified as "an absence of effective systems of higher education, vocational education and training (VET), and life-long learning that would provide young people and adults with the knowledge and skills needed to acquire good-quality jobs" (Obradović et al., 2019, p 11).

Attributable to unemployment or minimum wages linked to precariousness, the prolonged stay in the parents' home even after graduating is a common practice among a great portion of young adults, leading to "the latest late" pattern of transition to adulthood. Fleeing from the vicious cycle of poverty, unemployment, economic crisis, political instability in the country and personal insecurity, and the inability to afford to live independently, a significant number of young people have left the country (Council of Ministers of Bosnia and Herzegovina, Directorate for Economic Planning, 2018). Research findings from 2019 show that the socio-economic environment has taken over the primacy of influence over heightened desire to emigrate from the individual characteristics that dominated a decade earlier (2009) (Čičić et al., 2019, p. 71). The same study confirms that younger respondents were exhibiting stronger migration aspirations than their older counterparts (ibid.).

Young persons' closeness to members of their primary family can be understood in relation to the importance of family in a traditional, patriarchal BiH society, but also in relation to, in average, later social maturation of young people in BiH. In any case, financial dependence and insecurity, together with the intimately close ties of a young person with the members of his/her immediate and extended family, create a specific family formation in BiH society. In this society, a young person is considered 'a child' who is not expected to financially contribute to the household in which he/she lives, or to be independent in any way. Although, seemingly, everyone benefits from this situation, it can be viewed as a specific manifestation of the family crisis in the contemporary BiH society. In this way, young person's parents are exhausted in their role of family providers,

---

[6] Of the total number of the enrolled students at all years of study in the academic year 2019/20, 59 percent are females (BHAS, 2020b).

Socio-Economic Challenges to Family Formation in Bosnia and Herzegovina • **13**

and the young man or women is (temporarily) stopped in his or her development towards an independent, responsible and mature individual who is ready to form a new family unit.

CONCLUSION

In spite of strong family ties, paradoxically, Bosnia and Herzegovina is among those world countries that have been recording very low fertility (below 1.3 children per woman since 2002), which alone should be of great concern. This suggests that the social climate for starting a family or having more than one or two children is far from being favorable.

Young people in Bosnia and Herzegovina face a plethora of social risks including unemployment, precarious work, suboptimal educational standards, dissatisfaction leading to various psychological consequences, and other social problems (Bartlett, 2013). Additionally, gender-based discrimination/inequalities are still present in some spheres of society. All these adversities may be considered severe influencing factors on family formation among persons from their mid-20s. In light of such circumstances, outmigration often serves as a coping strategy for a significant percentage of young adults who have either left the country or have the intention to emigrate in the foreseeable future. These negative trends have been profoundly affecting the reproductive capacity of the society, and ultimately birth rates, causing more progressive population ageing, and a series of long-term disruptions to demographic structures. Since an efficient and comprehensive policy response is missing, familism is a sort of compensation for it, but impoverishment of many families in the transitional and post-conflict BiH society reduces their ability for more generous financial support to their adult offspring. Hence, systematic addressing of structural disadvantages related to starting a family needs to be placed at the top of the political agenda from local to state-level authorities, in order to avoid a very pessimistic (and at the same time realistic) future demographic scenario.

REFERENCES:

Aboim, S., & Vasconcelos, P. (2019). Reassessing (de)standardization: Life course trajectories across three generations. *Portuguese Journal of Social Science 18*(3), 299–318.

Agency for Development of Higher Education and Quality Assurance. (n.d.). *List of accredited higher education institutions*. http://hea.gov.ba/akreditacija_vsu/Default.aspx

Agency for Statistics of Bosnia and Herzegovina (BHAS). (2017). *Census: Households and families*.

Agency for Statistics of Bosnia and Herzegovina (BHAS). (2018). *Household Budget Survey 2015*. Thematic Bulletin 15.

Agency for Statistics of Bosnia and Herzegovina (BHAS). (2019). *Labour force survey 2019*: Thematic Bulletin 10.

14 • MIRZA EMIRHAFIZOVIĆ & ANDREA PUHALIĆ

Agency for Statistics of Bosnia and Herzegovina (BHAS). (2020a). *Demography 2019*: Thematic Bulletin 02.

Agency for Statistics of Bosnia and Herzegovina (BHAS). (2020b). *Demography and social statistics: Education statistics—Higher education in the school year 2019/2020* (First release). https://bhas.gov.ba/data/Publikacije/Saopstenja/2020/ EDU_05_2019_Y2_1_BS.pdf

Bartlett, W. (2013). *Analiza nedostataka u oblasti politika socijalne zaštite i inkluzije u Bosni i Hercegovini* [Analysis of flaws in politics of social protection and inclusion in Bosnia and Herzegovina]. UNICEF.

BiH Council of Ministers, Directorate for Economic Planning. (2018). *Bosna i Hercegovina: izvještaj o razvoju. Godišnji izvještaj 2017.* Vijeće Ministara BiH, Direkcija za ekonomsko planiranje. https://www.google.com/url?sa=t&rct=j&q=&esrc=s&so urce=web&cd=&cad=rja&uact=8&ved=2ahUKEwja1cjAk7DwAhVkxosKHVTfB QEQFjACegQIBBAD&url=http%3A%2F%2Fwww.dep.gov.ba%2Frazvojni_doku menti%2Fizvjestaji%2F%3Fid%3D2036&usg=AOvVaw2Jivciiw7gyojw69XJLec0

Billari, F. C., & Liefbroer, A. C. (2010). Towards a new pattern of transition to adulthood? *Advances in Life Course Research, 15*(2–3), 59–75. https://doi.org/10.1016/j. alcr.2010.10.003

Čičić, M., Trifković, M., Husić-Mehmedović, M., Efendić, A., Turulja, L., & Emirhafizović, M. (2019). *Emigration study Bosnia and Herzegovina. Special editions* (Volume CLXXXII). Academy of Sciences and Arts of Bosnia and Herzegovina.

Council of Ministers of Bosnia and Herzegovina, Directorate for Economic Planning. (2018). *Bosna i Hercegovina: izjveštaj o razvoju. Godišnji izvještaj 2017* [Bosnia and Herzegovina: development report. Annual report 2017]. Vijeće Ministara BiH, Direkcija za ekonomsko planiranje. https://www.google.com/url?sa=t&rct=j &q=&esrc=s&source=web&cd=&cad=rja&uact=8&ved=2ahUKEwja1cjAk7Dw AhVkxosKHVTfBQEQFjACegQIBBAD&url=http%3A%2F%2Fwww.dep.gov. ba%2Frazvojni_dokumenti%2Fizvjestaji%2F%3Fid%3D2036&usg=AOvVaw2Jiv ciiw7gyojw69XJLec0

Đugum, A. (2019, October 8). Sva lica nezaposlenosti u BiH [All the faces of unemployment in Bosnia and Herzegovina (BiH)]. *Radio free Europe* [Radio Slobodna Evropa]. https://www.slobodnaevropa.org/a/nezaposlenost-bih-bijeda-siromast-vo/30206122.html

Elzinga, C. H., & Liefbroer, A. C. (2007). De-standardization of family-life trajectories of young adults: A cross-national comparison using sequence analysis. *Eur J Population, 23*, 225–250. https://doi.org/10.1007/s10680-007-9133-7

Emirhafizović, M. (2018). Kad demografska zima zakuca na vrata: Denatalitet i prirodna depopulacija u Bosni i Hercegovini [When demographic winter knocks the door: Natural decrease and depopulation in Bosnia and Herzegovina]. *Context: Journal of Interdisciplinary Studies, 5*(1), 7–24.

Emirhafizović, M., & Zolić, H. (2010). *Strategy for Reduction of Negative Demographic Trends in the Sarajevo Canton.* Unpublished raw data.

Eurostat. (2019a). *Enlargement countries—Statistics on migration, residence permits, citizenship and asylum.* https://ec.europa.eu/eurostat/statistics-explained/index. php?title=Enlargement_countries_-_statistics_on_migration,_residence_permits,_ citizenship_and_asylum

Socio-Economic Challenges to Family Formation in Bosnia and Herzegovina • 15

Eurostat. (2019b). *Key figures on enlargement countries—2019 edition.* Retrieved December 12, 2019, from: https://ec.europa.eu/eurostat/documents/3217494/9799207/KS-GO-19-001-EN-N.pdf/e8fbd16c-c342-41f7-aaed-6ca38e6f709e

Eurostat. (2020). *Enlargement countries—Education statistics.* https://ec.europa.eu/eurostat/statistics-explained/index.php?title=Enlargement_countries_-_education_statistics#Early_leavers_from_education_and_training

Flere. S. (2015). Youth and family in south east Europe. In K. Hurrelmann & M. Weichert (Eds.), *Lost in democratic transition? Political challenges and perspectives for young people in south east Europe: Results of representative surveys in eight countries.* Friedrich Ebert Stiftung Regional Dialogue SEE.

Frątczak. E. (2004, February 20–21). *Family and fertility in Poland: Changes during the transition period* [Paper presentation]. The PIE International Workshop on Demographic Changes and Labor Markets in Transition Economies, Tokyo, Japan. https://www.ier.hit-u.ac.jp/pie/stage1/Japanese/seminar/workshop040220/Fratczak.pdf

Halilibašić, M., Domljan, V., Oruč, N., & Balavac, M. (2015). *Dijagnoza tržišta rada* [Labor market diagnosis]. Ekonomski institut Sarajevo.

Institute of Statistics of the Federation of BiH (FZS). (2014). *Statistical yearbook.* https://docs.google.com/gview?url=http://fzs.ba/wp-content/uploads/2016/06/SG2014.pdf

Institute of Statistics of the Federation of BiH (FZS). (2019). *Demographics.* https://docs.google.com/gview?url=http://fzs.ba/wp-content/uploads/2020/06/DEMOGRAFSKA-STATISTIKA-2019-SB-307.pdf

Institution of the Human Rights Ombudsman of Bosnia and Herzegovina. (2019, July 22). *Report to the Committee on Economic, Social And Cultural Rights* (CESCR). https://www.ombudsmen.gov.ba/documents/obmudsmen_doc2019072211565148eng.pdf

Khare, S., Ronnås, P., & Shamchiyeva, L. (2010). *Towards the European Union—Key problems of social inclusion in Bosnia and Herzegovina (BiH).* International Labour Office. https://www.ilo.org/wcmsp5/groups/public/ed_emp/documents/publication/wcms_144424.pdf

Kolenović Đapo, J., & Brkić Šmigoc, J. (2020). *Values in Bosnia and Herzegovina: Overview of the main findings of the 2019 European values study.* Friedrich Ebert Stiftung.

Ministry of Civil Affairs of Bosnia and Herzegovina (Commission for the coordination of YOUTH ISSUES in Bosnia and Herzegovina). (n.d.). *Data on youths in Bosnia and Herzegovina* (BiH). http://www.mladi.gov.ba/index.php?option=com_content&task=%20view&id=46&lang=en

Ministry of Security of Bosnia and Herzegovina (Sector for Immigration). (2020). *Bosnia and Herzegovina: Migration profile for the year 2019.* Ministry of Security of Bosnia and Herzegovina. https://msb.gov.ba/PDF/220720202.pdf

Obradović, N., Jusić, M., & Oruč, N. (2019). *ESPN thematic report on in-work poverty—Bosnia and Herzegovina.* European Social Policy Network (ESPN). European Commission. file:///C:/Users/User/AppData/Local/Temp/ESPN_BA_TR1_2018-19%20on%20in-work%20poverty_final.pdf

Papić, Ž., & Fetahagić. M (2019). *Prema Evropskoj Uniji-Ključni problemi socijalnog uključivanja u BiH* [Towards the European Union—Key problems of social inclusion in Bosnia and Herzegovina (BiH)]. Fondacija za socijalno uključivanje u Bosni i Hercegovini. https://www.ibhi.ba/Documents/Publikacije/2019/Prvi_policy_papir_finalna_verzija.pdf

16 • MIRZA EMIRHAFIZOVIĆ & ANDREA PUHALIĆ

Prlić, L. (2016). *Zakon o liječenju neplodnosti biomedicinski potpomognutom oplodnjom u Bosni i Hercegovini* [Treatment of infertility by biomedical assisted fertilization in Bosnia and Herzegovina]. Forum lijeve inicijative. Olaf Palme International Center.

Republic Institute of Statistics of SR Bosnia and Herzegovina. (1991). *Statistical yearbook of Socialist Republic of Bosnia and Herzegovina.* Republički zavod za statistiku.

Republic Institute of Statistics RS. (2016). *Demographic statistics.* Statistical Bulletin no. 9.

Republic Institute of Statistics RS. (2019). *Statistički godišnjak 2019* [Statistical yearbook of Republika Srpska 2019.]. https://www.rzs.rs.ba/static/uploads/bilteni/godisnjak/2019/05stn_2019.pdf Preuzeto: Novembar, 2020.

RS Institute of Statistics. (2020). *Demographic statistics.* Statistical Bulletin. https://www.rzs.rs.ba/static/uploads/bilteni/stanovnistvo/BiltenDemografskaStatistika_2020_WEB.pdf

RS Law on Child Protection 2012 (BiH). Službeni glasnik Republike Srpske, br. 37/2012.

RS Law on Child Protection 2017 (BiH). Službeni glasnik Republike Srpske, br. 114/17.

Šabanović, E. (2018, January 19). *Poverty in Bosnia and Herzegovina—Basic facts.* https://www.elval.org/en/siromastvo-u-bosni-i-hercegovini-osnovne-cinjenice/

Sobotka, T., Zeman, K., Di Lego, V., Goujon, A. , Hammer, B., Loichinger, E., Sauerberg, M., & Luy, M. (2018). *European demographic data sheet 2018.* Wittgenstein Centre (IIASA, VID/OEAW, WU). http://edds2018.populationeurope.org/download/files/eds2018_key_findings.pdf

Turčilo, L., Osmić, A., Kapidžić, D., Šadić, S., Žiga, J.., & i Dudić, A. (2019). *Studija o mladima- Bosna i Hercegovina 2018–2019* [Youth Study Bosnia and Herzegovina 2018/2019]. Friedrich-Ebert-Stiftung.

UCLA Health (n.d.). *Infertility: Symptoms, Treatment, Diagnosis.* https://www.uclahealth.org/obgyn/infertility

UNDP & The World Bank. (2018). *Roma at a glance: Bosnia and Herzegovina* [Factsheet]. https://www.eurasia.undp.org/content/rbec/en/home/library/roma/regional-roma-survey-2017-country-fact-sheets.html

UNICEF. (2016). *Glasovi mladih: Istraživanje o mladima u BiH* [Voices of youth—Research into youth in BiH]. Prism Research & Consulting.

United Nations (UN). (2015). *World fertility patterns 2015: Data booklet.* https://digitallibrary. un.org/record/826484

United Nations Development Programme (UNDP). (2013). *Rural development in Bosnia and Herzegovina: Myth and reality.* National Human Development Report. http://hdr.undp.org/sites/default/files/nhdr_en_web_30102013.pdf

World Bank & The Vienna Institute for International Economic Studies. (2019). *Western Balkans labor market trends 2019.* Retrieved 5, March 2021 from https://documents1.worldbank.org/curated/en/351461552915471917/pdf/135370-Western-Balkans-Labor-Market-Trends-2019.pdf

Žiga, J., Turčilo, L., Osmić, A., Bašić, S., Džananović Miraščija, N., Kapidžić, D., & Brkić Šmigoc, J. (2015). *Youth study Bosnia and Herzegovina.* Friedrich Ebert Stiftung.

CHAPTER 2

FAMILY FORMATION IN CHANGING ECONOMIC AND SOCIETAL CONDITIONS IN THE CZECH REPUBLIC

Vera Kucharova

Research Institute of Labour and Social Affairs, Prague

1. NATIONAL CONTEXT

The Czech Republic (former Czechoslovakia), along with several other Central European countries, experienced turbulent post-war development, which can be summarized as the road from capitalism through the totalitarian version of socialism and back to capitalism. Each of these stages influenced the form of social organization both at the macro and micro levels and, naturally, included a formative influence on the setting of family relationships.

The first stage commenced with the end of the Nazi totalitarian regime which first instilled in the society the necessity for schizophrenic behavior via a strict separation of life within and outside the family; a fully subordinating ruling regime. This first stage of the post-war period, which provided a welcome "breath"

Family Formation Among Youth in Europe: Coping With Socio-Economic Disadvantages,
pages 17–38.
Copyright © 2022 by Information Age Publishing
www.infoagepub.com
All rights of reproduction in any form reserved.

of freedom was, however, destined to last a mere three years and ended in the February 1948 coup that ushered in a further period of, this time communist, totalitarianism.

For the next 20 years, despite some minor deviations from the basic totalitarian format, the schizophrenia referred to above returned to the society. During this time, however, a new generation emerged that exhibited dual behavior, one at home and the other for the public face involving the adoption of certain standards and norms. Exceeding these norms posed a serious threat to day-to-day career, study, and lifestyle choices.

It should be added that the regime managed to maintain this situation relatively well, compared to other so-called "peoples' democracies", through relatively successful economic development and responsive social policies. However, the absence of market mechanisms resulted in the relaxation of both the work ethics and pressure to perform well at work and, at the same time, supported the development of the black economy, which suited certain groups in society. Most of the society became accustomed to the fact that one's political views played a more important role than knowledge that certain goods were rarely available in the shops, or that people were not allowed to travel abroad.

However, 20 years later, it appeared that the system had exhausted itself. The so-called Prague Spring of 1968 was accompanied by an unprecedented surge in civic initiatives and an easing of political and economic pressures that promised the end of totalitarianism. For a short time, society breathed freedom once more; suddenly it was possible to express oneself freely and to travel abroad and finally see for oneself what it looked like "out there". This euphoria, however, ended suddenly with the invasion of the Soviet Bloc forces in August 1968.

The so-called "normalization" period commenced in the beginning of the 1970s, i.e., the enforced return to the totalitarian system. Although it did not lead to political executions, as in the early 1950s, people were once again forced from their employment positions and studies for political reasons and, again, it was dangerous to express one's views in public.

In the 1970s (as since the 1950s), the private family life was mostly a sort of shelter, a sphere of relative freedom which strengthened intergenerational and intra-generational relations. The marriage rate was rather high (only 6% of men and 3% of women remained single their whole life), the average age of marriage was low (men 25, women 22 years old at first marriage) as well as the average age of childbirth (the average age at first birth was about 22 years) (CZSO, 2007).

The period of "normalization", however, ended in the memorable year of 1989 and with it ended the whole tragic attempt to build the so-called socialism. Apart from the short 3-year period between 1945 and 1948 and less than two years between 1968 and 1969, the society was now provided with an opportunity to develop freely for the first time since 1938. However, it has to be taken into account that the totalitarian period influenced a number of generations that were forced to adapt to sudden changes in circumstances and to raise their children accordingly, and that such habits were, naturally, very difficult to break. The generation born after 1990, therefore, was the first generation not to experience (and hopefully will never experience) totalitarianism in whatever form. Thus, this generation is the first that can bring up their children without the burden of totalitarian thinking; the question is, however, what thinking they will replace it with based on their own experiences.

The return to capitalism was generally welcomed. People were provided with the opportunity not only to express themselves freely, but also to engage in private business activities, travel and study—experiences they have been denied for decades. However, it is now evident that for various reasons not everybody has a comparable opportunity to make use of these changes. At the same time, with freedom came responsibility, which was previously largely assumed by the state. It soon became clear that the absence of responsibility for one's own actions was one of the most important legacies of the totalitarian period. Even today, there are social groups that automatically seek assistance from the state where they might be expected to rely on their own initiative. The Czech society is currently polarized both politically and economically. Certain social groups seem to be unable to accept the changes brought about by globalization and the advent of a knowledge and performance-based economy. Whether the causes are objective or subjective in nature, it is important that the state (which is no longer lacking in resources as it was in the past) be prepared to provide care for these social groups.

2. DEMOGRAPHIC TRENDS RELEVANT TO FAMILY FORMATION

The average population of the Czech Republic increased for the seventh consecutive year in 2018 to 10,690 thousand (as of 31 December 2019; CZSO, 2020b). Immigration made a significant contribution to the population increase, even though the increase in immigration per 1,000 inhabitants declined between 2007 and 2018 (from 8.1 to 3.6) due to a slowing down of the increase in the domestic population per 1,000 inhabitants from 1.0 to 0.1 (ibid.)[1]. Between 2008 and 2018, the average age of the population increased by 2.0 years and the median age by 3.4 years. As of 31 December 2018, for every 100 persons aged 20 to 64 there were 66 persons aged 0 to 19 and 65 years and over (ibid.). The value of this so-called index of economic dependence has been gradually increasing over the last ten years. The population of the Czech Republic is highly homogeneous. According to the 2001 census, 94% of the population were of Czech nationality. According to the 2011 census, 69% of the population claimed Czech nationality, with 25% of the population declining to answer the voluntary question on nationality (CZSO, 2014).

---

[1] Both indicators decreased up to 2013—the year in which they were negative. They subsequently increased until last year, whereupon there was again a year-on-year decrease in the domestic population.

TABLE 2.1. Selected Demographical Data

	2007	2008	2009	2010	2011	2012	2013	2014	2015	2016	2017	2018	2019	2020
Population, 31 December (thousands)	10,381	10,468	10,507	10,533	10,505	10,516	10,512	10,538	10,554	10,579	10,610	10,650	10,694	10,702
Age (%):														
0–14	14.2	14.1	14.2	14.4	14.7	14.8	15.0	15.2	15.4	15.6	15.7	15.9	16.0	16.1
15–64	71.2	71.0	70.6	70.1	69.1	68.4	67.6	67.0	66.3	65.6	65.0	64.5	64.1	63.8
65 and more	14.6	14.9	15.2	15.5	16.2	16.8	17.4	17.8	18.3	18.8	19.2	19.6	19.9	20.2
Aging index (65+ / 0–14 v %)	102.4	105.1	107.0	107.8	110.4	113.3	115.7	117.4	119.0	120.7	122.1	123.2	124.6	125.5
According to Marital Status (v %):														
Single	38.8	39.2	39.6	40.0	40.2	40.6	40.9	41.3	41.6	41.9	42.1	42.4	42.6	43.1
Married	44.2	43.8	43.3	42.7	42.0	41.5	41.0	40.5	40.1	39.8	39.5	39.3	39.1	38.7
Divorced	9.7	9.8	10.0	10.2	10.5	10.7	10.9	11.1	11.2	11.3	11.4	11.4	11.5	11.5
Widowed	7.3	7.2	7.1	7.1	7.3	7.2	7.2	7.1	7.1	7.0	7.0	6.9	6.9	6.8
Marriages	57,157	52,457	47,862	46,746	45,137	45,206	43,499	45,575	48,191	50,768	52,567	54,470	54,870	45,415
Mean Age of Single Bridegrooms	31.2	31.4	32.0	32.2	32.2	32.3	32.3	32.3	32.4	32.2	32.2	32.2	32.1	—
Mean Age of Single Brides	28.6	28.8	29.2	29.4	29.6	29.6	29.8	29.8	29.8	29.9	29.8	29.8	29.8	—
Marriages per 1,000 Inhabitants of Mid-Year Population	5.5	5.0	4.6	4.4	4.3	4.3	4.1	4.3	4.6	4.8	5.0	5.1	5.1	5.2
Divorces														
Mean duration of marriage at divorce (years)	12.3	12.3	12.5	12.7	12.9	12.8	13.0	13.1	13.0	13.1	13.2	13.4	13.5	—

Share of divorced partners with minor children (%)														
	59.1	58.1	57.8	57.3	56.3	57.5	57.1	56.8	57.5	58.9	59.0	58.4	59.0	58.5
Total divorce rate (%)	48.7	49.6	46.8	50.0	46.2	44.5	47.8	46.7	46.5	45.2	47.2	44.8	44.8	—
Divorces per 1,000 inhabitants of mid-year population														
	3.0	3.0	2.8	2.9	2.7	2.5	2.7	2.5	2.5	2.4	2.4	2.3	2.3	2.0

Births

Live Births	114,632	119,570	118,348	117,153	108,673	108,576	106,751	109,860	110,764	112,663	114,405	114,036	112,231	110,200
Outside Marriage	39,537	43,457	45,954	47,164	45,421	47,088	48,000	51,267	52,976	54,733	56,091	55,338	54,093	4,781
Outside Marriage (%)	34.5	36.3	38.8	40.3	41.8	43.4	45.0	46.7	47.8	48.6	49.0	48.5	48.2	48.5

Live Births by Age of mother:

Up to 19 Years	3,534	3,610	3,614	3,356	3,073	3,063	2,825	2,734	2,619	2,637	2,653	2,443	2,283	2,178
More Than 40 Years	1,670	1,889	1,987	2,100	2,220	2,442	2,769	3,075	3,683	3,949	4,273	4,701	4,767	4,781
Mean Age of Mothers at Childbirth														
	29.1	29.3	29.4	29.6	29.7	29.8	29.9	29.9	30.0	30.0	30.0	30.1	30.2	—
Mean Age of Mothers at Childbirth—1st Child														
	27.1	27.3	27.4	27.6	27.8	27.9	28.1	28.1	28.2	28.2	28.2	28.4	28.5	—
Total Fertility Rate	1.438	1.497	1.492	1.493	1.427	1.452	1.456	1.528	1.570	1.630	1.687	1.708	1.709	—
Live Births per 1,000 Inhabitants of Mid-Year Population														
	11.1	11.5	11.3	11.1	10.4	10.3	10.2	10.4	10.5	10.7	10.8	10.7	10.5	10.3
Abortions	40,917	41,446	40,528	39,273	38,864	37,733	37,443	36,956	35,761	35,921	35,012	32,952	31,797	30,368

(continues)

TABLE 2.1. Continued

	2007	2008	2009	2010	2011	2012	2013	2014	2015	2016	2017	2018	2019	2020
Induced Abortions	25,414	25,760	24,636	23,998	24,055	23,032	22,542	21,893	20,403	20,406	19,415	18,298	17,757	16,886
Total Abortion Rate	0.54	0.54	0.53	0,51	0.52	0.51	0.52	0,51	0.51	0.51	0.51	0.50	0.48	-
Abortions per 1,000 Inhabitants of Mid-Year Population														
	4.0	4.0	3.9	3.7	3.7	3.6	3.6	3.5	3.4	3.4	3.3	3.1	3.0	2.8
Induced Abortions per 1,000 Inhabitants of mid-Year Population														
	2.5	2.5	2.3	2.3	2.3	2.2	2.1	2.1	1.9	1.9	1.8	1.7	1.7	1.6
Deaths	104,636	104,948	107,421	106,844	106,848	108,189	109,160	105,665	111,173	107,750	111,443	112,920	112,362	129,289
Deaths per 1,000 inhabitants of mid-year population														
	10.1	10.1	10.2	10.2	10.2	10.3	10.4	10.0	10.5	10.2	10.5	10.6	10.5	12.1
Infant Mortality	3.1	2.8	2.9	2.7	2.7	2.6	2.5	2.4	2.5	2.8	2.7	2.6	2.6	2.3
Neonatal Mortality	2.1	1.8	1.6	1.7	1.7	1.6	1.4	1.6	1.5	1.7	1.8	1.6	1.6	1.6
Migration														
Net Migration	83,945	71,790	28,344	15,648	16,889	10,293	−1,297	21,661	15,977	20,064	28,273	3, 629	44,270	26,927
Net Migration per 1,000 Inhabitants of Mid-Year Population														
	8.1	6.9	2.7	1.5	1.6	1.0	−0.1	2.1	1.5	1.9	2.7	3.6	4.1	2.5
Natural Increase	9,996	14,622	10,927	10,309	1,825	387	−2,409	4,195	−409	4,913	2,962	1,116	−131	−19,089
Natural Increase per 1,000 Inhabitants of Mid-Year Population														
	1.0	1.4	1.0	1.0	0.2	0.0	−0.2	0.4	−0.0	0.5	0.3	0.1	−0.0	−1.8
Total Population Growth	93,941	86,412	39,271	25,957	18,714	10,680	−3,706	25,856	15,568	24,977	31,235	39,745	44,139	7,838
Total Population Growth per 1,000 Inhabitants of Mid-Year Population														
	9.1	8.3	3.7	2.5	1.8	1.0	−0.4	2.5	1.5	2.4	2.9	3.7	4.1	0.7

Source: Czech Statistical Office. Česká republika od roku 1989 v číslech - aktualizováno 12.12.2019. (Czech Republic in Numbers since 1989—updated May, 14. 2021). https://www.czso.cz/csu/czso/ceska-republika-od-roku-1989-v-cislech-aktualizovano-1452021

Long-term changes in the population structure according to marital status continued in the period 2007–2018 (CZSO 2020b, d). With respect to the population aged over 15, while the number and share of single and divorced persons is on the increase, the number of married and widowed persons is decreasing, both absolutely and relatively.[2]

Marriage Rates

The decreasing marriage rate trend dating back to 2007 bottomed out in 2013 (when a historical minimum of marriages was recorded) and the number of newly-formed marriages has been increasing steadily for the last 5 years (CZSO, 2020d), by 26% in 2013–2019 (CZSO, 2020b). The year-on-year increase in 2018 was 3.6% (0.7% in 2019) to 54,870 marriages, the highest number since 2007 (CZSO, 2018, 2020d). The number of marriages of both single and divorced persons is increasing as is, to a lesser extent, the number of widowed persons remarrying. Moreover, the marriage rate is continuously increasing.[3]

The average age of marriage of single persons has stagnated at 32.2 years for men and 29.8 years for women (CZSO, 2020b), and more than half of those who marry are aged between 25 and 34 (i.e., 50.7% of men and 56.2% of women in 2018). In terms of five-year age groups (CZSO, 2019b), while men in the 25–29 group predominated in 2008, the 30–34 age group has predominated since 2009. In the case of women, the 25–29 age group has predominated for the last 10 years and in 2018 it accounted for 33.5% of all brides. The age structure of those who marry has changed over time; the number of persons aged 35 and over is increasing and the number aged 25 years and under is decreasing (ibid.) (in line with the development of population age structure in general).

Birth Rate

The total fertility rate (TFR) increased for the seventh consecutive year (up to 2018) (CZSO, 2020b). In 2008, the TFR stood at 1.50 children; this was followed by a period of stagnation and in 2011, it even decreased to 1.43. In 2018, it increased to 1.71 children per woman. The same figure was last recorded in 1992, with a higher figure recorded for the previous year (ibid.). The net reproduction rate developed in a similar way, i.e., 0.724 in 2008 followed by a decrease to 0.689 in 2011, and an increase to 0.829 girls born per woman in 2018 (CZSO, 2018). Positive developments were recorded concerning the total induced abortion rate (which decreased to 0.28 children) (CZSO, 2019b) and the infant mortality rate (which decreased to 2.6 per 1,000 live births) (ibid.).

---

[2] Over the past decade the number of single persons has increased by 3 percentage points, while those living in a married relationship has decreased by 4 percentage points (CZSO 2020b).

[3] Should the 2018 marriage rate persist, 59% of men and 67% of women will enter their first marriage before the age of 50, and 45% of divorced men and 43% of divorced women will remarry (Křesťanová, Kurkin, 2019, p. 194).

24 • VERA KUCHAROVA

The time of the decline in the TFR between 2008 and 2011 saw a decrease particularly in the fertility rate of women aged 20–30 (CZSO, 2018). With the exception of 2009, women aged 30 have consistently registered the maximum fertility rate, the level of which has not changed significantly, i.e., there were 124.6 live births per 1,000 women in 2008 and 128.4 ten years later (ibid.).

The average age of mothers at childbirth increased slightly to 30.1 years in 2018 (after two years of stagnation at 30.0 years) and the average age at first birth to 28.4 years (CZSO, 2019b).

Over the last decade, the highest number of live births was recorded in 2008 (119,570) followed by a decline until 2013 (to 106,751) (ibid.). Conversely, the period 2014 to 2017 witnessed a continuous year-on-year increase until 2018 which saw a decline in the birth rate. The number of live births in 2018 was 5,500 less than in 2008, due mainly to a decrease in the number of women of reproductive age.

Whereas, traditionally, the majority of mothers have been married women, their predominance has been decreasing over the long term (CZSO, 2018). While in 2008 the proportion of married mothers was 63.7%, it had fallen to just 51.5% in 2018. The second largest group consists of single mothers. The proportion of live births to single mothers was 43.8%, while in 2008 it was only 29.7%. The number of live births to unmarried women has increased with respect to all birth orders over the last 10 years, with the highest relative increase concerning second births (by 45.1%) (ibid.).

One of the most important influences in terms of children born to unmarried women concerns the mother's educational attainment over the last ten years. The higher the educational attainment, the lower the incidence of births out of wedlock (ibid.). A further important determinant of differentiation in the proportion of children born out of wedlock relates to the age of the mother. The highest value of this indicator traditionally concerns women under 19 years of age (93.6% in 2018) and is significantly lower for older age groups (55.6% for women aged 20–29 and 41.0% for those aged 30–39 years) (ibid.).

Households

The only reliable source of data on the number and structure of households and families is the census, which is usually conducted every ten years (the last one in 2011). Two-parent families live in more than three-fifths of all private households,[4] one-parent families live in one-tenth of them, the rest live predominantly in one-person households (SILC-EU 2019 data, in: CZSO, 2020c). Almost one fifth of two-parent families take the form of unmarried cohabitation (OECD, 2020). The majority of persons younger than 20 with children live as single parents (80%), while with respect to older persons the two-parent family

---

[4] Private households accounted for about 80% of all households; the remaining 20% consisted mainly of single person households.

Family Formation in the Czech Republic • 25

TABLE 2.2. Development of the Structure of Private Households

	2007	2011	2012	2013	2014	2015	2016	2017	2018	1019
Number of households (thousands)	4,043	4,181	4,255	4,282	4,304	4,325	4,348	4,372	4,395	4,453
Structure of Households (%)										
Two-parent families	64.1	63.9	60.4	60.3	60.3	60.7	61.2	61.5	61.1	60.3
One-parent families	11.2	11.4	11.5	11.0	10.9	10.3	9.4	9.4	9.2	9.1
Non-family households	0.9	1.0	0.9	0.9	1.0	1.1	1.0	0.8	0.9	0.8
Individuals	23.8	23.7	27.2	27.8	27.9	27.9	28.4	28.3	28.7	29.8
Total	100	100	100	100	100	100	100	100	100	100
Households With Dependent Children (%)										
Two-parent families	84.2	83.3	82.5	83.7	82.7	83.4	84.9	85.1	84.8	-
One-parent families	15.7	16.3	17.0	15.9	16.9	16.0	14.6	14.5	14.8	-
Non-family households	0.1	0.4	0.4	0.4	0.4	0.6	0.5	0.4	0.4	-
Total	100	100	100	100	100	100	100	100	100	-

Definition of private households: A private household is a set of persons who share a dwelling and basic expenditure (on nutrition, household operation, maintenance of the dwelling, etc.).
Source: CZSO. Focus on Women and Men—2020. Czech Statistical Office. https://www.czso.cz/csu/czso/focus-on-women-and-men-2020

26 • VERA KUCHAROVA

model prevails, i.e., 56% of cases in the 20–24 age group and 75% in the 25–29 age group. More young women live with their children without a partner than men do. Whereas in recent years, the share of unmarried cohabitation is known to have increased, no accurate data is available. This form of household in the Czech Republic is more common with respect to younger and less educated persons and those living in larger cities.

Approximately 15% of all private households consist of extended families, most often families with one child or, conversely, families with four or more children (CZSO, 2020c).

Migration

The number of immigrants arriving in the Czech Republic reached 58,100 in 2018 (CZSO, 2018). The number of immigrants has been increasing since 2015 (by 66%). The most recent year in which more immigrants were recorded than in 2018 was 2008 (77,800). Concerning emigrants in the period 2008–2018, the highest number of them was registered in 2013 (30,900) and the lowest in 2011 (5,700) and 2008 (6,000)[5] (CZSO, 2019b).

In 2018, the population growth resulting from foreign immigration was 38,600, the highest increase since 2008 (71,800) (ibid.). Over the last 10 years, only in 2013 did the immigration/emigration balance show a negative value (–1,297) (ibid.). The volume of foreign migration (the sum of the number of immigrants and emigrants) stood at 77,700 in 2018, the highest value since 2009 (ibid.).

The proportion of men in the total number of immigrants was bigger than that of women in the entire period, 59.5% in 2018 (CZSO, 2018). Intensity of immigration decreased during the last ten years in all age groups, namely in the group of people aged 19–24. The share of children aged 0–14 decreased between 2008 and 2018 to 9.3% (ibid.).

3. NORMATIVE FRAMEWORK

The Czech society is generally very liberal with respect to partnerships, marriage and parenthood. Moreover, it is also tolerant of various non-traditional forms of cohabitation and family behavior, including divorce. While persons with higher levels of education are more liberal in their attitudes, they tend to behave relatively conservatively in their own lives, i.e., they are more likely to marry and have lower incidence of children born outside marriage.

Gender equality has ceased to be perceived as an ideological tool employed by the communist regime, and Western feminist approaches now exert the biggest influence in this respect. They were supported by NGOs and, with a short delay, reflected in the state family policy. The gender pay gap and the employment gap

---

[5] Due to differences in the data sources in 2008–2011 and after 2011, the data may not be fully comparable.

Family Formation in the Czech Republic • **27**

as phenomena are currently being subjected to intense discussion (Vohlídalová, 2017), as well as reconciling family, private life and employment. While gender equality is supported in both the public and private spheres (CVVM, 2020a), especially among younger people, it does not always translate into the real division of work and family responsibilities.

The importance of marriage and the understanding of partnership in the Czech population are changing (CVVM, 2020b). While the high perceived value of family persists, its form is gradually being modified. Although the value of family has traditionally been supported by all socio-demographic groups in the population, marriage is no longer seen as an imperative by younger generations. Today, it is not expected that children be born only to married couples, and the planned motherhood of single mothers is generally accepted; moreover, the degree of tolerance for raising children by same-sex couples is on the increase. Conversely, with respect to the role of marriage as a guarantee of enhanced economic security, marriage continues to be seen in a positive light (ibid.).

While the family as an intimate domain retains its autonomy to some extent, family cohesion is becoming increasingly relaxed due to the influence of trends towards individualization. As a result of the adoption of some functions of the family by other institutions, people are attaching greater importance to social support for the family. All these changes are exerting a significant impact on family formation (the starting and stability of a family, mother's age at first birth, (in) dependence of young people on the family of orientation, lifelong childlessness). The preferred, ideal and real life-start age is increasing, i.e., the age at the start of economic activity and parenthood. The declared ideal maternal age at first birth has increased by around four years over the last ten years and is now approaching thirty years of age (mothers 25–29, fathers 30 or more) (ibid.). Most Czechs continue to regard the two-child family as the ideal (ibid.).

The level of tolerance for "alternative" forms of family life is high in the Czech Republic. Unmarried cohabitation, with respect to both young couples and older divorced or widowed persons, is perceived as a form of habitation equivalent to marriage. This is supported by legislation that ensures equal rights for children of parents of all marital statuses and forms of cohabitation. The share of non-cohabitation partnerships is increasing and a number of alternative forms of relationship are emerging.

Abortion is generally well tolerated, perhaps partly due to its dramatic decline after 1989, which was due primarily to the widespread availability of previously difficult to obtain quality contraception. At present, the right of women to free choice is supported by almost 70% of the population (the proportion has remained unchanged since 2010) (CVVM, 2019b). This view is supported particularly by young people and by women.

28 • VERA KUCHAROVA

4. SOCIO-ECONOMIC CONDITIONS

Education

About 290 thousand students studied at 64 private and public universities in the Czech Republic in 2018 (CZSO, 2019e). The number of students at Czech universities increased steadily up to 2010, since when the number has been decreasing every year. The decrease (of almost one third compared to 2010) relates principally to bachelor study programs (bachelor degree students make up 58% of all university students). Doctorate students constitute 7.4% of all university students (ibid.). Women account for more than half of university students (56%) and graduates (60%) (CZSO, 2019f). Every seventh university student is a foreigner.

The number of secondary schools, classes and pupils has also decreased over the last 10 years (CZSO, 2019e). A total of 421,000 students attended secondary schools in the 2018/19 academic year, i.e., 143,500 fewer than in 2008/09, the reason for which consisted of a significant decline in the birth rate in the 1990s. The proportion of the so-called early-school leavers is more or less stable in the population and can be differentiated on a regional basis (Chamoutová, Kleňha et al., 2019, p. 75). While in those regions with the highest levels of education, especially Prague and Central Bohemia, this group is marginal (2% of students), in the region with the lowest level of education (Northwest Bohemia) this group constitutes 10% of all secondary school students.

Labor Market

Whereas in 2004 the Czech economy was in a state of economic recession, with a general unemployment rate (ILO definition) in excess of 8%, the unemployment rate at the end of 2018 stood at just 2.2% with a continuing downward trend (CZSO, 2020b). Between these two extremes, economic growth peaked in 2008, at which time the unemployment rate stood at 4.4%. The Czech Republic has witnessed economic growth and an associated decline in unemployment since 2014.

In addition to the current, apparently temporary, shortage of labor, the basic problem facing the Czech labor market consists of its regional imbalance (ibid.). Alongside regions with a permanently low unemployment rate (Prague and Central and Eastern Bohemia), a number of regions are struggling with three-fold or even higher rates (Northwest Bohemia and North Moravia). The difference is primarily due to the historical predominance of heavy industry and the corresponding educational structure of the labor force in these regions. A further important problem facing the Czech labor market consists of the large intergenerational differences in the educational structure of the workforce. While, with respect to older generations, the proportion of those with tertiary education is less than 20%, the proportion of the youngest generation with this level of education is roughly twofold (CZSO, 2019c). Individual generations are thus presented with different opportunities in the labor market, which is increasingly requiring a skilled labor

Family Formation in the Czech Republic • **29**

TABLE 2.3. Basic Data on Employment and Education

		2007	2010	2015	2018	2019	2020
Children in Pre-Primary Education		285,419	314,008	367,361	362,756	363,776	364,909
University students	total	316,176	388,991	346,909	298,686	311,367	288,915
Students	Higher professional education [1]	27,650	28,749	26,946	19,883	18,416	17,954
Employment rate (%)	total	55,6	54,2	56,4	59,2	59,2	59,1
Employment rate (%)	sex males	65,5	63,7	65,1	67,5	67,4	67,3
	females	46,4	45,1	48,1	51,3	51,3	51,3
Rate of economic activity (%)	total	58,8	58,4	59,4	60,6	60,4	60,3
Rate of economic activity (%)	sex males	68,3	68	68	68,7	68,5	68,5
	females	49,8	49,3	51,3	52,8	52,6	52,5
Unemployment rate (%)	total	5,3	7,3	5	2,2	2,0	2,0
Unemployment rate (%)	sex males	4,2	6,4	4,2	1,8	1,7	1,8
	females	6,7	8,5	6,1	2,8	2,4	2,3
Share of unemployed persons (%)	total [5]	.	7,4	6,2	3,1	2,9	4,0
Share of unemployed persons (%)	sex males	.	7,7	6,1	3,0	2,8	3,9
	females	.	7,1	6,4	3,2	2,9	4,1
Labor force (thousands persons)	total	5,198.3	5,268.9	5,309.9	5,415.4	5,412.2	5,378.1
Labor force (thousands persons)	sex males	2,929.7	2,989.1	2,962.7	3,000.3	3,002.5	2,992.3
	females	2,268.7	2,279.8	2,347.3	2,415.1	2,408.7	2,385.8

Source: CZSO Public database. https://vdb.czso.cz/vdbvo2/faces/en/index.jsf?page=statistiky

force. Those under 29 years currently account for around a quarter of the total number of the unemployed among women and one third among men (ibid.).

Those with the lowest levels of qualifications have for many years constituted one of the groups in the labor market most vulnerable to unemployment, including long-term unemployment. The proportion of this group is below 5% of the economically active population for all generations (ibid.). The unemployment rate of low-skilled persons currently stands at over 10% and is twice as high in problem regions (CZSO, 2019i). Active employment policy programs have only rarely been successful. Conversely, the unemployment rate of those with a tertiary education is around one percent; while regional differences are apparent, the most important factor with regard to the employment of this group is the structure of the area of study.

Housing

Housing constitutes the most basic and an increasingly difficult problem confronted by young people who wish to start a family. Younger generations are currently facing the sharply increasing housing prices, accompanied by a decrease in the overall availability of housing. The difference in the value of the housing of poorer and wealthier households is often substantially greater than the difference in their incomes (Sunega & Lux, 2017). The number of young people who are unable to afford their own homes without financial or other assistance from older generations is on the increase. The inequalities in terms of home ownership have been exacerbated by both unequal access to owner-occupied housing and the disproportionate development of the prices of apartments and houses between 2008 and 2018, namely after 2016 (CZSO, 2019a). Today, the unavailability of housing concerns not only owner-occupied but also rented housing. Moreover, further problems faced by young people with respect to rented housing include the limited availability of short-term leases and the low level of tenant protection.

The forms of housing of young people under 29 differ markedly from the average, i.e., rented housing predominates (52%) while 20% of young people live in their own flat and 13% live in their own house (CZSO, 2020c). One-tenth of young people live with relatives or friends. While for the earning population in general housing costs represent on average 13% of the household income, they account for 20% of the income of young people.

Poverty and Social Exclusion

9.6% of Czechs are at risk of income poverty,[6] a level which has remained, with only one fluctuation in 2017, since 2014 (ibid.). The level was the same in 2007 (CZSO, 2008). Most households survive on their income relatively easily or at least with little difficulty. However, for 17.6% of the population, this presents

---

[6] Applying a poverty line of 60% of median equalized disposable income.

a significant problem. The rate of material deprivation in 2019 stood at 2.7% (compared to 6.1% in 2009) (CZSO, 2020c). It was similar in the age group 18–24 years (2.9%), but it amounts to 9.0 % in the case of one-parent families.

Young people are more at risk of poverty than other age groups (ibid.). 11% of those aged under 18 (the same as in 2013) are currently at risk of poverty compared to 17% in 2007, while 10% of those aged 18–24 live below the poverty line (compared to 11% in 2013 and 12% in 2007) (CZSO, 2008).

5. INSTITUTIONAL FRAMEWORK

The introduction of the new Civil Code (in force since 2014) brought about changes to family law. Tax changes to the advantage of families with children were introduced in several stages. Paternity leave was introduced in 2018 (MoLSA, 2020c). Changes to the parental allowance (since 2008) enabled by the introduction of a flexible benefit claiming system allow parents to choose different duration of parental leave while receiving the same total amount of money (MOLSA, 2020d). Child-day care was extended by a new type in 2014 (MPSV, 2020a).

Fiscal-tax treatment of household types: A system of tax relief for families with children was established in 2005 (MoLSA, 2020b; MPSV, 2020b). Child tax credits have been increasing since 2008 and, since 2015, the deduction from the tax differs according to the number of children[7] (Höhne & Šťastná, 2020, p. 45). Low-income parents are entitled to claim a tax bonus.[8] In 2015, tax credit was introduced for children enrolled in pre-school facilities. The importance of the family benefits[9] has decreased, with the exception of the relatively high parental allowance (CZSO, 2019g). In 2011 and 2012, the entitlement conditions for certain social benefits were tightened. The resulting deficit was offset in the following years. In 2018, the amount of child benefit was increased for families with income from gainful employment or its substitution (MPSV, 2020c).

Treatment of marriage and cohabitation: Marriages can be concluded in the Czech Republic via civil or religious ceremony. As far as the legal background is concerned, issues concerning the family are enshrined in the Civil Code (effective from 1 January 2014) (Act No. 89/2012 Coll.). Marriage is not directly legally favored over cohabitation (CVVM, 2020b). However, unmarried partners do not enjoy the same protection under the Civil Code and are not covered by some other legal provisions equally as their married counterparts. Children are guaranteed equal rights (inheritance, maintenance, parental responsibility, etc.) regardless of whether their parents are married, whether they live in the same household, etc.

---

[7] Since 1 January 2006, instead of tax deductions from the assessment base, a direct deduction from tax was introduced (6,000 Czech crowns per year/child in 2006, and since 2015, at three levels according to the order of a child, i.e., the first, the second and the third and higher orders; now the amounts are 15,204/19,404/24,204 Czech crowns)

[8] The taxpayer receives a tax bonus if his/her tax benefits are higher than the calculated income tax payable.

[9] Mainly within the system of the State social support.

32 • VERA KUCHAROVA

Since 2006, the Czech legal system recognizes the so-called registered partnership which entails similar rights and mutual obligations as marriage, but is intended exclusively for persons of the same sex (Act No. 115/2006 Coll.). It does not provide an alternative to marriage for heterosexual couples.

Relevant Social Policy Provisions

Social policy provisions aim both at social prevention and social assistance for families or individuals in need (MoLSA, 2020b). The former is provided namely by social counselling, covering primary social counselling and professional social counselling, and also through residential services. The latter includes various types of social care services for people with lower self-sufficiency and for their families. The mentioned forms of assistance are predominantly free of charge. Social services are provided among others in cooperation of municipalities or regions and NGOs.

Families in material needs are assisted through a system of financial support (MoLSA, 2020a). The entitlement is based on income testing. This system includes Allowance for Living (insufficient income), Supplement for Housing (income insufficient to cover justified housing costs), Extraordinary Immediate Assistance (individual form of insufficiency).

6. COUNTRY-SPECIFIC CHALLENGES TO FAMILY FORMATION

In recent years, the main trends with respect to demographic processes that commenced after 1989, characterized by the diversification of family forms, have continued. The average ages at marriage and at childbirth are increasing, the intensity of marriage is fluctuating at a low level and the intensity of the divorce rate is high (CZSO, 2020d). The share of unmarried cohabitation as a lifelong alternative to marriage is increasing, as is the proportion of children born outside marriage. However, a clear discrepancy is evident between declared values (family as the most important value, two children prevail in reproduction plans) and actual reproductive behavior.

The economic conditions for family formation are favorable. The Czech economy has, on the whole, been growing for almost 20 years (CZSO, 2020a) and is currently characterized by a very low unemployment rate. Total household incomes are increasing. Around one-tenth of households (but 30% of single-parent households) are threatened by income poverty. Income inequality remains low in the Czech Republic and has not changed significantly since 2005 (CZSO, 2020c). The rate of material deprivation is decreasing. The share of families receiving social benefits has declined (CZSO, 2019g), the contribution of tax deductions to the family budget has increased. A drawback of the state financial support is that it focuses primarily on poor families and on families in the early stages of parenthood, while those with school-age children are not specifically supported despite them being more at risk of poverty (ibid.; OECD, 2020). Single-parent families suffer from a significantly worse financial situation (CZSO, 2020c)—around one-third of single parents do not receive income from employment. The absence of one of the parents in the family implies a greater deterioration in the income situation than in the case of couples not being married.

The dynamic development of housing costs in both the owner and rental sectors (MMR, 2019a) has led to a decrease in availability, including for the middle class. The strong preference for owner-occupied housing continues (Vobecká et al., 2014). The ability of families to secure housing is weakest in the early stages of the family cycle. One-fifth of the population lives in overcrowded conditions (Eurostat, 2020). Moreover, the number of families living in substandard housing, mainly single or multi-child families, is on the increase. One-tenth of households spend more than 40% of their income on housing (MMR, 2019b). Unsuccessful efforts to introduce a social housing act is complicating the solution to the spatial exclusion of certain groups of people (Kuchařová et al., 2020, p. 92).

The participation of men and women in the labor market is strongly influenced by parenthood (OECD, 2020). The lowest employment rates relate to women with children aged up to two years, both as a result of the general parental preference for long periods of parental leave (for mothers) and the lack of non-family day care facilities and flexible forms of employment. Single parents particularly suffer from more difficult conditions in this respect.

While parents today prefer the egalitarian role-sharing family model (CVVM, 2020a), in practice, the "traditional" strategies for the reconciliation of work and family life persist (Kuchařová et al., 2020, p. 145), particularly in the early stages of the family cycle and despite the impact on the gender pay gap. The main reasons consist of the normative settings of the Czech society, the maternity and parental allowance systems, a lack of accommodating attitudes on the side of employers and the limited availability of childcare services.

The Czech society has largely abandoned efforts aimed at supporting family stability and is more concerned with helping and supporting families following their break-up. While in such cases most parents make efforts to agree on the upbringing and care of their children, in recent years the intensity of parental disputes over their children has been on the increase along with the various associated negative consequences for the children concerned (ibid.). One of the main deficiencies with respect to services for children and families consists of the insufficient legislative anchoring of preventive and support services, instability and the diverse quality of the services on offer.

The numbers of foster parents and children in foster care have more than doubled over the past decade; however, there remains a shortage of long-term foster parents in particular (Kuchařová et al., 2019, p. 183).

Approximately one-tenth of the Czech population and less than one-twentieth of the child population consists of persons with disabilities (Kuchařová et al., 2019, p. 206–207). Up to the age of 29, such persons live predominantly with their parents as the main caregivers. While the needs of caring families are very heterogeneous, they are not approached in an individual manner. The system of services for families with disabled members is highly fragmented both regionally and in terms of quality. Families with disabled members are entitled to social benefits; however, they often do not adequately cover the increased costs faced by families with disabled persons.

Conceptually, the Czech family policy is not sufficiently anchored in legislation and the objectives thereof usually depend on the ruling political parties. Policy measures are often implemented in a non-systemic way and several measures that have been introduced recently clearly include populist motives. During the economic crisis (around 2011), the level of family support was reduced in order to make savings in the state budget (Kuchařová et al., 2019, pp. 64–65). Family policy lacks a systematic link between its various components, e.g. between financial support and the provision of services, between support for benefits and tax deductions, between family policies of the state and the regions, etc. The Czech family policy has been criticized, for example, for the financial support for families that focuses mainly on poor families and families with very young children, and no support provided for the prevention of social failure of families. In terms of the objectives of state family policy measures, they can be assessed as being universal in the sense that they target essentially the same forms of family arrangements. Rather than being based on a strict definition of the family, they are concerned with the various forms thereof.

7. CONCLUSION

In terms of the basic legal norms (Civil Code, Charter of Fundamental Rights and Freedoms, etc.) and their normative value, the Czech society is open to various types of family relationships and the adoption of different forms of family arrangements. Public policy aims primarily to ensure that children growing up under whatever family conditions enjoy the same and favorable conditions for their lives and development to adulthood.

Practically, however, the socio-economic conditions of single-parent families, in particular, differ significantly from two-parent families. While universal family policy measures exert a number of positive impacts, in terms of the long-term context of living in different types of families, those living in single-parent and unmarried cohabitation families are disadvantaged compared to families in which the parents are married, especially in the areas of income tax, pension insurance, property settlement following separation, including housing and inheritance issues. Given the relatively high degree of instability of unmarried partnerships, this leads to considerable life complications for many unmarried parents compared to their married counterparts.

On the other hand, the state has created assistance systems that act to compensate for some of the disadvantages associated with those who have chosen "alternative" forms of family life. The 2017 Family Policy Concept (MPSV, 2017) emphasizes that its key principle is to create an environment in which families can

Family Formation in the Czech Republic • **35**

freely pursue their decisions and beliefs with regard to family values, approaches to caring, and family and personal life objectives, with the overriding intention of strengthening family autonomy.

REFERENCES

Act No. 115. (2006). *Coll.—Zákon o registrovaném partnerství* [Civil Union Act]. https://public.psp.cz/en/sqw/sbirka.sqw?cz=115&r=2006

Act No. 89. (2012). *Coll.—Občanský zákoník* [Civil Code]. https://www.zakonyprolidi.cz/cs/2012-89 [English translation: http://www.czechlegislation.com/law-no-89-2012-coll-civil-code/]

Chamoutová, D., Kleňha, D., Koucký, J., Trhlíková, J., Úlovec, M., & Vojtěch, V. (2019). *Uplatnění absolventů škol na trhu práce—2018.* [School-leavers on the labour market—2018]. Praha, Czech Republic: Národní ústav pro vzdělávání. http://www.nuv.cz/file/3652/

CVVM. (2014). *Jaké hodnoty jsou pro nás důležité—červen 2014?* [Which values are important for us?—June 2014]. https://cvvm.soc.cas.cz/media/com_form2content/documents/c2/a1782/f9/ov140717.pdf

CVVM. (2017). *Czech public opinion on the rights of homosexuals—May 2017.* https://cvvm.soc.cas.cz/en/press-releases/other/relations-attitudes/4358-attitudes-of-czech-society-towards-homosexuals-and-their-rights-may-2017

CVVM. (2019a). *Evaluation of some social conditions—October 2019.* https://cvvm.soc.cas.cz/en/press-releases/economical/work-income-living-level/5056-evaluation-of-some-social-conditions-october-2019

CVVM. (2019b). *Public opinion on abortion, euthanasia and prostitution—May 2019.* https://cvvm.soc.cas.cz/en/press-releases/other/relations-attitudes/4959-public-opinion-on-abortion-euthanasia-and-prostitution-may-2019

CVVM. (2020a). *Názory veřejnosti na roli muže a ženy v rodině—únor 2020.* [Public opinion on the role of men and women in family—February 2020]. https://cvvm.soc.cas.cz/cz/tiskove-zpravy/ostatni/vztahy-a-zivotni-postoje/5185-nazory-verejnosti-na-roli-muze-a-zeny-v-rodine

CVVM. (2020b). *Postoje českých občanů k partnerství, manželství a rodičovství—únor 2020.* [Czech citizens' opinions on marriage and the family—February 2020]. https://cvvm.soc.cas.cz/media/com_form2content/documents/c2/a5175/f9/ov200325.pdf

CZSO. (2007). *Vývoj obyvatelstva České republiky—2006* [Population trends in the Czech Republic—2006]. Czech Statistical Office. https://www.czso.cz/csu/czso/vyvoj-obyvatelstva-ceske-republiky-2006-jmfk8fw73c

CZSO. (2008). *Household income and living conditions in the Czech Republic—2007.* Czech Statistical Office. https://www.czso.cz/csu/czso/household-income-and-living-conditions-in-the-czech-republic-2007-f73vbtlnf6

CZSO. (2014). *Národnostní struktura obyvatel—2011.* [Population by nationality]. Czech Statistical Office. https://www.czso.cz/csu/czso/narodnostni-struktura-obyvatel-2011-aqkd3cosup

CZSO. (2018). *Vývoj obyvatelstva České republiky—2018.* [Population trends in the Czech Republic—2018]. Czech Statistical Office. https://www.czso.cz/csu/czso/vyvoj-obyvatelstva-ceske-republiky-2018

36 • VERA KUCHAROVA

CZSO. (2019a). *Ceny sledovaných druhů nemovitostí—2016 až 2018.* [Prices of observed types of real estate]. https://www.czso.cz/csu/czso/ceny-sledovanych-druhu-nemovitosti-2016-az-2018

CZSO. (2019b). *Czech demographic handbook—2018.* Czech Statistical Office. https://www.czso.cz/csu/czso/czech-demographic-handbook

CZSO. (2019c). *Focus on women, on men.* Czech Statistical Office. https://www.czso.cz/csu/czso/focus-on-women-and-men-iolyqig690

CZSO. (2019d). *Příjmová chudoba ohrožuje necelou desetinu obyvatel.* [Income poverty threatens almost one tenth of population]. Czech Statistical Office. https://www.czso.cz/csu/czso/prijmova-chudoba-ohrozuje-necelou-desetinu-obyvatel

CZSO. (2019e). *Školy a školská zařízení—školní rok 2018/2019.* [Schools and school institutions—school year 2018/2019]. Czech Statistical Office. https://www.czso.cz/csu/czso/skoly-a-skolska-zarizeni-skolni-rok-20182019

CZSO. (2019f). *Terciární vzdělávání: Studenti a absolventi vysokoškolského a vyššího odborného vzdělávání—2017.* [Tertiary education: students and school-leavers of universities and higher vocational schools—2017]. Czech Statistical Office. https://www.czso.cz/csu/czso/terciarni-vzdelavani-studenti-a-absolventi-vysokoskolskeho-a-vyssiho-odborneho-vzdelavani-2017

CZSO. (2019g). *Vybrané údaje o sociálním zabezpečení—2018.* [Selected social security data—2018.] Czech Statistical Office. https://www.czso.cz/csu/czso/vybrane-udaje-o-socialnim-zabezpeceni-2018

CZSO. (2019h). *Vývoj ekonomiky České republiky—4. čtvrtletí 2019.* [The Czech economy development—4th quarter 2019]. https://www.czso.cz/csu/czso/vyvoj-ekonomiky-ceske-republiky-4-ctvrtleti-2019

CZSO. (2019i). *Zaměstnanost a nezaměstnanost podle výsledků VŠPS—4. čtvrtletí 2019.* [Employment and unemployment as measured by the labour force survey—4. quarter of 2019]. Czech Statistical Office. https://www.czso.cz/csu/czso/zamestnanost-a-nezamestnanost-podle-vysledku-vsps-ctvrtletni-udaje-4-ctvrtleti-2019

CZSO. (2020a). *The Czech economy development—Year of 2019.* Czech Statistical Office. https://www.czso.cz/csu/czso/the-czech-economy-development-year-of-2019

CZSO. (2020b). Česká republika od roku 1989 v číslech. [The Czech Republic in numbers since 1989]. Czech Statistical Office. https://www.czso.cz/csu/czso/ceska-republika-od-roku-1989-v-cislech-aktualizovano-1552020#01

CZSO. (2020c). *Household income and living conditions—2019.* Czech Statistical Office. https://www.czso.cz/csu/czso/household-income-and-living-conditions-2019

CZSO. (2020d). *Population development charts 1950–2019.* Czech Statistical Office. https://www.czso.cz/csu/czso/population-development-charts

CZSO Public database. (2020, June). Czech Statistical Office. https://vdb.czso.cz/vdbvo2/faces/en/index.jsf?page=vystup-objekt&f=TABULKA&z=T&udIdent=262357&pvo=UD-1575011025074&&str=v10002&kodjaz=203#w=

Eurostat. Database. (2020, June). *Database.* https://ec.europa.eu/eurostat/data/database

Höhne, S., & Šťastná, A. (2020). Bulletin No 35. Vývoj hlavních ekonomických a sociálních ukazatelů České republiky 1990–2019. [Main economic and social indicators of the Czech Republic 1990–2019]. VÚPSV, v. v. i. https://www.vupsv.cz/download/bulletin-no-35-kveten-2020/?wpdmdl=7082&refresh=5ee68be2875641592167394

Křesťanová, J., & Kurkin, R. (2019). Populační vývoj v české republice v roce 2018. [Population development in the Czech Republic in 2018]. *Demografie 61*(3), 190–

210. https://www.czso.cz/csu/czso/demografie-review-for-population-research-no-32019

Kuchařová, V., Barvíková, J., Höhne, S., Janurová, K., Nešporová, O., Paloncyová, J., Svobodová, K., & Vidovićová, L. (2019). *Česká rodina na počátku 21. století: Životní podmínky, vztahy a potřeby* [Czech family at the beginning of the 21st century: Living conditions, relationships and needs]. Sociologické nakladatelství (SLON): VÚPSV, v.v.i..

Kuchařová, V., Barvíková, J., Höhne, S., Nešporová, O., Paloncyová, J., & Vidovićová, L. (2020). *Zpráva o rodině 2020* [Report on family 2020]. MPSV—VUPSV, v.v.i. https://www.mpsv.cz/documents/20142/225508/Zpr%C3%A1va+o+rodin%C4%9B+2020.pdf/c3bdc63d-9c95-497d-bded-6a15e9890abd

MMR—Ministry of Regional Development. (2019a). *Bydlení v České republice v číslech (srpen 2019)* [Housing in the Czech Republic in numbers /August 2019/]. Praha, Czech Republic: Ministerstvo pro místní rozvoj. https://www.mmr.cz/getmedia/44278f53-e63a-4dc5-8694-922df2853088/BvCZ-online-CZ.pdf.aspx?ext=.pdf

MMR—Ministry of Regional Development. (2019b). *Selected data on housing (June 2018)*. Praha, Czech Republic: Ministerstvo pro místní rozvoj. https://www.mmr.cz/getmedia/e9c0b9f8-11ff-48f9-9cfa-82e49f23e7ff/Selected-Data-on-Housing-2018-(June-2019).pdf.aspx?ext=.pdf

MoLSA—Ministry of Labor and Social Affairs. (2020a, June). *Assistance in Material Need*. https://www.mpsv.cz/web/en/assistance-in-material-need

MoLSA—Ministry of Labor and Social Affairs. (2020b, June). *Family*. https://www.mpsv.cz/web/en/family#ssf

MoLSA—Ministry of Labor and Social Affairs. (2020c, June). *Sickness insurance*. https://www.mpsv.cz/web/en/sickness-insurance#3

MoLSA—Ministry of Labor and Social Affairs. (2020d, June). *State social support*. https://www.mpsv.cz/web/en/state-social-support.

MPSV—Ministry of Labor and Social Affairs. (2017). *Koncepce rodinné politiky 2017* [Family policy concept 2017]. MPSV. https://www.mpsv.cz/documents/20142/225508/Koncepce_rodinne_politiky.pdf/5d1efd93-3932-e2df-2da3-da30d5fa8253

MPSV—Ministry of Labor and Social Affairs. (2020a, June). *Dětské skupiny* [Children's groups]. https://www.mpsv.cz/web/cz/detske-skupiny

MPSV—Ministry of Labor and Social Affairs. (2020b, June). *Podpora rodiny* [Support of families]. https://www.mpsv.cz/web/cz/podpora-rodiny

MPSV—Ministry of Labor and Social Affairs. (2020c, June). *Státní sociální podpora* [State social support]. https://www.mpsv.cz/web/cz/statni-socialni-podpora

MPSV—Ministry of Labor and Social Affairs. (2020d, June). *Působnost MPSV* [Responsibilities of MoLSA]. https://www.mpsv.cz/web/cz/pusobnost-mpsv

OECD. (2020, June). *Family Database* http://www.oecd.org/els/family/database.htm

Sunega, P., & Lux, M. (2018). Rovní v příjmech, nerovní v majetku? Nerovnosti ve vlastnickém bydlení v ČR [Equal in incomes, unequal in wealth? housing wealth inequalities in the Czech Republic). *Sociologický časopis / Czech Sociological Review, 54*(5), 749–780. https://sreview.soc.cas.cz/pdfs/csr/2018/05/04.pdf

Vobecká, J., Kostelecký, T., & Lux, M. (2014). Rental housing for young households in the Czech Republic: Perceptions, priorities and possible solutions. *Sociologický časopis/Czech Sociological Review, 50*(3), 365–390. http://dx.doi.org/10.13060/00380288.2014.50.3.102

38 • VERA KUCHAROVA

Vohlídalová, M. (2017). *Genderové rozdíly v odměňování očima veřejnosti v České republice.* [Gender pay gap in public opinion in the Czech Republic]. Sociologický ústav AV ČR, v.v.i. https://www.soc.cas.cz/sites/default/files/publikace/genderove_rozdily_v_odmenovani_akt_mv.pdf

CHAPTER 3

DISADVANTAGES IN FAMILY FORMATION NATIONAL REPORT

Germany

Dirk Hofäcker
University of Duisburg-Essen, Germany

1. NATIONAL CONTEXT

With more than 83 million inhabitants, Germany is currently the largest European country in terms of *population size* (Eurostat, 2020a). Its population has been constantly growing from the 1950s to the mid-1990s, and has since then mostly stagnated (BIB, 2016, p. 6). 19.3 million have a *migrant background*, out of which 13.2 million were immigrants themselves and 6.1 were born in Germany as children of immigrants (Göttsche, 2018, p. 28). 36% of children in Germany nowadays have a migration background (ibid., p. 33). Various immigration waves have shaped the German population: the migration of foreign workers in the 1950s/60s (mostly from Southern European countries, Turkey and the former Yugoslavia), the migration of ethnic German repatriates (mostly from the former Soviet Union) in the 1980s/1990s, and the migration of asylum seekers from the Middle East and North African countries since 2014 (ibid., p. 28ff.). Migrants in

---

Family Formation Among Youth in Europe: Coping With Socio-Economic Disadvantages,
pages 39–54.
Copyright © 2022 by Information Age Publishing
www.infoagepub.com
All rights of reproduction in any form reserved.

40 • DIRK HOFÄCKER

Germany thus nowadays make up a heterogeneous group of people with very different geographical origins and migration histories. Overall, even though notable advances have been made in the integration of migrants, their educational level and labor market integration on average still remains below that of the native German population (ibid., p. 42) and they have fewer financial resources at their disposal (Schacht & Metzing, 2018, p. 274ff.).

As many other European countries, Germany can be described as an *ageing society*. Currently, 18% of the population is below 20 years old, while 21% are aged 65 and over. Until 2060, the number of "older persons" is projected to rise to 32%, while that of the younger will decrease to 16% (BIB, 2018, p. 12). German policies are increasingly anticipating this demographic change and the related repercussions: on the one hand, "active ageing" policies increasingly aim to prolong working lives. In fact, in recent decades, Germany has been among the countries where employment rates among the older population have increased most substantially (Ebbinghaus & Hofäcker, 2013). On the other hand, family policies have increasingly become oriented at facilitating work-family reconciliation for women, in order to promote both women's employment and birth rates (see section 5 below).

Throughout the last two decades, Germany had a largely stable *economy*. GDP rates have been almost continuously growing since the 1990s, with the financial crisis in 2008/2009 constituting the only major exception. Yet, even after this short downturn, the economy soon recovered (Mucha, 2018, p. 131). In consequence, life satisfaction in Germany is high with 93% of the population reporting to be "satisfied" or "very satisfied" with their lives overall—10 percentage points more than the EU average. 79% perceive the overall labor market situation in their country as being "good" and 72% appear to be equally satisfied with their personal situation (EU-28: 42% and 61% respectively; Scheuer, 2018, p. 434).

One very particular characteristic of the German case are its *regional differences*: even more than a quarter of a century after the reunification, there continue to be East-West differences in various respects (see Statistische Ämter des Bundes und der Länder, 2015). This holds particularly for the overall *economic situation and the labor market*: The economic situation in the former GDR deteriorated dramatically after the reunification, reflected in severe declines in employment and unemployment rates of more than 18% in the mid-2000s, almost twice as much as in the Western part. More recently, however, labor market figures have increasingly started to converge (ibid., p. 63).

There are also differences in the composition of the *population*: there has been a considerable out-migration, particularly of young people, and disproportionately women (Deschermeier, 2017), in search of labor, from East to West Germany, resulting in both the population decline and significantly older population in East Germany. Apart from a few urban centers, population density in Eastern Germany is clearly lower (BiB, 2017a). There are also substantial differences in the share of migrants in the population, which is clearly higher in Western Germany than in the Eastern (BiB, 2017b).

Due to the still pronounced differences observable between the Eastern and Western part of Germany, this report subsequently differentiates between the two parts where applicable.

2. DEMOGRAPHIC TRENDS RELEVANT TO FAMILY FORMATION

The development in family-related structures and processes in Germany has often been described as reflecting a destabilization of the traditional "middle class family model". This entailed both a move away from one clearly dominant family type to a plural coexistence of various different family models ("pluralization of family forms") as well as "deinstutionalization" of processes of marriage and family formation (Peuckert, 2019, p. 7).

The notion of **pluralization of family forms** implies that the relative importance of the "normal family model" (Peuckert, 2019, p. 18; Tyrell, 1979)—typical for the German middle-class in the 1950s to 1960s and referring to a married heterosexual couple with children, living in a long-term, monogamous relationship within a joint household—has decreased over time. This is reflected already in the distribution of *household types*: while in 1972, around 39% of all German households consisted of married couples with children, this figure has decreased to 22% in 2007; in East Germany, they constitute an even lesser share (16.5% in 2007; figures from Peuckert 2019, p. 18). This decline cannot be explained by falling fertility rates in Germany alone (see below for details). Even within the group of family households (i.e., parent-child constellations in private households), the relative share of households with married couples has suffered from a "loss of its monopoly" (Meyer, 2014, p. 430), as it dropped from 81.4% (1996) to 69.7% (2017; figures from Adam & Degen, 2018, p. 13f.).

Parallel to this "standard family type," various other household forms have expanded, differing from the standard model in both parental constellation and family status. Due to increasing rates of family dissolution (see below), the relative share of *single parent households* in family households has risen from 13.8% in 1996 to 18.9% in 2017. In the same time span, the relative share of *civil unions* (i.e., unmarried couples) with children has more than doubled from 4.8% to 11.4% (2017). For many young people, entering a civil union has turned into a normal "probation period" for a relationship before entering marriage, after which young people decide whether they enter into marriage or not (Meyer, 2014, p. 430). Deviations from the "normal family model" are also observed in various other respects: partnerships or marriages are no longer exclusively heterosexual, particularly after the legalization of *same-sex-marriages* in Germany in 2017; official statistics refer to 130,000 couples in 2018 (among them 37,000 married; Statistisches Bundesamt, 2019a).

It is important to note that the trend towards pluralization of new household types is not equally distributed among the German population; as shown earlier, the trend is more pronounced in the Eastern part of Germany, strongest in early stages of life, and disproportionately observed among higher social classes (Peuckert, 2019, p. 8). Yet, despite the sharp increase of new family types, they oftentimes still represent a minority. Or, as German family sociologists have expressed it, "[…] the nuclear family models nowadays face increasing competition as an ideal of life. Yet, for the majority, it continues to be a natural benchmark for their individual life orientation" (Meyer, 2014; own translation).

A number of the previously described changes in family types are strongly related to changes in the **institutionalization of marriage**, reflected in marriage and divorce rates. After the "Golden Age of Marriage" in the 1960s, *marriages* in the Western part have declined both in absolute numbers (from 521,400 in 1960 to 331,900 in 2016), as well as in relative rates per 1000 inhabitants (from 9.4 to 5.0 in the same time period). East Germany saw a similar decline in crude marriage rates from 9.7 to 4.9 in the same period (BIB, 2020a). A part of this decline may be due to the fact that marriages have increasingly been postponed to later ages: whereas the mean age of marriage was around age 23 in the 1960s (West: 23.7; East: 22.6), it is now over age 30 (West: 30.2; East: 31.6; ibid.). This postponement is in line with a general trend in the postponement of pivotal life course transitions due to educational expansion (such as the attainment of a first job, leaving the parental home etc.; Peuckert, 2019, p. 7; see also section 4). In line with this shift to later ages, the binding nature of marriage also seems to have declined as the share of people that *ever* marry is now at around on third (69% of men; 63% of women) as compared to the 1970s when marriage was almost universal (93% of men; 87% of women; ibid., p. 34).

Parallel to declining rates of marriages, they have also become more unstable as the raw divorce rate doubled since the 1960s in the West (1960: 8.8/1000; 2016: 20.2). In the East, these rates have been traditionally higher; following a temporary high in the late-1990s (31.5 in 1986) they have now converged with Western figures (17.7 in 2016; all figures: BiB, 2020b). Marriages are most vulnerable in their early stages (i.e., between 5 and 10 years of duration), even though the risk has declined somewhat across recent cohorts and at least partly shifted to later ages (i.e., duration of 20 years and longer; BiB, 2020b). In around 50% of cases, underage children are affected by a divorce (ibid.).

Figure 3.1 gives an overview of trends in the total **fertility** rate in Germany as a whole, and split by East and West, since the 1960s. As in many other modern societies, Germany has witnessed a sharp drop of fertility in the last half-decade, yet with some notable variations. Following the "baby boom" of the 1950s and early 1960s, fertility rates declined sharply, a trend attributed to various factors such as the availability of contraceptives, changes in the value of children, the lack of work-family reconciliation measures (Geissler, 2014, p. 35) and a societal lack of consideration of family matters (Kaufmann, 2005).

While the decline initially occurred in both parts of Germany, explicit population policy measures incentivizing childbirth led to a temporary trend reversal between the mid-1970s and mid-1980s in the Eastern part. The breakdown of

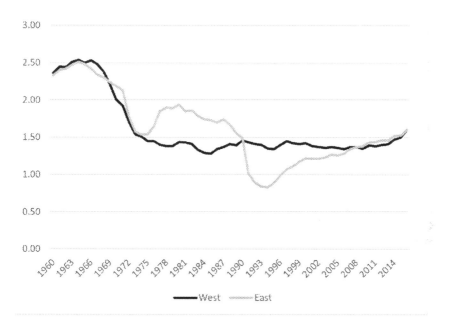

FIGURE 3.1. Total Fertility Rates in Germany (West/East) 1960–2018. Source: BiB 2020c

the former GDR and the process of German reunification subsequently initiated a "demographic crisis" (Geissler, 2014, p. 34) with fertility rates falling even below 1.0 in the former GDR, followed by a gradual recovery since the late 1990s. More recently, fertility rates have been on the rise again, surpassing a TFR of 1.5 in both parts of Germany. This increase, on the one hand, reflects higher fertility rates among migrant women, but may also be traced back to the combined effect of increasing birth rates in higher age groups, favorable economic situation, and positive effect of recent family policy measures (Pötzsch, 2018, p. 81f.).

A consistent trend in both parts of Germany has been the postponement of the *age of first births*. While these occurred around age 27 (West: 27.8; East: 26.4) in the 1970s, they have risen to more than age 30 (BiB, 2020c). For migrants, births happen on average two years earlier, even though variations across migrant groups can be observed (Peuckert, 2019, p. 167ff.). Furthermore, mothers with higher education particularly tend to postpone births to later ages (ibid., p. 174f.).

Over time, first births have increasingly decoupled from marriage. While in 1960, only around 6.3% of children in the West and 11.6% of children in the East were born *outside marriage*, this number has increased substantially. In 2016, non-marital births accounted for a third of children in the West (30.4%) and more than 50% (57.1%) in the East (BiB, 2020c). The higher number of out-of-wedlock births in the former GDR is related to higher acceptance of non-marital cohabitation, but also to special privileges for unmarried mothers, e.g. in terms of housing or childcare access (Peuckert, 2019, p. 189).

A final notable feature of German fertility patters, and one reason for the low TFR, is the relatively high share of women who remain *childless*. Among cohorts born in the 1970s, it currently stands at around 22% in the Western and 18% in the Eastern part. Childlessness is also more widespread among academics, women living in urban regions, and those in full-time employment, while it is lowest in married couples and among migrants (Statistisches Bundesamt, 2019b). Experts expect that the share of childless women may rise further up to a quarter (Lück et al., 2016).

3. NORMATIVE FRAMEWORK

For most Germans, the family as such is highly important. When being asked about their central domain of life, 79% of respondents of a representative survey in 2016 chose the family, even reflecting a minor increase as compared to a study ten years prior (BMFSFJ, 2017, p. 11).

While (as shown above) family forms have increasingly become pluralized, Germans still orient their *image of a "typical family"* around this notion. As a representative survey by Lück and Ruckdeschel (2019) shows, it is only a heterosexual couple with children that is equally regarded a "family" –irrespective of their marital status. Single-parent families and particularly couples without children are encompassed by this notion to a far lesser degree.

Despite the relatively low fertility and high levels of childlessness, many young people aged 18–30 years have a distinct *desire to have children*. More than 90 percent of childless couples have a desire for children, with most of them aspiring for 2 children. This pattern has remained remarkably stable over time; in recent years, the desire for more than 3 children has even increased (BMFSFJ, 2017, p. 26).

While family formation and partnership apparently still enjoy a lot of popular support, the consideration of *marriage* as a central life course transition is clearly declining. When being asked within the Population Policy Acceptance Study whether they consider "marriage as an outdated institution," around a quarter of all German respondents reported they do. Notably, this share was significantly higher among 20–29-year-old men (West: 38%; East: 41%) and women (West: 27%; East: 32%; figures according to Peuckert, 2019:37f.) than among the older population.

In terms of general *gender role attitudes*, Germany has long been considered to follow the classical norms of a "strong male breadwinner model" (Lewis & Ostner, 1994) in which men are responsible for ensuring the household income and women are largely expected to be responsible for care and household work. Yet, public support for this model has declined throughout the last decades. While in 1988, around 37% of Western Germans still supported a suchlike gendered distribution of work, this share has more than halved until 2012 (14.5%). Despite this move away from the normative framework of a gendered division of labor, there are still reservations towards out-of-home childcare that may facilitate an equal sharing of labor. In 2012, for example, around a third of West Germans still agreed that "a pre-school child is likely to suffer if his or her mother works". In Eastern Germany, which during the communist times was close to a dual earner model based on full-time employment of both parents, support for a male breadwinner was never strong (8.5% in 1994, 7% in 2012) and only around 16.4% nowadays expect negative effects of maternal work (own calculations based on ISSP data).

Yet, despite this attitudinal move away from a male breadwinner model, the *actual division of labor* among the genders is often still largely traditional. A report based on a time-use survey in 2012/3 concluded that "household chores within family households, such as cooking, laundry, and cleaning are still predominantly taken over by women" (Statistisches Bundesamt, 2017, p. 82; own translation). Similar asymmetries are reported for childcare activities (Walper & Lien, 2017).

4. SOCIO-ECONOMIC CONDITIONS

After the mid-2000s, the German **labor market** has gone through a long boom period, with *unemployment* rates declining almost continuously from more than 10% in 2005 to less than 4% in 2018 (see Figure 3.2). Among others, this trend can be traced back to labor market activation measures (particularly the so-called 'Hartz reforms'), modest wage policies and a generally favorable economic climate (Sperber & Walwei, 2015). This trend even continued throughout the financial market crisis of 2008, where unemployment rates only modestly increased, but continued to fall thereafter. Following this boom, the ratio of unemployment to vacant jobs is now at a record low within the last 25 years (Bossler et al., 2018).

One further notable feature is that the *labor market performance of youth* closely followed the overall labor market trend. Unlike in many other countries, youth unemployment rates are only marginally higher than overall unemployment rates (see Figure 3.2). There are, however, some signs of negative developments: *youth employment* fell slightly throughout the crisis as the employment rate of 15–24-year-olds fell from around 44 percent in 2007 to less than 42 percent in 2013 and has not recovered since (Brenke, 2017). Furthermore, even though youth unemployment rates in Germany are among the lowest in Europe, youth initially find it difficult to establish themselves firmly in the labor market, which is reflected in the high shares of *fixed-term employment* in early career (51.7% among 15–24-year-old Germans in 2018; OECD, 2020b).

Another notable characteristic of the German labor market is its *gendered* nature, particularly around family formation. Employment rates of men and women in Germany generally have converged throughout recent years (79.7% for men and 72.1% for women in 2018; OECD, 2020a). Yet, among women with at least one child aged 0–14 years, only 30% are full-time employed while 39% work only part-time (OECD, 2020b). Notably, survey data suggest that a number of the latter women would like to work more but are hindered from doing so due to the lack of childcare infrastructure (see section 4 below; Lietzmann & Wenzig, 2017).

Educational level has continuously improved in Germany: in 2014, 34.7% left school with a higher education entrance qualification, 45.9% obtained a sec-

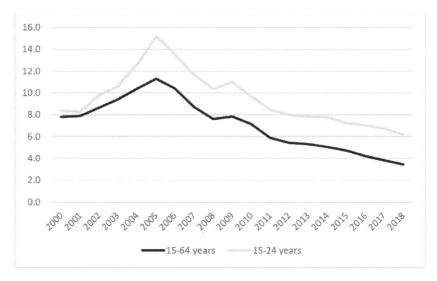

FIGURE 3.2. Unemployment Rates, Germany 2000–2018 (total working age population and youth). Source: OECD, 2020a

ondary school certificate ("Mittlere Reife") and 17.6% a lower secondary degree (Deutscher Bundestag, 2017, p. 162). Throughout recent years, women have been outperforming men in educational attainment (Eurostat, 2020b). At the other end, *early school leavers* (without even a basic educational degree) make up 6.0% (men: 7.2% women 5.5%). Despite the increased efforts to reduce this share, numbers have stagnated or even risen recently (Autorengruppe Bildungsberichterstattung, 2018, p. 121). Young people with *migration background* on average obtain lower educational degrees (Statistisches Bundesamt, 2019a, p. 89), even though considerable differences between migrant groups can be observed (Geißler & Weber-Menges, 2008, p. 17).

In a report on **housing** conditions based on 2006, the authors described the German situation as "expensive, comfortable and usually rented" (Noll & Weick, 2014). This characterization still applies to German housing conditions today.

Housing is "expensive," in as far as the cost for housing still posed a considerable financial burden for 15.8% of German households in 2016 (i.e., they made up for more than 40% of household disposable income). Among income poor households, this even applies for half of the population (50.3%). Both figures are clearly higher than the EU average of 11.9 and 39% respectively (Eurostat, 2018, p. 72f.). Housing cost burdens are higher for households with children than for those without, higher for tenants than for owners, and particularly high among single parent families (Statistisches Bundesamt, 2019, p. 169).

Housing is also "comfortable" with regards to both the spatial dimension and the standard of living. The average number of rooms per person (1.8) is somewhat larger in Germany than in the EU overall (1.6; Eurostat, 2018, p. 61). The average living space per person was 43.8 m² in 2014 with only moderate differences between West (44.7 m²) and East Germany (40.1 m²; Statistisches Bundesamt, 2020). This follows considerable convergence between the two parts. Overcrowding rates in Germany are consequently low (7.2%; EU-28: 15.5%; Eurostat, 2020c). Only 3.7% are not able to keep their home adequately warm; less than half of the percentage in EU-28 (8.7%; Eurostat, 2018, p. 63).

Finally, housing in Germany is characterized by high shares of rented apartments and only low rates of tenure. By 2018, only around half of Germans owned their dwelling, clearly less than in Europe overall (69.3%). Tenants made up the remaining 48.5%, around 40 percent paid rent at a market price while roughly 8 percent paid rent at a reduced price or fee (Eurostat, 2020c).

The age at which young people become *independent* in terms of housing varies considerably between educational levels. Surprisingly, it is the higher educated that leave their parental home earliest at around age 21, even though they start their first employment considerably late (age 25 on average). In between, they are frequently either supported by parents, public credits for education and training, or own employment. In contrast, the lower educated leave latest (age 25), and only significantly after they have established themselves on the job market (1st job is attained on average at age 20; Berngruber, 2015).

With 16.0% in 2018, the share of the population in Germany that is at-risk-of-**poverty** (i.e., those that have less than 60% of median equivalized income at their disposal) is about one percentage point lower than in the EU-overall (EU-28: 17.1%; Eurostat, 2020c). Notably, the risks of poverty vary according to several sociodemographic characteristics (see Kott, 2018, p. 234):

- *Age*: Young people, particularly, those between age 12 and 17, are at a somewhat higher poverty risk than the overall population (18.7% in 2016). Furthermore, poverty risks among retirees is slightly higher (18%).
- *Gender*: Poverty risks are somewhat higher among women (17.8%) than men (15.2%).
- *Education:* Among the lower educated, 29.4% are at-risk-of-poverty, while this applies only to 9.8% of the higher educated.
- *Family status and household type*: Poverty risks are lower for households with children (13.5%) than for those without (18.7%). Single parent families face a particularly high poverty risk (32.6%).
- *Employment status*: While around 9.5 of those employed face relative income poverty, this is true for 70.5% of the unemployed. The higher the overall work intensity is within a household, the lower is the poverty risk.
- *Migration background*: The risk of poverty is about two times higher for those with a migration background as compared to the indigenous population (Göbel & Krause, 2018, p. 248).

From a dynamic perspective, falling into poverty does not necessarily mean permanent impoverishment. Between 2012 and 2016, 41.9% of those in the low-

48 • DIRK HOFÄCKER

est income quintile managed to move into a higher one. Yet, throughout recent decades, rates of upward moves have decreased while the risk to move into lower quintiles has increased (ibid., p. 252)

5. INSTITUTIONAL FRAMEWORK

Germany has long been considered a prime example of a "strong male breadwinner" model, not only in attitudinal (see above) but also in socio-political terms. This orientation was reflected in a comparatively generous financial protection for care-taking mothers and a long parental leave of up to three years, as well as a joint taxation model which incentivized the caring role of the mother. At the same time, early child care was particularly underdeveloped, often allowing only for additional part-time work by women (Hofäcker, 2004).

Through a series of reforms, especially between 2013 and 2017, German family has recently modernized in various respects, and now exhibits a number of approaches to equally support a dual earner model.

German family policy encompasses a number of different measures that are relevant to the process of family formation (see BMFSFJ, 2020 for an overview):

- Prior to giving birth, mothers-to-be receive a *maternity allowance* of up to 13 Euro per day; if they were previously employed and the daily wage was higher than 13 Euro, the employer is expected to pay a respective top-up.
- For each child, families receive a *child allowance* of between 219 and 250 Euro per child, depending on the number of children. Benefits are paid up to the age of 18 and can be extended in case of vocational education or unemployment. As an alternative to direct benefits, parents can also decide for *tax abatements* for their dependent children. Families with low income can receive a supplementary child allowance.
- Together, both parents are entitled to a *parental allowance* ("Elterngeld") of 14 months if they stop working. The distribution of leave can be freely decided, but one partner can take only a maximum of 12 months. Parental allowance is income-dependent and ranges between 300 and 1.800 Euro per month. Especially for higher-income couples, the upper ceiling makes it attractive for the lower-earning partner (usually the mother) to take (most of) the leave. The so called "Elterngeld plus" makes it possible to receive the allowance for twice the time with half of the benefits if one partner works part-time. If *both* partners work simultaneously between 25 and 30 hours, four additional months can be taken. The reform of the previous parental allowance and the inclusion of at least two "daddy months" has significantly improved the share of fathers taking a leave. At the same time, since then, women have also found it easier to return to employment earlier (Bujard, 2013).
- Following the introduction of a public child care guarantee for pre-school children, *child care* in Germany has recently improved significantly. While coverage of public child care at 3–6 years has always been next to univer-

sal, early child care for the 0–2-year-olds has more than doubled from an enrolment rate of 16.8% in 2005 to 37.2% in 2017. Notably, early child care take-up is significantly lower for parents with migration background (BMFSFJ, 2017, p. 58). Better availability of childcare indeed has a positive effect on women's readiness to return to the labor market early (Diener & Berggruber, 2018). Yet, even with these higher rates, Germany occupies at best a mid-position in cross-national comparison (OECD, 2020c). Another shortcoming in childcare is that it is still not always offered full-day: only around 21.4 % of toddlers, 53.2% of pre-school children and 52.8% of school children up to the age of 12 effectively have access to formal childcare of 30 hours and more (Eurostat, 2018, p. 107). In the early family stage, women are thus often either forced to reduce their working hours or to purchase mostly expensive private childcare to work full-time.

- While the above measures have improved the opportunities for work-family-reconciliation of both sexes, the German tax system still sets incentives for an asymmetric division of paid work and care work among spouses. Germany still applies the so-called "*tax splitting*" in which the income of both spouses is added, then divided by two and assessed for taxation. Due to tax progression in Germany, this incentivizes a division of work in which spouses have large income differences. Recent studies show that this mode of taxation effectively suppresses women's employment in married couples (Bick & Fuchs-Schündeln, 2017).

6. CHALLENGES TO FAMILY FORMATION IN GERMANY

Taken together, the situation in Germany regarding family formation may best be described as paradoxical. On the one hand, Germany provides a number of favorable conditions for family formation. Throughout recent years, the German economy has been stable (section 1), employment rates are high and unemployment is at a record low (section 4). A general welfare state provides good levels of protection, family policy effectively protects young people from falling into a poverty (section 5), and a career break is protected through both dismissal protection and public transfers (section 2). Overall life satisfaction in Germany is high (section 1), daily costs of life, particularly for housing, are affordable and poverty is modest from a European perspective (section 4). At the same time, fertility in Germany is low, well beyond the net reproduction rate of approximately 2.08 children, and has only slightly recovered in the last few years (section 2). This is even more surprising, given the continued centrality of family life and the orientation at a classical family model with two children (section 3). How can this paradox between seemingly good conditions for family formation and low fertility be explained? And what could be possible challenges for the future in order to improve the situation?

One possible explanation for the paradox may be that, despite the seemingly good labor market situation in Germany, young people have long-lasting difficulties in establishing themselves safely in the labor market. As shown here (section 4) and elsewhere (e.g. Buchholz & Kolb, 2011), young people in Germany are particularly affected by insecure atypical employment up until their late-20s, as employers disproportionately channel flexibilization pressures towards them. Under these conditions, young people find it difficult to make long-term binding decision for their lives, such as forming a permanent partnership and making the transition to adulthood (Blossfeld et al., 2005). In consequence, this behavioral pattern promotes a postponement of family formation, and in some cases even its abandonment, reflected in the high level of childlessness in Germany (section 2). Following this line of argument, German policy would be well-advised to promote more security in early employment career, e.g. through strengthening employment protection for atypical work forms and promoting permanent contracts.

Another possible explanation for the low fertility figures would be the incomplete transition of Germany from a male breadwinner to a dual earner model. The previous discussions have shown that even though family policies have put an increasing emphasis on work-family reconciliation, there are still apparent contradictions within the German family policy model, as some policy measures still support a traditional division of labor (e.g. tax splitting system, not fully income-dependent parental leave benefits and deficiencies in full-day childcare; see section 5). Due to these structural constraints, career-oriented women, in particular, frequently see themselves in a position to decide for either family formation (often involving a career break) or career continuation (involving the postponement of family formation). Looking at the situation from this perspective, policies in Germany would be well advised to implement a more "holistic" infrastructure in which all policies in terms of cash, care and time are synchronized among each other (Bujard, 2011). This would entail a further expansion of childcare coverage and opening hours, a move towards a more individualized tax system and further reforms in the parental leave payments. However, as earlier research has shown (e.g. Borck, 2010), such structural reforms need to go hand in hand with changes in the cultural dimension. As our discussions in section 3 have shown, German gender norms have noticeably liberalized in recent years. Yet, there still appears to be certain normative skepticism concerning out of-home- child care, which suggest that the described changes may be achievable rather in the medium- than in the short-term.

REFERENCES

Adam U., & Degen, F. (2018). *ifb-Familienreport Bayern: Tabellenband Deutschland. ifb-Materialien 2-2018* [ifb Family Report Bavaria: Tables for Germany. ifb materials No 2-2018]. Staatsinstitut für Familienforschung an der Universität Bamberg.

Autorengruppe Bildungsberichterstattung. (2018). *Bildung in Deutschland 2018: Ein indikatorengestützter Bericht mit einer Analyse zu Wirkungen und Erträgen von Bildung* [Education in Germany 2018: An indicator-based report, with an analysis of educational effects and educational gains]. wbv.

Berngruber, A. (2015a). Ohne Moos nix los? Wann und warum junge Erwachsene zum ersten Mal aus dem Elternhaus ausziehen [No mon, no fun? When and why adults leave their parental home for the first time]. In S. Walper, W. Bien, & Th. Rauschenbach, Th. (Eds.), Aufwachsen in Deutschland heute. dji-survey aid:a 2015 (pp. 55–58). Deutsches Jugendinstitut.

BiB [Bundesinstitut für Bevölkerungsforschung]. (2016). *Bevölkerungsentwicklung: Daten, Fakten, Trends zum demografischen Wandel* [Population development: Data, facts and trends about demographic change]. Bundesinstitut für Bevölkerungsforschung.

BiB [Bundesinstitut für Bevölkerungsforschung]. (2017a). *Fakten: Fertilität, Bevölkerungsdichte in Deutschland nach Kreisen, 2017* [Facts: Fertility and population density in Germany by administrative district, 2017]. Retrieved December 17, 2020, from https://www.bib.bund.de/DE/Fakten/Fakt/B77-Bevoelkerungsdichte-Kreise.html

BiB [Bundesinstitut für Bevölkerungsforschung]. (2017b). *Regionale Unterschiede: Ausländische Bevölkerung in Deutschland (Kreisebene), 2017* [Regional differences: Foreign population in Germany (district level), 2017]. Retrieved December 17, 2020 from: https://www.bib.bund.de/DE/Fakten/Fakt/B84-Auslaendische-Bevoelkerung-Kreise.html?nn=9995760

BiB [Bundesinstitut für Bevölkerungsforschung]. (2020a). *Fakten: Lebensformen und Haushalte* [Facts: Ways of life and households]. Retrieved March 14, 2020 from: https://www.bib.bund.de/DE/Fakten/Lebensformen/Lebensformen-Haushalte.html

BiB [Bundesinstitut für Bevölkerungsforschung]. (2020b). *Fakten: Rohe Ehescheidungsziffer für West- und Ostdeutschland (1950–2018)* [Facts: Crude divorce rates for East and West Germany (1950–2018)]. Retrieved December 17, 2020 from: https://www.bib.bund.de/DE/Fakten/Fakt/L128-Ehescheidungen-West-Ost-ab-1950.html?nn=10197516

BiB [Bundesinstitut für Bevölkerungsforschung]. (2020c). *Fakten: Fertilität* [Facts: Fertility]. Retrieved March 14, 2020, from https://www.bib.bund.de/DE/Fakten/Fertilitaet/Fertilitaet.html

Bick, A., & Fuchs-Schündeln, N. (2018). Taxation and labor supply of married couples across countries: A macroeconomic analysis. *Review of Economic Studies, 85*(3), 1543–1576.

Blossfeld, H.-P., Klijzing, E., Mills, M., & Kurz K. (Eds.). (2005). *Globalization, uncertainty and youth in society.* Routledge.

BMFSFJ [Bundesfamilie für Senioren, Familie, Frauen und Jugend]. (2020). *Familienleistungen* [Family benefits]. Retrieved December 17, 2020 from : https://www.bmfsfj.de/bmfsfj/themen/familie/familienleistungen

BMFSFJ [Bundesfamilie für Senioren, Familie, Frauen und Jugend]. (2017). *Familienreport 2017* [Family report 2017]. Trends, Berlin BMFSFJ.

Borck, R. (2010). Kinderbetreuung, Fertilität und Frauenerwerbstätigkeit [Child care, fertility and women's employment]. *Vierteljahrshefte zur Wirtschaftsforschung, 79*(3), 169–180.

Bossler, M., Gütztgen, N., Kubis, A., & Moczall, A. (2018). *IAB-Stellenerhebung von 1992 bis 2017: So wenige Arbeitslose pro offene Stelle wie nie in den vergangenen 25 Jahren: iab Kurzbericht 23/2018.* Institut für Arbeitsmarkt- und Berufsforschung (iab).

Brenke, K. (2017). Jugendliche in Europa: rückläufige Arbeitslosigkeit, aber weiterhin große Probleme auf dem Arbeitsmarkt [Young people in Europe: Declining unemplyoment, but still considerable labour market problems]. *DIW Wochenbericht Nr. 44.2017,* 985–1008.

52 • DIRK HOFÄCKER

Buchholz, S., & Kolb, K. (2011). Selective flexibilization and deregulation of the labour market: The German answer to increased needs for employment flexibility and its consequences for social inequalities. In H.-P. Blossfeld, S. Buchholz, D. Hofäcker, & K. Kolb (Eds.), *Globalized labour markets and social inequality in Europe* (pp. 25–45). Palgrave Macmillan.

Bujard, M. (2013). Wie wirkt das Elterngeld? [How effective is parental allowance?] In *Analysen & Argumente 123.* Konrad Adenauer Stiftung.

Bujard, M. (2011). *Familienpolitik und Geburtenrate Ein internationaler Vergleich* [Family policy and birth rates: An international comparison]. Bundesministerium für Familie, Senioren, Frauen und Jugend.

Deschermeier, P. (2017). Bevölkerungsentwicklung in den deutschen Bundesländern bis 2035 [Population developments in German federal states until 2035]. *IW-Trends, 44*(3), 63–80.

Deutscher Bundestag. (2017). *Bericht über die Lebenssituation junger Menschen und die Leistungen der Kinder- und Jugendhilfe in Deutschland—15. Kinder- und Jugendbericht, Drucksache 18/11050* [Report on the living conditions of young people and child and youth services in Germany—15th report on children and youth, printed doument 18/11050]. Deutscher Bundestag.

Diener, K., & Berggruber, A. (2018). Die Bedeutung öffentlicher Kinderbetreuung für die Erwerbsentscheidung und den Erwerbsumfang von Müttern beim beruflichen Wiedereinstieg [The importance of child care for employment-related choice and the extent of women's employment when re-entering the labour market]. *Zeitschrift für Familienforschung, 30*(2), 123–150.

Ebbinghaus, B., & Hofäcker, D. (2013). Reversing early retirement in advanced welfare economies: Overcoming push and pull factors. *Comparative Population Studies—Zeitschrift für Bevölkerungswissenschaft, 38*(4), 807–840.

Eurostat. (2020a). *Demography and migration.* Retrieved March 22, 2020, from: https://ec.europa.eu/eurostat/web/population-demography-migration-projections/data/main-tables

Eurostat. (2018). *Living conditions in Europe—2018 edition.* Publications Office of the European Union.

Eurostat. (2020b). *Education and training.* Retrieved March 15, 2020, from: https://ec.europa.eu/eurostat/web/education-and-training/data/database

Eurostat. (2020c). *Income and living conditions.* Retrieved March 22, 2020, from https://ec.europa.eu/eurostat/web/income-and-living-conditions/data/database

Geißler, R. (2014). *Die Sozialstruktur Deutschlands, 7., grundlegend überarbeitete Auflage. Mit einem Beitrag von Thomas Meyer* [The social structure of Germany, 7th revised edition; with a contribution by Thomas Meyer]. Springer VS.

Geißler, R., & Weber-Menges, S. (2008). Migrantenkinder im Bildungssystem: doppelt benachteiligt [Children of migrants in the educational system: doubly disadvantaged]. *Aus Politik und Zeitgeschichte, 49*, 14–22.

Goebel, J., & Krause, P. (2018). Einkommensentwicklung—Verteilung, Angleichung, Armut und Dynamik [Income development—Distribution, convergence, poverty and recent dynamics]. In Bundeszentrale für politische Bildung (Ed.), *Datenreport 2018: Ein Sozialbericht für die Bundesrepublik Deutschland* [Data report 2018: A social report for the German Federal Republic] (pp. 239–253). bpb.

Göttsche, F. (2018). Bevölkerung mit Migrationshintergrund [The population with a migrant background]. In Bundeszentrale für politische Bildung (Ed.), *Datenreport 2018: Ein Sozialbericht für die Bundesrepublik Deutschland* [Data report 2018: A social report for the German Federal Republic] (pp. 28–42). bpb.

Hofäcker, D. (2004). Typen europäischer Familienpolitik: Vehikel oder Hemmnis für das adult worker model? [Types of European family policy—Vehicle or obstacle for the adult worker model]. In S. Leitner, I. Ostner, & M. Schratzenstaller, M. (Eds.), *Wohlfahrtsstaat und Geschlechterverhältnis im Umbruch. Was kommt nach dem Ernährermodell? Jahrbuch für Europa- und Nordamerika-Studien 7/2003* [Welfare state and gender relations on the move: What follows after the male breadwonner model. Yearbook for European and North American Studies 7/2003] (pp. 257–284). VS Verlag für Sozialwissenschaften.

Kaufmann, F.-X. (2005). *Schrumpfende Gesellschaft. Vom Bevölkerungsrückgang und seinen Folgen* [The shrinking society. About population decline and its consequences]. Suhrkamp.

Kott, K. (2018). Armutsgefährdung und materielle Entbehrung [Risk of poverty and material deprivation]. In Bundeszentrale für politische Bildung (Ed.), *Datenreport 2018: Ein Sozialbericht für die Bundesrepublik Deutschland,* Bonn: bpb, pp. 231–238.

Lewis, J., & Ostner, I. (1994). *Gender and the Evolution of European Social Policies; Arbeitspapiere des Zentrums für Sozialpolitik No. 4/1994* [Working papers of the Centre for Social Policy No. 4/1994]. Zentrum für Sozialpolitik.

Lietzmann, T., & Wenzig, C. (2017). Arbeitszeitwünsche und Erwerbstätigkeit von Müttern: Welche Vorstellungen über die Vereinbarkeit von Beruf und Familie bestehen, iab Kurzbericht 10/2017 [Preferred working times and employment of mothers: Which ideas about work-family-reconciliation do exist? iab Short Report 10/2017]. Institut für Arbeitsmarkt- und Berufsforschung (iab).

Lück, D., Panova, R., Naderi, R., & Bujard, M. (2016). Kinderlosigkeit und Kinderreichtum—Ein differenzierter Blick auf das Geburtengeschehen in Deutschland [Childlessness and abundance of children—A differentiated view on fertility trends in Germany]. *Bevölkerungsforschung aktuell, 37*(1), 2–10.

Lück, D., & Ruckdeschel, K. (2019). Familie—was bedeutet das heute? Familienleitbilder in Deutschland sind vielfältig, aber im Kern stabil [Family—What does that mean nowadays? Family models in Germany are diverse, but basically stable]. *Bevölkerungsforschung aktuell, 40*(2), 2–7.

Meyer, T. (2014). Der Wandel der Familie und anderer privater Lebensformen [The change of the family and private forms of life]. In Geißler, R. (Ed.), *Die Sozialstruktur Deutschlands, 7., grundlegend überarbeitete Auflage. Mit einem Beitrag von Thomas Meyer* [The social structure of Germany, 7th revised edition; with a contribution by Thomas Meyer] (pp. 413–454). Springer VS.

Mucha, T. (2018). Volkswirtschaftliche Gesamtrechnungen [National accounts]. In Bundeszentrale für politische Bildung (Ed.), *Datenreport 2018: Ein Sozialbericht für die Bundesrepublik Deutschland* [Data report 2018: A social report for the German Federal Republic] (pp. 129–137). bpb.

Noll, H.-H., & Weick, S. (2014). Housing in Germany: Expensive, comfortable and usually rented. Analysis of the housing conditions and quality in comparison to other European countries. *ISI-Informationsdienst Soziale Indikatoren, Selected English Articles, 4,* 1–6.

OECD. (2020a). *OECD statistics.* https://stats.oecd.org/ (Retrieved March 18, 2020).

OECD. (2020b). *OECD family Data Base: Table LMF 1.2 "Maternal employment."* Retrieved March 15, 2020 from: http://www.oecd.org/social/family/database.htm

OECD. (2020c). *OECD family data Base: Table PF 3.2 "Enrolment in childcare and preschool."* Retrieved March 15, 2020 from: http://www.oecd.org/social/family/database.htm

Peuckert, R. (2019). *Familienformen im sozialen Wandel, 9., vollständig überarbeitete Auflage* [Family forms and social change", 9th revised edition]. Springer VS.

Pötzsch, O. (2018). Aktueller Geburtenanstieg und seine Potenziale [The current rise in births and its potentials]. *WISTA—Wirtschaft und Statistik, 3,* 72–89.

Schacht, D., & Metzing, M. (2018). Lebenssituation von Migrantinnen und Migranten und deren Nachkommen [Living conditions of migrants and their offspring]. In Bundeszentrale für politische Bildung (Ed.), *Datenreport 2018: Ein Sozialbericht für die Bundesrepublik Deutschland* [Data report 2018: A social report for the German Federal Republic] (pp. 272–279). bpb.

Scheuer, A. (2018). Lebensqualität und Identität in der Europäischen Union [Quality of life and identitiy in the Europen Union]. In Bundeszentrale für politische Bildung (Ed.), *Datenreport 2018: Ein Sozialbericht für die Bundesrepublik Deutschland* [Data report 2018: A social report for the German Federal Republic] (pp. 433–439). bpb.

Sperber, C., & Walwei, U. (2015). Trendwende am Arbeitsmarkt seit 2005: Jobboom mit Schattenseiten? [The trend reversal on the labour market since 2005: Job boom with negative side effects?]. *WSI Mitteilungen, 8,* 583–592.

Statistische Ämter des Bundes und der Länder. (2015). *25 Jahre Deutsche Einheit* [25 years of German unity]. Statistisches Bundesamt.

Statistisches Bundesamt. (2019a). *Statistisches Jahrbuch 2019: Deutschland und Internationales* [Statistical yearbook 2019: Germany and international data]. Statistisches Bundesamt.

Statistisches Bundesamt. (2019b). *Kinderlosigkeit, Geburten und Familien: Ergebnisse des Mikrozensus 2018* [Childlessness, births and families: Results from the German micro-census]. Statistisches Bundesamt.

Statistisches Bundesamt. (2020). *Wohnen* [Living]. Retrieved March 22, 2020 from: https://www.destatis.de/DE/Themen/Gesellschaft-Umwelt/Wohnen/_inhalt.html

Tyrell, H. (1979). Familie und gesellschaftliche Differenzierung [Family and social differentiation]. In H. Pross (Ed.), *Familie -wohin?* [Family—Whereto?] (pp. 13–77). Rowohlt.

Walper, S., & Lien, S.-C. (2017). Aktive Vaterschaft im Kontext unterschiedlicher Familienphasen und Erwerbskonstellationen [Active fatherhood in the context of different family phases and work constellations]. In Statistisches Bundesamt (Ed.), *Wie die Zeit vergeht: Analysen zur Zeitverwendung in Deutschland: Beiträge zur Ergebniskonferenz der Zeitverwendungserhebung 2012/2013 am 5./6. Oktober 2016 in Wiesbaden* [How time flies: Analyses of time use in Germany. Contributions to the Conference on the German Time Use Survey 2012/2013, Wiesbaden, October 5/6, 2016] (pp. 91–116). Statistisches Bundesamt.

Wolf, A. (2016). *Das wirtschaftliche Süd-Nord-Gefälle in Deutschland: Aktuelle Befunde und Ursachen; HWWI Policy Paper 99* [The economic north-south-divide in Germany: Recent findings and its causes. HWWI policy paper 99]. Hamburgisches WeltWirtschaftsInstitut (HWWI).

CHAPTER 4

DISADVANTAGES IN STARTING A FAMILY IN HUNGARY

Márton Medgyesi
TÁRKI and Centre for Social Sciences

1. NATIONAL CONTEXT

After four decades of the communist regime, Hungary engaged in a transition process to democracy and market economy around 1990, similarly to other countries of Eastern Europe. As Kornai (2006) describes, the transition in Eastern Europe was a remarkably fast (10–15 years long) and peaceful process during which these countries adopted economic and political institutions of the Western civilization. The beginning of the transition process has proven difficult for Hungary as the country experienced structural shocks and the resulting recession continued until the middle of the decade. This period of transitional recession was characterized by a double-digit decline in GDP, a heavy increase in unemployment, income inequality and poverty (Fábián et al., 2014).

In the second half of the 1990s, Hungary recovered from recession and enjoyed growth rates above the EU average until EU accession in 2004. The massive redistribution programs, implemented after the 2002 elections, however, led to high budget deficits and the slowdown of economic growth already in 2006.

Family Formation Among Youth in Europe: Coping With Socio-Economic Disadvantages,
pages 55–65.
Copyright © 2022 by Information Age Publishing
www.infoagepub.com
All rights of reproduction in any form reserved.

56 • MÁRTON MEDGYESI

The economic crisis found Hungary with a vulnerable economy and the country had to ask for an IMF loan in 2009 to avoid state bankruptcy. Unemployment and poverty increased during the crisis years, while inequality increased in 2012, after the government introduced changes to the personal income taxation system. After 2014, economic growth resumed, employment rose and wages increased, partly as a consequence of labor shortage due to emigration. In the same time, the decisions of the Orban government (in power since 2010), including recentralization of public administration, renationalization in the economy and the weakening of institutional control over the government, meant that, over the past decade, Hungary has been moving away from the European model.

2. DEMOGRAPHIC TRENDS
RELEVANT TO FAMILY FORMATION

For over 30 years, between the mid-1970s and 2011, the number of marriages in Hungary was declining, the greatest fall occurring between 1990 and 2011, when the crude marriage declined from 6.4 (per thousand inhabitants) to 3.6 in 2011, one of the lowest values in the EU. In the past few years, this tendency reversed and the marriage rate increased to 5.3 in 2016 (Gregor, 2018). One factor behind the declining marriage rates was the postponement of marriage. Between 2000 and 2016: age at first marriage increased from 24.7 to 29.7 for women and from 27.2 to 32.5 for men (Murinkó & Rohr, 2019). The weakening of the institution of marriage between 1990 and 2011 can also be seen in the increased number of divorces in Hungary. The frequency of divorce (measured by total divorce rate) increased between 1990 and 2008 from 31% to 46%, indicating that almost half of all marriages ended in divorce. During the following years, this trend has reversed—and parallel to the increase in marriages—the total divorce rate declined and reached 42% in 2016 (Makay & Szabó, 2019). In a European comparison, Hungary was among the countries with middle-level divorce rate in 2015.

With regard to other forms of partnership status, demographic statistics show an increase in cohabitation and a comparatively small-scale rise in the proportion of singles. Between 2000 and 2016, the proportion of population in cohabitation aged 15 or older increased from 6.6% to 13% (Murinkó & Rohr, 2019). It is clear that an increasing number of couples choose cohabitation as a long-term alternative to marriage: between 2000 and 2016, the proportion of those who have never been married among those cohabiting increased from 53% to 70%.

Total fertility dropped from 1.84 in 1990 to below 1.3 by 1999 and stagnated around this very low level until the years following the economic crisis. In 2011, the value of the total fertility rate (1.23) was among the lowest in EU. Despite the improvement that has taken place since 2011, the total fertility rate in Hungary (1.49 in 2018) remains among the lowest in the EU. The mean age at birth has increased considerably (from below 26 to 30) during the period of declining fertility (Kapitány & Spéder, 2015), thus fertility decline is partly a consequence of postponement of childbearing. Fertility rates adjusted for postponement remained broadly stagnant

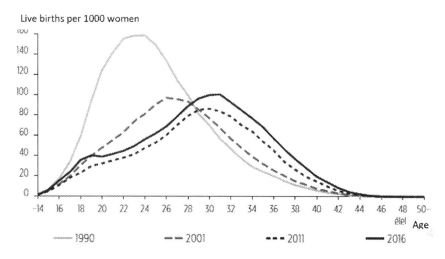

FIGURE 4.1.   Unconditional Fertility Rates by Age, Hungary. Source: Kapitány, 2018

until 2005 and started to decline afterwards. According to birth order, the most important decline has been observed in case of second births, while declining first birth (increasing childlessness) was less important. The following figure from Kapitány (2018) shows clearly the tendency of fertility postponement. The modal age of fertility was in the range of 23–24 in 1990, while in 2016 women most frequently gave birth after the age of 30. Moreover, it is clear that in recent years the age profile of fertility has developed a bimodal character: there is an emerging pattern of early fertility around the age of 18–20. Live births per 1000 women aged 15–19 was 24.9 in 2016, which is more than double the EU average (10.7).

The declining fertility contributed to population decline and changing age distribution. The population of Hungary peaked at 10,709 thousand in 1980 but has been declining ever since, falling below ten million in 2011. The declining fertility combined with (to some extent) declining mortality has also had an effect on the age structure, bringing about the ageing of the population. The generational balance shifted significantly from the young to the older generations. The share of children (0–14 years) declined from 22% in 1980 to less than 15 percent by 2019. At the same time, the share of the 65+ population has increased from 12 percent in 1980 to 23 percent in 2019.

3. NORMATIVE FRAMEWORK

In Hungary, family (and children) is among the most important values, deeply embedded in the societal value system. Based on data from the European Values Study, Hungary is among the countries—together with Malta, Cyprus and North-

58 • MÁRTON MEDGYESI

ern Ireland—with the highest share of people (over 90%) agreeing that family is a priority value (the EU average 85%). As far as the most important values and necessities for a good marriage and family life are concerned, Hungary is very similar to the EU average, listing fidelity, capacity for discussing and solving problems, and having children in families among the top 3 priorities (Rosta & Tomka, 2010). Moreover, more Hungarians than the EU average deny the statement that marriage is an outmoded institution (Rosta & Tomka, 2010; Török, 2010).[1]

Results of many of the above mentioned studies have confirmed that despite modernization, individualization and transition, traditional family values and attitudes are strongly embedded in the Hungarian society: there is a—non-religious—conservatism (Pongrácz & S.Molnár, 2000); those who were more concerned about the status, employment of women and related family conflicts, especially after the transition, belonged to the traditional value oriented group (S. Molnár & Dobossy, 2000); and—quite surprisingly—there is no significant difference between young and old generations, therefore "familialism" (meaning family centric ideas and attitude) is very strong (see, for example, Dupcsik & Tóth, 2008; Tóth & Dupcsik, 2007).

As demonstrated by Kapitány and Spéder (2018), the preferred number of children showed a high level of stability in Hungary. Both the ideal number of children and the planned number of children remained essentially stable in the decade and a half from 2001 to 2016. The ideal number of children in 2016 was put at 2.2 for both men and women, and the planned number of children was 2.0 for women and 1.9 for men. Falling fertility is thus not a consequence of the declining importance of having children and the desired number of children, but of an increase in unrealized fertility plans.

4. SOCIO-ECONOMIC CONDITIONS SINCE THE ECONOMIC CRISIS

The economic crisis resulted in an increase in unemployment among young people in many countries of the EU (Eurofound 2012). Between 2008 and 2011, youth unemployment primarily grew in those countries most affected by recession, e.g., Greece, Spain, Latvia, Lithuania and Ireland. In these countries, the overall unemployment rate of the active-age population (aged 15–64) increased by 8–10 percentage points, while in the age group 15–24, it grew even more markedly (by 15 percentage points in Ireland and 23 percentage points in Greece). Furthermore, the increase in youth unemployment also concerned countries with a less pronounced increase in overall unemployment. E.g., in Hungary, the overall unemployment rate increased from 7.5% in 2007 to 11% by 2010, while in case of the 15–29 age group, unemployment increased from 12% to 19%. Between 2011 and 2014, the unemployment rate and youth unemployment grew further in the

---

[1] Source: European Values Study (EVS) 2008 results and publications in Hungary, e.g., Rosta and Tomka (2010) and Török (2010).

Southeast European countries. However, in the Baltic states, Ireland, the United Kingdom and Hungary, unemployment fell in this period, as did youth unemployment. After 2014, unemployment rates have been decreasing in the majority of EU Member States. In Hungary, youth unemployment rate was 6 points above the 7.8% overall rate in 2014; by 2017, this gap reduced to 3 points. Overall, thus, youth seem to have been more influenced by both the recession and the economic upturn in Hungary and typically also in other EU countries.

The deteriorating labor market situation of young people between 2008 and 2014 was reflected in the increased risk of poverty: youth income poverty[2] increased in nearly all EU Member States between 2008 and 2014 (Medgyesi, 2018). The most substantial increase was seen in countries with a strong increase in youth unemployment. In Ireland, the share of the poor among young adults increased from 13% to 25%, but the rate of increase was not much lower in Spain, Greece or Romania. In Hungary, income poverty among the young increased from 16% in 2008 to 20% in 2015 (see Figure 4.2). In about half of the EU Member States, the poverty rate increased to a larger extent among young people than in the total working-age population.

Since 2014, the increase in the youth poverty rate has come to an end in most countries. The proportion of the poor has grown significantly only in Cyprus (by 5 percentage points) and Spain (2 percentage points). However, there has been a decrease of 5 percentage points in Ireland and a comparable decline has been observed also in Hungary (see Figure 4.2). In the rest of the countries, the poverty rate has changed by less than 2 percentage points. Nonetheless, youth poverty rates in the majority of EU Member States are above the poverty rates for the total active-age population. Moreover, educational indicators show that human capital investment continues to be relatively low in areas with higher occurrence of poverty. The effects of poverty and the deficiencies of the Hungarian school system lead to a high level of school dropout. The rate of early school leavers in 2018 was 12.5%, which is relatively high in Europe and above the EU average (10.6%).

The situation of the young tends to be vulnerable not only on the labor market, but on the housing market as well. Hungary has a housing system which is dominated by owner-occupied housing and limited opportunities for private rental and social housing. During the years of economic growth before the crisis, many families took out loans denominated in foreign currencies (EUR, CHF) to finance homeownership due to lower interest rates. Unfortunately, the crisis brought about a depreciation of the Hungarian currency (HUF) which resulted in a jump of the debt burden for these families and many of them became unable to repay their debts.

---

[2] As measured by the rate for those with less than 60% of the median equivalized household income.

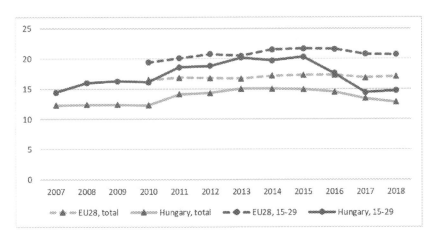

FIGURE 4.2. Trends in the At-Risk-Of-Poverty Rate in Hungary and the EU28 (%).
Source: Eurostat database, table ilc_li02, extracted 12.03.2020.

5. INSTITUTIONAL FRAMEWORK

The Hungarian government has a relatively generous set of family policy measures (Makay, 2019) to subsidize family formation and childbearing. The Hungarian system of cash family benefits provides a variety of benefits that are available under different eligibility conditions. Some of the benefits are linked to employment and payment of social security contributions (e.g., parental leave policies CSED, GYED and family tax allowance), while others are not (e.g., maternity benefit, GYES, education allowance), and some benefits are means-tested (e.g., regular child protection benefit). Since 2010, there has been a clear increase in the importance of employment-related benefits within family cash benefits. The significant increase in the amount of family tax allowance[3] made it one of the most important family benefits, and the amount of other employment-related benefits also increased with the rise in wages. At the same time, however, the government has long failed to increase the amount of universal benefits, like child allowance. Moreover, child allowance has been subject to school attendance condition (Makay, 2019, Szikra, 2014). The population policy package adopted in 2014 included measures to encourage mothers with young children to return to the labor market. Parents can return to work while continuing to receive GYES or GYED after the first birthday of the child. A more pro-natalist measure has also been

---

[3] The government increased the generosity for tax deductions for families with children in 2011. In 2020, families who have tax liabilities high enough to fully take advantage of the system can benefit from the following deduction of personal income taxes (and social security contributions): 1 child families 10.000 HUF/child a month (30 €), for 2 child families 20.000 HUF/child a month, for 3 child families 33.000 HUF/child a month (100 €).

introduced, namely that if the family has another child while still receiving one of the child-raising allowances, they can now receive both benefits. In 2015, the government introduced a new housing allowance program (CSOK) for families, which is a non-refundable state subsidy for the purchase or construction of new or used residential property, the amount of which depends on the number of children. The maximum benefit to married couples with three or more children is equivalent to a $36,000 grant to buy a new home, and a capped-interest loan for part of the home value. As a result of successive modifications, the aid scheme continued to expand in the following years.

In recent years, the government has aimed to improve not only cash benefits for families but also services. By using EU development funds, the government has set itself the goal of improving day care and significantly increasing the number of places, primarily to increase the employment of mothers with young children. As a result of the introduction of compulsory kindergarten education from the age of 3, participation in day care within the age group of 4–6 years has become virtually complete (96% of the age group attended kindergarten in 2016). The number of nursery seats has increased in recent years, to 46,475 in 2017. This has also been reflected in the increase in the number of people under 3 years receiving formal day care, which increased from 10% in 2013 to 15.6% in 2016 (Eurostat database), but still far behind the EU28 countries' 33% average. Not only is there a small number of nursery places in the country, but their distribution is uneven: a quarter of young children live in settlements without nurseries.

Literature suggests that cash and in-kind support for families with children can have a positive impact on fertility and child development (see, e.g., Szabó-Morvai et al., 2019). Cash support for families with children decreases the costs associated with childbearing and improves the income situation of families with children. In addition, these measures might also mitigate the adverse effects of poverty on child development. Child-related welfare benefits not only affect the child generation but also the activity of the parent generation. Welfare grants can encourage parents with young children to stay at home with their children, but with the right setting of incentives, parents can also be encouraged to return to the labor market.

Fertility has increased in recent years, with overall fertility rates rising from 1.24 in 2011 to almost 1.5 in 2017. At the same time, it is difficult to get an accurate picture of the impact of changes in family support on fertility, as these changes took place at the same time as economic growth and household incomes increased. Effects of earlier reforms of family benefits have shown a modest but significant positive effect of cash benefits on fertility in Hungary. Gábos et al. (2009) showed that during the period between 1950 and 2005, fertility tended to be higher in years with higher expenditure on family benefits. Aassve et al. (2006) demonstrated that the abolition of earnings-related paid parental leave induced a radical fall or postponement of parenthood among the more educated women. Spéder et al. (2020) studied the effects of the introduction of GYET in 1993 and the introduction of the tax allowance on families with children in 1999. They have shown that longer parental leave under the GYET benefit has induced low status parents to have more children, while the increase in tax relief encouraged those with high educational attainment to have a third child. Szabó (2017) also found a significant effect of the tax deduction on birth of the third child, especially in case of women with higher education. Szabó-Morvai et al. (2019) find a significant positive effect in the first to third year in case of three types of family policies: family tax credit, nursery school development and home ownership support. They interpret their results supporting findings of previous literature, which suggests that fertility decisions are affected primarily by employment, subsistence and housing prospects.

6. COUNTRY-SPECIFIC CHALLENGES TO FAMILY FORMATION

Hungary is a country with middle-level income inequality when compared to other countries of the EU (Fábián et al., 2014). On the other hand, the level of social mobility tends to be relatively low and success of youth in education or on the labor market is strongly affected by the parental background (OECD, 2018). In the domain of education, this has been repeatedly demonstrated by international comparative studies: e.g., the OECD PISA study has shown that Hungary is among the OECD countries with the strongest effect of parental socio-economic status on child test scores (OECD, 2019). Another study comparing the correlation of parental and child educational attainment also found that Hungary has a low level of educational mobility (Hertz et al., 2008). Other studies demonstrate that, in Hungary, the correlation between parental and child earnings is relatively strong. While this is to a large extent connected to strong intergenerational correlation of educational attainment, it is clear that the strong effect of parental background also extends to the labor market (OECD, 2018).

In countries where parental background has a strong effect on life chances of children, child poverty is a severe problem. According to Eurostat data, the proportion of children (below 18 years of age) in income poverty increased in Hungary in the years following the economic crisis until 2014, but then the indicator dropped from 25% in 2014 to 15% in 2017. Similar development has been described for those affected by severe material deprivation, and the proportion of those affected by income poverty or social exclusion, which is a combination of the two indicators (and the proportion of people living in households with very low labor intensity). The value of the latter indicator rose from 33% to 44% between 2008 and 2014, before dropping to 32% by 2017. The proportion of children affected by income poverty or social exclusion is higher than that of the general population (26% in 2017). In Hungary, the rate of income poverty among children in 2017 was lower than the EU28 average (20%), but the proportion of people experiencing income poverty or social exclusion was higher than the EU average (25%). Poverty and child poverty in Hungary have a strong territorial aspect and an ethnic dimension as well. Severe poverty is concentrated in small settlements in the Northern and North-Eastern regions of the country. The ethnic dimension of poverty concerns the population of Roma ethnicity. Poverty rates in this population exceed by far the average rates: in 2017, 48% of Roma were characterized by income poverty, while the corresponding figure was 12.8% for non-Roma (Bernát, 2019).

These social cleavages are also manifested in the patterns of family formation and fertility. As Kapitány (2018) demonstrates, fertility among women below age 20 is concentrated among the low educated and in the regions more affected by poverty. Consequently, in Hungary, problematic patterns of family formation include not only the postponement of childbearing and the resulting decline in fertility, but also too early childbearing which is more frequent among the low educated and which might severely constrain life chances of the women and children concerned.

The low performance of the education system, rising unemployment and increasing debt burden during the crisis years have induced many young people to emigrate: this, of course, has a negative effect on family formation and fertility in Hungary. Year 2011 marked a turning point in the trends of emigration, as labor markets of Germany and Austria fully opened up towards citizens of the new Member States (Gödri, 2015). These two became the main destination countries of Hungarian emigrants; until Brexit, emigration to the United Kingdom has been of the same magnitude and some new destination countries have also emerged (e.g., the Netherlands). Despite the significant return migration, the number of Hungarian citizens residing in European countries has been steadily increasing. According to statistics of the receiving countries, the number of active age (between 20 and 65 years) Hungarians residing in other EU countries stood around 330 thousand in 2017, which is nearly three times their number in 2009 (Hárs & Simon, 2019a). Among Hungarians residing abroad, men and younger age groups are over-represented. Between 2006 and 2010, graduates were most likely to work abroad, but since 2014, the probability of working abroad increased for those with vocational education and they became the group with the highest likelihood of working in other countries (Hárs & Simon, 2020).

7. CONCLUSION

The economic crisis clearly had a negative impact on Hungarian young adults: youth unemployment and poverty among young adults have increased and many families became unable to repay housing loans. Since 2014, however, economic growth has resumed, unemployment declined and wages have also increased. The total fertility rate declined during the crisis period, but it increased between 2011 and 2016, and marriage rates have also increased from their relatively low levels after the crisis. The government expanded family benefits, but mostly those that are conditioned on working status (tax deductions, social insurance benefits), while benefits that are available for all children, including the poor, were not raised. Studies on effects of specific policies show that the government efforts presumably had some positive effect on fertility, but not fully in the intended way.

64 • MÁRTON MEDGYESI

Despite focusing major subsidies on middle-class families, the data clearly show a polarization of fertility trends: fertility not only increased for middle-class families but early fertility (teenage pregnancy) also increased among the low educated. Emigration, which has increased since the economic crisis, also puts a downward pressure on family formation and fertility.

REFERENCES

Aassve, A., Billari, F. C., & Spéder, Zs. (2006). Societal transition, policy changes and family formation: Evidence from Hungary. *European Journal of Population/Revue européenne de Démographie, 22*(2), 127–152.

Bernát, A. (2019). Integration of the Roma in Hungary in the 2010s. In I. Tóth, & I. Gy. (Eds.), *Hungarian Social Report 2019* (pp. 195–214). Tárki.

Dupcsik, Cs., & Tóth, O. (2008). Feminizmus helyett familizmus [Familialism instead of Feminism]. *Demográfia, 51*(4), 307–328.

Eurofound. (2012). *Young people not in employment, education or training: Characteristics, costs and policy responses in Europe*. Eurofound.

Fábián, Z., Gábos, A., Kopasz, M., Medgyesi, M., Szivós, P., & Tóth, I.Gy. (2014). *Hungary: A country caught in its own trap.* In B. Nolan, W. Salverda, D. Checchi, I. Marx, I., A. McKnight, I.Gy. Tóth, & H. van de Werfhorst (Eds.), *Changing inequalities and societal impacts in rich countries. Thirty countries' experiences,* Oxford University Press.

Gábos, A., Gál, R. I., & Kézdi, G. (2009). The effects of child-related benefits and pensions on fertility by birth order: A test on Hungarian data. *Popul. Stud. 63*, 215–231.

Gödri, I. (2015). International migration In J. Monostori, P. Őri, & Zs. Spéder, (Eds.), *Demographic portrait of Hungary*. Hungarian Demographic Research Institute.

Gregor A. (2018): A hazai ifjúság demográfiai jellemzői és az azt alakító tényezők [Demographic characteristics of Hungarian youth and driving factors]. In A. Nagy (Ed.), *Margón kívül-magyar ifjúságkutatás 2016* [Out of the margin—Hungarian youth survey—2016]. Excenter Kutatóközpont

Hárs, Á., & Simon, D. (2019a). Increasing outward migration—opportunities, hopes and labour market impacts. In I. Gy. Tóth, (Ed.), *Hungarian Social Report 2019* (pp. 137–161). Tárki.

Hárs, Á., & Simon, D. (2020). Outward migration of youth—Young people working abroad. In K. Fazekas. M. Csillag, Z. Hermann, & Á. Scharle (Eds.), *The Hungarian labour market 2019.* KRTK Budapest.

Hertz, T., Jayasundera, T., Piraino, P., Selcuk, S., Smith, N., & Verashchagina, A. (2008). The inheritance of educational inequality: International comparisons and fifty-year trends. *The B.E. Journal of Economic Analysis & Policy, 7*(2), 1–48.

Kapitány, B. (2018). Bimodális (kétcsúcsú) termékenységi görbe Magyarországon—leíró eredmények és lehetséges okok [Bimodal fertility curve in Hungary—Descriptive results and potential causes]. *Demográfia, 61*(2–3), 121–146. DOI: 10.21543/Dem.61.2-3.1

Kapitány, B., & Spéder, Zs. (2015). Fertility. In J. Monostori, P. Őri, & Zs. Spéder, (Eds.), *Demographic portrait of Hungary 2015.* Hungarian Demographic Research Institute.

Disadvantages in Starting a Family in Hungary • 65

Kapitány, B., & Spéder, Zs. (2018). Fertility. In J. Monostori, P. Őri, & Zs. Spéder, (Eds.). *Demographic portrait of Hungary 2018.* Hungarian Demographic Research Institute.

Kornai, J. (2006). The great transformation of Central Eastern Europe. Success and disappointment. *Economics of Transition 14*(2), 207–244.

Makay, Zs. (2019). The family support system and female employment. In J. Monostori, P. Őri, & Zs. Spéder, (Eds.). *Demographic portrait of Hungary 2018.* Hungarian Demographic Research Institute.

Makay, Zs., & Szabó, L. (2019). Divorce. In J. Monostori, P. Őri, & Zs. Spéder, (Eds.). *Demographic portrait of Hungary 2018.* Hungarian Demographic Research Institute.

Medgyesi, M. (2018). Inequality of outcomes and opportunities among the young. In R. Carmo, C. Rio, & M. Medgyesi (Eds.), *Reducing inequalities* (pp. 115–134). Palgrave Macmillan.

Murinkó, L., & Rohr, A. (2019). Marriage and partnerships. In J. Monostori, P. Őri, & Zs. Spéder, (Eds.), *Demographic portrait of Hungary 2018.* Hungarian Demographic Research Institute.

OECD. (2018). *The broken social elevator.* OECD.

OECD. (2019). *Where all students can succeed. PISA 2018 results* (Volume II). OECD.

Pongrácz, T., & Molnár, S. E. (2000). Kísérlet a "tradícióőrző" és az attól elszakadó „modernizálódó" családi értékek empirikus vizsgálatára [An attempt at the empirical investigation of traditional and modernised family values]. In Zs. Spéder & P. P. Tóth (Eds.), *Human Relations. In honour of László Cseh-Szombathy.* Századvég.

Rosta, G., & Tomka, M. (Eds). (2010). *What do Hungarians value.* OCIPE.

S. Molnár, E., & Dobossy, I. (2000). "Tradíciókövető" és "modernizálódó" szemléletmód a rendszerváltozás után jelentkező családi problémák érzékelésében [Traditional and modernised approach in the perception of family problems after transition]. In Zs. Spéder & P. P Tóth (Eds.), *Human relations. In honour of László Cseh-Szombathy.* Századvég.

Spéder, Zs., Murinkó, L., & Oláh, L. Sz. (2020). *Cash support vs. tax incentives: The differential impact of policy interventions on third births in contemporary Hungary. Population Studies,* DOI: 10.1080/00324728.2019.1694165

Szabó, B. (2017). *Fertility effects of the family tax break extension in Hungary.* MA Thesis, Central European University. https://www.etd.ceu.edu/2017/szabo_bence.pdf

Szabó-Morvai, Á., Balás, G., Bördős, K., & Herczeg, B. (2019). *Evaluation of family policy measures and their impact on fertility.* Hétfa Institute.

Szikra, D. (2014). Democracy and welfare in hard times: The social policy of the Orbán Government in Hungary between 2010 and 2014. *Journal of European Social Policy, 24*(5), 486–500. https://doi.org/10.1177/0958928714545446

Török, P. (2010). *Family and education in the light of the European values.* Retrieved 10 January 2017 from: http://folyoiratok.ofi.hu/sites/default/files/article_attachments/upsz_2011_1–5_11.pdf

Tóth, O., & Dupcsik, Cs. (2007). Családok és formák - változások az utóbbi ötven évben Magyarországon [Families and Forms. Changes in Hungary during the last fifty years]. *Demográfia, 50*(4), 430–437.

CHAPTER 5

FAMILIES IN ISRAEL

Coping and Adjustment

Tali Heiman, Dorit Olenik-Shemesh, and Merav Regev-Nevo

The Open University of Israel

For most Israelis, the family is the center around which life revolves. The emphasis on family life in Israel is evident across all cultural and religious sub-groups composing the Israeli society: it can be seen in high marriage rates, fertility rates and the cultural ideals surrounding them. Nevertheless, is there such a thing as an 'All-Israeli' family? In this chapter, we draw a picture of the Israeli family shaped by tradition and modernity, reviewing data regarding family types and patterns, marriage and divorce, fertility and the place of children in the Israeli family, as well as regarding other factors surrounding family as a social institution.

1. NATIONAL CONTEXT

Perhaps more than any other modern state, Israel can be said to have a (relatively) short history but a very long past. The modern state of Israel was founded in 1948, one of many states established following WWII and the disintegration of the British empire and it has been at the center of strife and international attention ever

Family Formation Among Youth in Europe: Coping With Socio-Economic Disadvantages, pages 67–82.
Copyright © 2022 by Information Age Publishing
www.infoagepub.com
All rights of reproduction in any form reserved.

68 • TALI HEIMAN, DORIT OLENIK-SHEMESH, & MERAV REGEV-NEVO

since. It is a unique place, incorporating western ideals with traditional religious values and a Mediterranean atmosphere.

Israel has a widely diverse, multi-cultural society composed of multiple national, religious and ethnic groups: Jews and Arabs, native-born Israelis and immigrants. The Jewish majority (approx. 74% in 2018) comprises secular Jews, who identify with Jewish nationality but generally do not adhere to religious norms and commandments and view religious practices as a matter of personal choice; National-Orthodox Jews, who keep with the Jewish religious commandments, but strive to be integrated in the general society when it does not conflict with their faith; and ultra-orthodox Jews who strictly observe the religious laws and generally prefer to avoid integration with other groups (Central Bureau of Statistics[2], 134/2019). The Arab minority (approx. 21%) consists mostly of Muslims, as well as prominent Christian and Druze groups—all of which tend to be moderately religious (Cohen, 2018; Katz, 2017).

A brief outline of five factors we deem especially influential for understanding the forces shaping the Israeli society and Israeli families will be given here for background and context; however, the reader should keep in mind that many further cultural variations exist in Israel that cannot be fully—or indeed, even partially—explored here.

Western Secular Individualism vs. Collectivism and Religiosity

Upon its establishment and ever since, Israel's leaders chose to define Israel as a Jewish and democratic state (Shetreet & Homolka, 2017). The tension between these two definitions is perhaps more evident in questions surrounding family life than in any other field. Israel strives to see itself as a modern, liberal, individualistic state; its liberal attitudes can be witnessed in its comparatively liberal approach towards the gay community, its policies regarding adoption and registration of children to gay and lesbians couples and its extensive recognition of single-parent families (Sperling, 2010). Yet, alongside this liberalism, it displays many traditional, religious values, accompanied by collectivistic perceptions of the appropriate relation between the individual and the group (Lavee & Katz, 2003; Ritblatt, 2003).

The Jewish Holocaust

Jewish history is fraught with pogroms and persecution, reaching a terrible climax in the Holocaust. In the Jewish-Israeli psychology, an increased Jewish reproduction is portrayed as a concrete and symbolic answer to these traumatic memories; indeed, as early as 1943, Yitzhak Halevi Herzog, the chief Rabbi of mandatory Palestine, has called upon the Jewish population to "be fruitful and multiply, and replenish the earth" (Steinfeld, 2015).

The Israeli-Arab Conflict

The war between the newly founded Jewish state of Israel and its close (and far) Arab neighbors broke out when the new state was but one day old. When a ceasefire was declared a year later, the young state of Israel found itself the sovereign of all the territories inside the 'Green Line', and of 156,000 Arabs that did not leave during the war and became the group we will refer to as Arab-Israelis. More Israeli-Arab wars were to follow (especially significant to the Israeli society were the six-day war in 1967, the Yom-Kippur war in 1973 and the 1st Lebanon war in 1982). Repeated warfare created a national schism in Israel, a division between Israeli Jews and Israeli Arabs, who form a permanent, non-assimilating minority. This division partially overlaps with the religious division between Jews, Muslim Arabs, Christian Arabs, Druze Arabs and other religious affiliations. Over the years, Israel signed peace accords with Egypt and Jordan, but ongoing outbursts of violence between Israeli and Palestinian forces keep Israeli Jews and Arabs conflicted. The ongoing-armed conflict is widely suggested as a further reason for the high fertility rates in Israel (Steinfield, 2015).

Immigration

Israel is an 'immigration country', made up largely of immigrants and their children. Between the years 1948–2016, about 3.2 million people migrated to Israel; in 2010, roughly 40% of the people living in Israel were international immigrants. In short, being an immigrant in Israel is quite normative.

These immigrants came from dozens of different countries, from Ethiopia to Russia, each bearing their unique cultural and socio-economical characteristics. Generally speaking, immigrants from Europe and North America tended to hold a western value system, be less religious and more economically successful, while immigrants from Asia and Africa (usually from Muslim-Arab countries) held a more collectivistic value system, were more conservative politically and religiously and less economically successful (Dobrin, 2015).

To serve its mission statement and offer a national home for all Jews around the world, Israel established separate courses for the immigration of Jews, as defined in the Law of Return, and for the immigration of non-Jews, as defined by the Law of Entrance to Israel. The Law of Return states that (practically) every Jew, or a person of Jewish descent (till the 3rd generation) that does not identify with another religion has the right to migrate to Israel, with their spouse, and confers immediate citizenship upon such immigrants alongside many other privileges intended to assist their assimilation into Israeli society (Law of return, 1950). The Law of Entrance to Israel, for immigrants from the diaspora, is complex and selective; it allows the entrance of "needed" people, such as tourists, volunteers and foreign employees, but with qualifications that make it highly unlikely they will gain citizenship, unless they have close family ties to Israeli citizens (DellaPergolla, 2013; Law of entrance, 1952; Sever, 2000).

Overall, there is more migration into Israel than emigration from Israel to other countries. The number of Israeli citizens leaving Israel every year has been steadily declining since 1990, and in 2017, the ratio of emigrants was 0.7 out of 1000 Israelis (Central Bureau of Statistics[3], 242/2019); it can be roughly estimated that overall, the Israeli population abroad equals approximately 15% of the Jewish population living in Israel (DellaPergola, 2013). Yet the characteristics of these emigrants are a concern for policy makers, as many of them are either young people or young families and many have tertiary education and advanced degrees (Cohen, 2009; DellaPergolla, 2013; Gould, 2007).

Geography

Israel is a small country—very small, in fact; it only covers 22,072 square kilometers. The country's small size allows frequent, face-to-face contact between relatives and encourages intra-family reliance and support (Lavee & Katz, 2003). Different national and religious holidays, as well as life-circle related events (i.e. births, marriages, etc.) are also primarily celebrated with the family, making even distant relatives closer (Halpern, 2001).

2. DEMOGRAPHIC TRENDS RELEVANT TO FAMILY FORMATION (BY AGE GROUPS, GENDER AND ETHNICITY)

Household Types and Cohabitation

Familial structure in Israel can greatly vary depending on the demographic group being observed, yet the traditional nuclear family—composed of a mother, a father and their biological children—is clearly predominant in all sub-cultures of Israeli society[5]. Overall, 62.2% of Israeli households are composed of couples (either married or unmarried) and offspring (either minors or adult); 24.9% of households are households without children; and 12.1% consist of single-parent families (Central Bureau of Statistics[4], 036/2019). 62.5% of Arab families are composed of parents and at least one minor child living with them, compared to 45.5% of Jewish families. In the Jewish population, there are many more households of couples without offspring of any age cohabitating—28%, compared to 11% in the Arab population. The percentage of single-parent households is similar in both the Jewish (11%) and the Arab (12%) population. In 2008, it was estimated that 2.8% of families (Jewish and other) in Israel are reconstituted families (Zionov, 2015).

As mentioned before, the Israeli population is highly varied not only regarding ethnicity, but also regarding religiosity within the same ethnic group. Different religious norms are of great influence for the family structure, influencing primarily the mean age of marriage and the number of children per family. In the Arab population, religious households contain 4.74 people on average, compared to 4 people in secular households; in the Jewish population, the difference is more marked, with secular households containing an average of 3.19 people, and ultra-orthodox households—5.29 (Central Bureau of Statistics, 036/2019).

Marriage Rates

Marriage rates in Israel are extremely high: 95% of cohabitating couples are married. Cohabitation without marriage is more widespread in the Jewish population - nearly 94.5% of such couples are Jewish (Central Bureau of Statistics, 181/2019). The typical cohabitating couple are not religious, are students or have tertiary education, are of European-American origin and third-generation Israeli (Manor & Okun, 2016). Cohabitation has been on the rise in the last decade, yet cohabitating couples form only 6% of Jewish couples and are somewhat younger than married couples—suggesting that future marriage is optional. This assumption is further supported by the fact that 23% of all couples cohabit before they marry, and that 67% of Jewish cohabitating couples are childless (Central Bureau of Statistics, 181/2019).

Calculating divorce rates in Israel is rather more difficult than might be expected, due to several of its unique characteristics—such as massive immigration and Israel's unique legislative system regarding family status (further explained below). Even so, it is clearly obvious that divorce rates have been climbing steadily since the 1970s, reached a peak in the beginning of the new millennium and seem to have stabilized since. Estimates suggest the Total Divorce Rate (TDR, calculated as the number of divorcees per 1000 inhabitants) in Israel is approx. 26%–27%, or perhaps slightly higher (Nahir, 2016). TDR has been relatively stable over the last two decades, making the Israeli family more stable than most families in the western world. As can be expected, TDR is greatly affected by the couples' cultural group—Jewish couples are far more likely to divorce than Muslim couples, who are in turn more likely to divorce than Christian or Druze couples (Central Bureau of Statistics, 2014).

Approximately, 11% of families with children aged 17 or younger are single-parent families, typically composed of mother and children (87% of such families). Some 18% of these mothers have never been married (Central Bureau of Statistics[6], 036/2019).

Mean Age of Marriage

The mean age for first marriage in the general population is 27.4 for men and 25 for women and has been steadily rising since 1970 (Central Bureau of Statistics[7], 244/2019). Overall, Jews marry at an older age than Muslim Arabs; the mean age for marriage is 27.7 compared to 26.4 for men, with the difference being more pronounced for women—25.8 compared to 22.4. In the Jewish population, 35% of women marry by the age of 21, with ultra-orthodox women twice as likely to marry compared to secular women (56% vs. 26%). 59% of Arab-Israeli women are also married by the time they are 21 years old.

Fertility Rates

In Israel, 33% of the population are children (0–17) (Central Bureau of Statistics[8], 349/2019). This stunning (and many times rather noisy) figure attests to the fact that Israel holds the fertility record in the OECD, with an average fertility rate of 3.11 children per woman. Muslim women have more children than Jewish women—3.29 compared to 3.11; however, whereas the fertility rates for Muslim women are steadily declining, fertility rates for Jewish women have been rising since 2006 (Central Bureau of Statistics, 073/2018). An interesting study by DellaPergolla (2009) shows that the increase in fertility rates in the Jewish-Israeli population is reflected in married Jewish women's perceptions of the ideal family; while in 1988 women indicated a personally intended family size of 3.5 children, in 2005 the intended family size has risen to 4.1 children.

It is important to note that within the Jewish population, great gaps exist between the fertility rates of secular and religious women. In 2015–2017, while average fertility rate for all Jewish-Israeli women was 3.28, the average fertility rate for ultra-orthodox women was 7.10; the average fertility rate for religious women was 4.02; and the average fertility rate for secular women was 2.22 children—much closer to the average in OECD countries (Central Bureau of Statistics[9], 073/2018).

Age of Mother at First Child

In 2016, the mean age of women when giving birth to their first child was 27.6, with Muslim women being the youngest at 23.8. 19% of Jewish women have their first child by the age of 21 compared to 41% of Arab women (Central Bureau of Statistics, 181/2019). Teen pregnancies are very rare in Israel—only 234 teenage girls under 17 (Muslims mostly) gave birth in 2018, 0.12% of births that year (Central Bureau of Statistics, 349/2019).

Births Outside Marriage

In 2016, 6.9% of the children born to Jewish women were born outside marriage. The unwed mothers tend to be older than married mothers, suggesting that having a child out of wedlock was an active choice (Central Bureau of Statistics, 073/2018).

3. NORMATIVE FRAMEWORK

Updated studies researching the norms regulating family life in Israel are limited. However, from the above data regarding marriage, divorce and fertility rates, we can see that, compared to other western countries, the Israeli society—both Jewish and Arab—is highly family oriented; some scholars describe it as the most familistic of postindustrial societies (Fogiel-Bijaoui, 2002; Hashiloni-Dolev, 2018).

What defines a family? In Israel, special importance is accorded to children who are perceived as the basis of family life (Almog & Bassan, 2018; Fogiel-Bijaoui, 2002). The Jewish-Israeli narrative promotes childbirth in many ways: as a divine dictate ("Be fruitful and multiply"), as personal fulfillment attributed to the joy of raising children, and as a national necessity, derived from the millions of Jews lost in the Holocaust alongside the fear of being outnumbered by the Arab population in Israel (Almog & Bassan, 2018; Okun, 2016; Steinfeld, 2015).

4. SOCIOECONOMIC CONDITIONS 2007–LATEST

The Israeli Economy

Labor market—When looking at the Israeli labor market, it is highly advisable yet again to consider different ethnic-religious groups, as the market in different groups can be strikingly different.

In total, unemployment rates in Israel are at an all-time low at 3.9%, with approximately 80% of people aged 25–64 working, suggesting a booming, growing economy—often referred to by the Israeli leaders as the "start-up nation" (Bank of Israel, 2019). Israel has, however, two major groups that do not fully participate in the work market for different cultural reasons: The Arab population, especially religious Muslim women; and ultra-orthodox Jewish population, especially men. In these two sub-groups, poverty, albeit (at times) freely chosen, is widespread. In fact, Israel's Prime Minister, Benjamin Netanyahu, was famously quoted saying, "If you leave out the Arabs and the ultra-orthodox, our situation is excellent" (*The Marker*, 6.4.12).

In the Jewish ultra-orthodox community, a somewhat reversed pattern is evident, with the women working (75.5% of ultra-orthodox women aged 25–64 were employed in 2018) and the men unemployed (47.8 employment rate in 2018) (Izenkot, 2018). This pattern exemplifies the "society of learners", the ultra-orthodox cultural ideal (Friedman, 1991; Kimmerling, 2005), wherein men are encouraged to dedicate their life to religious studies, while women are entrusted to work and support them financially. Other sources of income are government subsidies and donations, and a vast network of inter-community charities further supports this unique way of life.

In most families in Israel, 68% of children between the ages of 0 and 17 (73.6% of Jewish children, 49.7% of Arab children) live in households with two working adults; and 93.1% of children (95% among Jews, 87.1% among Arabs) live in households with at least one working adult (Central Bureau of Statistics, 349/2019). A survey conducted in 2016 by the Central Bureau of Statistics found that 41% of Israeli employees were dissatisfied by the work-family balance in their lives; 36% struggled to properly meet familial demands over the previous year. 22% worked in their free time to meet the organization's demands (Central Bureau of Statistics, 1712/2018). Ultra-orthodox Jews and Arab-Israelis appear to cope more easily with the work-family conflict, perhaps because their closely-knit familial communities offer better support for working parents (Cohen, 2018).

Education (tertiary and early school leavers)—Education is of top priority in the Jewish culture and, for countless generations, education was viewed as the key to social mobility and socioeconomic status (Botticini & Eckstein, 2012). Nowadays, Israel spends approximately 6% of its Gross Domestic Product (GDP) on education, primary to tertiary. Compulsory education starts at the age of 3 and ends at 15; free education is provided by the state till the age of 18. In the school year of 2017–2018, 2.5% of pupils from 7th to 12th grade dropped out of school; for every girl dropping out of school nearly 3 boys do; the percentage of dropping out is a little bit higher in the Arab population than in the Jewish population (3.2% vs. 2.2%); (Central Bureau of Statistics, 349/2019).

Israel also boasts 62 academic institutions (9 universities), most of which are public, and a relatively high percentage of people with tertiary education. The age for acquiring tertiary education in Israel is relatively high because of compulsory army service at age 18. For that reason and other cultural reasons, the average male student starting his BA is age 24.7 and the average female student is age 23.3 (Central Bureau of Statistics, 168/2018).

A recent OECD report has shown that in 2018, 48% of 55–64 years old Israelis completed a tertiary degree compared to an average of 27% across OECD countries (OECD, 2019). Israel is rapidly losing that advantage as tertiary education becomes more widespread, as can be derived from the fact that 48% of 25–34 years old Israelis had tertiary education in 2018—in comparison to 44% across OECD countries.

Despite these optimistic and impressive numbers, stratification in Israeli society is perhaps never more evident than when examining the subject of education—which shows an economic gap, a socio-cultural gap and a gender gap. Students who come from lower social-economic classes are less likely to apply, less likely to begin their schooling and more likely to drop out than students with a stronger socio-economic background (Central Bureau of Statistics, 168/2018). As for the gender gap, women in Israel—as in other countries - form the majority in tertiary education, with a gender gap of 20% in 2018. In 2018, there were 1.4 female BA students for every male student, and 1.5 MA students for every male student (Central Bureau of Statistics, 168/2018).

Housing—Housing in Israel is at the core of an ongoing socio-economic crisis, as housing costs have been rapidly rising since 2008 and are extremely high in comparison to the average income.

Israel has experienced dramatic house prices rises in the past decade. Despite domestic political uncertainty, security threats, and the global financial meltdown, Israel's house prices have risen by 118% (82% in real terms) from 2006 to 2017.

In 2018, an Israeli with an average income needed to save 146 monthly salaries to purchase a property. A similar, more moderate trend can be seen in the rental market, where costs have risen approx. 37% between 2008 and 2018. The soar-

Families in Israel • 75

ing housing prices contribute to the fact that many Israelis continue to live with their parents long after they come of age—some 32% of Israelis aged 25–23 do so (Central Bureau of Statistics, 2018).

The housing crisis evident across Israel affects all socio-economic classes, but like with all economic inequalities, its effects on the lower socio-economic classes are more evident and devastating (Central Bureau of Statistics[10], 5.34/2018). On average, 67.6% of all Israelis live in their own property; but while 81.4% of the 10th decile own their home, only 41.4% of the 1st decile do.

Poverty and Social Exclusion

Though minimum wages and the average salary are on the rise and inequality has been steadily declining since 2009, poverty is still abundant in Israel compared to other OECD countries. In 2017, 18.4% of families living in Israel were poor—466,400 families, including 1,780,000 people, of whom 814,000 were children. These alarming ratios represent an improvement in poverty rates since 2012, yet Israel is still at the head of the poverty scale of OECD countries. Inequality is also relatively high in the OECD context, as seen in the Gini index which measured 0.34 in 2016; the major source for inequality is the rise in labor income inequality (Eckstein & Larom, 2016).

Poverty rates increase with the number of children per family and decrease with the number of breadwinners. As mentioned before, poverty is especially prominent among Israeli-Arabs and ultra-orthodox Jews. 43.1% of ultra-orthodox families are poor; 47.1% of Israeli-Arab families are poor. Over half of these families have children, and though the number of poor children lessened, their poverty deepened. Another population prone to poverty is that of single-parent families: in 2015, 21.8% of such families were poor, compared to 17% in the general population. In the 1990s, a law was passed extending welfare for such families, especially in the form of income assurance (The law of Single Parent Families, 1992). This reduced poverty among single-parent families, but deepened their reliance on welfare as strict limitation was imposed on the salary single parents are entitled to if they wish to keep their welfare benefits.

6. INSTITUTIONAL FRAMEWORK

Key Policy Developments and Legislation 2007–Latest

Family law in Israel is a highly complex legislative field. Israel's family legislation is separate from other legislative fields both in its origins and in its courts of law. The origins for this split can be found in the Ottoman law, which confers jurisdiction over marriage and divorce to religious courts (Fournier, et al., 2012)—meaning that each Israeli citizen, to this day, must marry and divorce according to religious law. However, Israel does recognize all formal marriage certificates from abroad—but not divorce!—meaning that gay couples or inter-religious couples who cannot marry in Israel can still be registered as a married couple; those who wish to marry but cannot do so under their religious law can therefore marry abroad and then register as a married couple in Israel.

Over the years, civil legislation was added to religious law. In 1995, a special court for family law was established to sit in judgement over all matters pertaining to family disputes, such as divorce settlements, financial disputes, custody etc. (The law of Family Courts, 1995). The jurisdictions of Rabbinical (Jewish) courts and civil courts still overlap, however, especially in matters relating to divorce; and civil marriage is not yet optional within Israel's boundaries.

Adoption and Surrogacy

Adoption is a rare event in Israel. Approximately 19,500 adoptees live in Israel, and the numbers of adopted children seem to be dropping as the years go by. For example, while in 2013 there were 122 adoptions where an Israeli child was adopted by Israeli parents, in 2017 only 72 such adoptions took place. International adoption is even rarer, with 17 such cases in 2017, compared to 69 in 2013.

Israeli adoption law favors married couples; though singles may adopt a child, they may do so only when no married couple is interested in adopting the child. The adopted child must belong to the same religion as his/her adopting parents. As adoption opportunities are quite scarce, those waiting for a healthy baby/toddler aged 2 or younger would usually have to wait several years. A six-month trial period is further imposed in every adoption before it can be approved by a court of law (The Law of Adoption, 1981).

Same-sex couples' right to adopt became an issue of hot public debate in 2017 and still awaits legislative action. Based on precedence, in same-sex married couples where one of the parents is the biological parent of the child, the second parent will be allowed to legally adopt the child. In 2016, a special committee appointed by the government in 2009 to revise adoption laws asked that the government decides whether the adoption status of same-sex couples should be made equal to that of heterosexual couples. The government objected, causing mass public protests until the Minister of Welfare declared that his office retracts its objection. Official legislation on the matter was not presented to the parliament, however, and is unlikely to pass as religious political parties strongly object to it.

Since the opportunities for adoption are so few, couples often turn to surrogacy. This option is available in Israel only to heterosexual couples, where the woman has been medically proven unable to conceive or carry a pregnancy (The Law of Surrogacy, 2018). Between 1996 and 2017, 193 surrogate births took place in Israel. Single women and same-sex couples may turn to surrogacy in other countries, though this solution has also become less available as over recent years many countries stopped allowing international surrogacy.

Fertility Problems

The emphasis on children and child-bearing is very evident when we observe the social treatment of non-parenthood: barrenness is perceived in Israel as a source for profound female suffering ("Give me children, or else I will die"; Genesis 30,1) and non-parenthood by choice is very rare and strongly condemned (Birenbaum-Carmeli, 2016). Assisted reproductive technologies (such as IVF) were adopted in Israel very early on. The world's fifth "IVF baby" was Israeli and Israeli women make abundant use of these technologies compared to women in other countries. Israel's world record on this issue is sustained by a unique public health policy posing very few restrictions on Israeli citizens' eligibility for publicly covered treatments (Collins, 2002; Gooldin, 2013; Shalev & Gooldin, 2006).

While we might intuitively expect such a pro-fertility public atmosphere to be accompanied by strong anti-abortion sentiments, abortions in Israel are also available and covered by national health insurance (Almog & Bassan, 2018; Steinfeld, 2015). The pro-fertility national sentiment is reflected in the fact that a special committee, which includes not only medical professionals but also social workers and religious advisors, must approve every abortion. Yet most requests for abortion are approved—in 2016, for example, nine out of every 100 known pregnant women requested abortion, with an approval rate of 99.3%. Jewish and Christian-Arab women were more likely to seek abortion (9.4 and 9.8 requests per 100 pregnancies respectively) than Muslim-Arab (7.1) and Druze (6) women. 9.1% of requests came from teenagers (19 or younger) (Central Bureau of Statistics, 375/2018).

Fiscal-Tax Treatment of Household Types: Treatment of Marriage and Cohabitation

Married couples and common-law couples (either heterosexual or homosexual) are eligible for many fiscal benefits, such as tax reductions, increase in certain social security payments and state assistance in respect of mortgage loans. Single parents—mothers, mostly—are also eligible for various benefits, such as tax reductions, extra sick leave to attend to ailing children and daycare subsidies; but even so, in 2017, 26.1% of single-parent families were poor.

The state also pays child benefits. Those have been at the center of much political and public debate, as they were designed to favor different social groups over the years—most notably ultra-orthodox Jews and Muslims, who typically have larger families. Until 2003, the sum of those benefits would rise as the number of children grew, meaning that the benefit paid for each consecutive child rose. This trend reached its peak in 2000, when the government passed legislation decreeing that the fifth child (and the children that followed) would receive a benefit five times higher than the first child. In 2003, legislation changed and these sums have been made relatively equal (the second, third and fourth child still receive more that the first and fifth child, and any number of children to follow).

78 • TALI HEIMAN, DORIT OLENIK-SHEMESH, & MERAV REGEV-NEVO

A new feature of child benefits is Child Development Accounts (CDAs). Beginning in 2017, all newborn Israeli citizens receive a saving account in their name, into which Israeli's social security bureau deposits 50 shekels monthly; the parents may double the sum if they so desire. Children can withdraw from this account only when they reach the age of 18.

6. COUNTRY-SPECIFIC CHALLENGES TO FAMILY FORMATION

Inter-Religious Marriages

As mentioned before, marriage in Israel itself may only be officially conducted by religious officials[11] and overseen by the relevant religious court, rendering inter-religious marriages practically impossible. In 2006, it was estimated that inter-religious marriages make up about 5% of all Israeli couples. This estimate, however, also considers marriages between a Jewish partner and a partner of no formal religion. True inter-religious marriages (for instance, between a Jew and a Muslim, or a Muslim and a Christian) seem to be extremely rare and arouse strong emotions in the Israeli public. A survey from 2016 shows that 97% of Israeli Jews would feel uncomfortable if their child married a Muslim; marriage with a Christian is slightly more acceptable—only 89% would be uncomfortable with that. Other religious groups in Israel do not favor inter-religious marriages much more: 88% of Christian parents and 82% of Muslim parents would also be uncomfortable with their child marrying a Jewish partner.

The Law of Matrimonial Partnership (2010) applies to heterosexual, cohabitating couples when both partners are without religion. The Law of Matrimonial Partnership does not apply to most Israeli citizens. It is important to note that being "without religion" is not a matter of private identity: a person cannot announce that he/she is "without religion"—to change the religious status, one must present evidence of the change in his/her religious affiliation. Matrimonial partnership offers legal aid almost exclusively to immigrants or offspring of immigrants. Only when both partners are officially "without religion" they can marry under Matrimonial Partnership Law. Common-law marriages that are optional in other western countries simply do not exist in Israel.

Gay Couples

Although religious courts do not allow same-sex marriage, public opinion surveys consistently show support for gay marriage. For example, a 2017 survey held among a representative sample of the Jewish population found 79% of respondents thought gay couples should be allowed to officially marry or to register as married. As mentioned before, the status of common-law couple can be applied to all couples, without regard to religion or gender. Thus in 2018, for example, 408 gay couples married abroad and were later registered as married couples in Israel (compared to only 10 in 2010, https://foi.gov.il/he/node/6601). It has been claimed that thousands of gay couples live in Israel and it has been suggested that the Israeli gay community also strives to uphold the same familial, parental cultural norms the heterosexual community does.

7. CONCLUSION

Can we speak of the "All-Israeli Family"? It seems we cannot. As can be seen from the data above, the typical familial structure in Israel greatly varies between national and religious groups. Only one factor seems to combine these different groups, from ultra-orthodox Jews to Muslims, from religious to secular cohabitating couples: children. Children are the defining factor of a family, as is said in a popular Hebrew proverb: "Children are joy, children are a blessing".

Children are also a major driving force behind the demographical changes expected to take place in Israel in the next decades. While the ratio of Jews and Arabs in Israel is not predicted to radically change, the ratio of ultra-orthodox Jews is constantly increasing and is expected to reach one third of the Jewish population by 2065 (Central Bureau of Statistics, 138/2017). However, only time will tell which side will triumph in the Israeli struggle between modernity and tradition.

REFERENCES

Almog, S., & Bassan, S. (2018). The politics of pro and non-reproduction policies in Israel. *Journal of Health and Biomedical Law, 14,* 27–80.

Birenbaum-Carmeli, D. (2016). Thirty-five years of assisted reproductive technologies in Israel. *Reproductive Biomedicine & Society Online, 2,* 16–23.

Botticini, M., & Eckstein, Z. (2012). *The chosen few: How education shaped Jewish history* (pp. 70–1492). Princeton University Press.

Cohen, A. (2018). *Cultures within cultures in Israel: Jewish and Arab cultures and the work-family interface.* https://www.researchgate.net/publication/322266377_Cultures_within_Cultures_in_Israel_Jewish_and_Arab_Cultures_and_the_Work-Family_Interface

Cohen, Y. (2009). Migration patterns to and from Israel. *Contemporary Jewry, 29,* 115–125.

Collins, J. A. (2002). An international survey of the health economics of IVF and ICSI. *Human Reproduction Update, 8,* 265–277.

DellaPergola, S. (2009). Actual, intended, and appropriate family size among Jews in Israel. *Contemporary Jewry, 29,* 127–152.

DellaPergola S. (2013) World Jewish Population, 2012. In: Dashefsky A., Sheskin I. (eds) American Jewish Year Book 2012. American Jewish Year Book, vol 109-112. Springer, Dordrecht.

Dobrin, N. (2015). *Equal opportunities in education: Demographic and socio-economic barriers, Working Paper No. 91.* Central Bureau of Statistics—Chief Scientist Department. http://www.cbs.gov.il/publications/pw91.pdf.

Fogiel-Bijaoui, S. (2002). Familism, post-modernity and the state: the case of Israel. *Journal of Israeli history, 21,* 38–62.

Friedman, M. (1991). *Haredi (Ultra-Orthodox) Society: Sources, trends and processes.* The Jerusalem Institute for Israel Studies.

Fournier, P., McDougall, P., & Lichtsztral, M. (2012). Secular rights and religious wrongs? Family law, religion and women in Israel. *William and Mary Journal of Women and the Law, 18,* 333–362.

Gooldin, S. (2013). 'Emotional rights', moral reasoning, and Jewish-Arab alliances in the regulation of in-vitro-fertilization in Israel: Theorizing the unexpected consequences of assisted reproductive technologies. *Social Science & Medicine, 83,* 90–98.

Gould, E. D. (2007). Israel's brain drain. *Israel's Economic Review, 5,* 1–22.

Halpern, E. (2001). Family psychology from an Israeli perspective. *American Psychology, 56,* 58–64.

Hashiloni-Dolev, Y. (2018). The effect of Jewish-Israeli family ideology on policy regarding reproductive technologies. In H. Boas, Y. Hashiloni-Dolev, N. Davidovitch, D. Filc, & S. J. Aufwachsen in Deutschland heute Lavi (Eds.), *Bioethics and biopolitics in Israel* (pp. 119–128). Cambridge University Press.

Katz, Y. J. (2017). Religious encounters in Israeli state education. *Religious Education, 112,* 329–333.

Kimmerling, B. (2005). *The invention and decline of Israeliness: State, society and the military.* University of California Press.

Lavee, Y., & Katz, R. (2003). The family in Israel: Between tradition and modernity. *Marriage & Family Review, 35,* 193–217.

The Law of Adoption. 1981. https://main.knesset.gov.il/Activity/Legislation/Laws/Pages/LawPrimary.aspx?t=lawlaws&st=lawlaws&lawitemid=2000075

The Law of Family Courts. (1995). https://www.knesset.gov.il/review/data/heb/law/kns13_familycourt.pdf

The Law of Single Parent Parent Families. (1992). https://main.knesset.gov.il/Activity/Legislation/Laws/Pages/LawPrimary.aspx?t=lawlaws&st=lawlaws&lawitemid=2001097

The Law of Surrogacy. (2018). https://fs.knesset.gov.il/20/law/20_lsr_504281.pdf

Manor, A., & Okun, B. S. (2016). Cohabitation among secular Jews in Israel: How ethnicity, education and employment characteristics are related to young adults' living arrangements. *Demographic Research, 35,* 961–990.

Okun, B. S. (2016). An investigation of the unexpectedly high fertility of secular, native-born Jews in Israel. *Population Studies, 70,* 239–257.

Rithblatt, S. N. (2003). Couple formation in Israel Jewish society. In R. R. Hamon & B. B. Ingolds (Eds.), *Mate selection across cultures,* (pp. 137–155). Sage.

Sever, R. (2000). And I brought you from the peoples: Immigration and assimilation. In J. Koop (Ed.), *Pluralism in Israel: From melting pot to salad bowl.* Maor-Wallach Press. (Hebrew)

Shalev, C., & Gooldin, S. (2006). The uses and misuses of in vitro fertilization in Israel: Some sociological and ethical considerations. *Nashim: A Journal of Jewish Women's Studies & Gender Issues, 12,* 151–176.

Shetreet, S., & Homolka, W. (2017). *Jewish and Israeli law—An introduction.* Walter de Gruyter GmbH & Co.

Sperling, D. (2010). Commanding the "Be fruitful and multiply" directive: Reproductive ethics, law, and policy in Israel. *Cambridge Quarterly of Healthcare Ethics, 19,* 363–371.

Families in Israel • **81**

Steinfeld, R. (2015). Wars of the Wombs: Struggles over abortion policies in Israel. *Israel Studies, 20,* 1–26.

References Websites in Hebrew:

Bank of Israel. (2019). https://www.boi.org.il/en/DataAndStatistics/Pages/Indicators.aspx?Level=2&IndicatorId=1&Sid=5

Central Bureau of Statistics.[2] https://www.fips.org.il/wpcontent/uploads/2016/02/divorce_all.pdf

Central Bureau of Statistics.[3] https://www.cbs.gov.il/he/mediarelease/DocLib/2019/242/01_19_242b.pdf

Central Bureau of Statistics.[4] https://www.cbs.gov.il/he/mediarelease/DocLib/2019/036/11_19_036b.pdf

Central Bureau of Statistics.[5] (2014). https://www.fips.org.il/wp-content/uploads/2016/02/divorce_all.pdf

Central Bureau of Statistics.[6] https://www.fips.org.il/wp-content/uploads/2016/02/divorce_all.pdf

Central Bureau of Statistics.[7] https://www.cbs.gov.il/he/mediarelease/DocLib/2019/244/11_19_244b.pdf

Central Bureau of Statistics.[8] https://www.cbs.gov.il/he/mediarelease/DocLib/2018/073/01_18_073b.pdf

Central Bureau of Statistics.[9] https://www.cbs.gov.il/he/publications/DocLib/pw/pw101/pw101.pdf

Central Bureau of Statistics.[10] https://www.cbs.gov.il/he/publications/DocLib/2018/5.%20ShnatonHouseholdsAndFamilies/st05_34x.pdf

Eckstein, Z., & Larom, T. (2016). https://www.idc.ac.il/en/research/aiep/Documents/policy-papers/Poverty-in-Israel-Reasons-and-Labor-Market-Policy.pdf

Housing in Israel. https://adva.org/wp-content/uploads/2019/07/SocialReport2018.pdf

Israeli Society.[5] https://www.cbs.gov.il/he/mediarelease/DocLib/2019/036/11_19_036b.pdf

Izenkot, G. (2018). https://fs.knesset.gov.il/globaldocs/MMM/838c30e8-98fc-e811-80e1-00155d0a98a9/2_838c30e8-98fc-e811-80e1-00155d0a98a9_11_10854.pdf

New Family. https://www.newfamily.org.il/blog/data-statistics/%D7%9E%D7%A9%D7%A4%D7%97%D7%95%D7%AA-%D7%97%D7%93-%D7%9E%D7%99%D7%92%D7%93%D7%A8%D7%99%D7%95%D7%AA-%D7%97%D7%93-%D7%9E%D7%99%D7%A0%D7%99%D7%95%D7%AA-%D7%A2%D7%95%D7%93-%D7%90%D7%99%D7%A8%D7%99/

Nahir. (2016). https://old.cbs.gov.il/publications/pw98.pdf

OECD. http://www.oecd.org/education/education-at-a-glance/EAG2019_CN_ISR.pdf

The Jewish Majority.[1] https://old.cbs.gov.il/reader/newhodaot/hodaa_template.html?hodaa=201911134

The Law of Adoption. (1981). https://he.wikisource.org/wiki/%D7%97%D7%95%D7%A7_%D7%90%D7%99%D7%9E%D7%95%D7%A5_%D7%99%D7%9C%D7%93%D7%99%D7%9D

The Law of Matrimonial Partnership. (2010). https://main.knesset.gov.il/Activity/Legislation/Laws/Pages/LawBill.aspx?t=LawReshumot&lawitemid=327858

Religious Officials https://www.pewforum.org/2016/03/08/intergroup-marriage-and-friendship/pf_2016-03-08_israel-12-04/

The Law of Return. (1950). (https://www.knesset.gov.il/laws/special/heb/chok_hashvut.htm

Zionov, (2015). https://www.cbs.gov.il/he/publications/DocLib/pw/pw89/pw89.pdf

CHAPTER 6

TRENDS AND CHALLENGES IN FAMILY FORMATION IN ITALY

An Overview

Rosy Musumeci

University of Turin

1. NATIONAL CONTEXT

Different national contexts can facilitate or, on the contrary, discourage youth's autonomy and thus family formation, as well as the assumption of parental responsibilities. For this reason the present section describes the main characteristics of the Italian national context by illustrating the main social, historical, political, and economic developments.

Italy has been a parliamentary republic since 2 June 1946. The country is subdivided into 20 regions (*regioni*), 14 metropolitan cities (*città metropolitane*) and 96 provinces (*province*), which in turn are subdivided in 7,960 municipalities (*comuni*) (2018). Five of the 20 regions have a special autonomous status that enables them to enact legislation pertaining to some local matters. On 1 January

Family Formation Among Youth in Europe: Coping With Socio-Economic Disadvantages,
pages 83–103.
Copyright © 2022 by Information Age Publishing
www.infoagepub.com
All rights of reproduction in any form reserved.

83

84 • ROSY MUSUMECI

2019, the total resident population was 60,359,546.[1] The average age was 45.4 years (2.2 years more than ten years earlier). The incidence of the 15–29 years old youth was 13.3%.[2]

Italy has an economy that ranked ninth-largest in the world in 2017 (World Bank, 2019) and it is regarded as one of the world's most industrialized nations and a leading country in world trade and exports (Dadush, 2013; Sensenbrenner & Arcelli, 2013). The country is known for its creative and innovative businesses (Martin Prosperity Institute, 2011), a large and competitive agricultural sector, and for its influential and high-quality automobile, machinery, food, design and fashion industries.

Gender imbalance continues to be strong in Italy. The female employment rate (aged 15–64) has grown over time but is still lower than the male rate (49.5% versus 67.6% in 2018). The traditional family model with the male breadwinner, although less widespread today than in the past (especially in the North of Italy) due to the growth of women's labor market participation, continues to be the predominant "ideal" model. However, there are some visible changes among the young generations in terms of gender role attitudes and behaviors that are more egalitarian than in the past generations (Rosina & Fraboni, 2004). One of the main indicators of these changes is the way men perceive and practice fatherhood—particularly with regard to small children—which in turn reflects in changes in men's ideals and practices of masculinity. An increasing number of contemporary Italian fathers express the need to be—and actually are—more involved in childcare than their forefathers (Bosoni, 2011; Sabbadini & Cappadozzi, 2011). However, gender differences still persist, for example, with regard to parental leave taking: the share of men who take parental leave has grown over the years but remains very low compared to the female share; moreover, they take shorter periods of parental leave than mothers do (Casamonti, 2021; Magaraggia, 2015). Furthermore, public discourse is permeated by the same ambiguity: on the one hand, the 'intimate' emotional bonds (Dermott, 2008) are increasingly acknowledged at social and cultural levels as crucial components of 'good fatherhood' as is the importance of father's presence for the children's wellbeing and proper socialization; on the other hand, the ideals about fathers as the main breadwinners persist.

Significant territorial inequalities are another important structural imbalance in Italy. It is historically (and presently) characterized by a territorial heterogeneity in labor market outcomes and level of poverty: southern regions are poorer and have lower employment rates and higher unemployment rates (especially for women) in comparison with the Northern ones, as well as a higher incidence of long-term unemployed and a higher rate of NEET young people. In 2018, in the South of Italy, the unemployment rate of 15–29 years old youth was 39.8%,

---

[1] Source: "Tavola indicatori demografici," available at URL: http://demo.istat.it/altridati/indicatori/index.html

[2] Source: author's calculation based on data available at URL: http://demo.istat.it/pop2019/index.html

while in the North it was 15.5%,[3] and the incidence of long-term unemployment was near five times higher than in the North (24.1% *vs* 5.5%). In 2017, the net family income when the main income earner is under 35 years was about 19,600 euro in the South of Italy, whereas 30,000 in the North. South Italy is considered also more traditional and less egalitarian regarding gender roles, attitudes, and behaviors.

High labor market segmentation and precarization is another typical trait of the Italian context. The mix of different regimes of employment protection and the liberalization of atypical, temporary contracts increased the segmentation of the labor market (Lucidi & Raitano, 2009), allocating the worst jobs to the most vulnerable categories, especially young people and women. The deregulation policies throughout the past decades have been highly selective, burdening the already disadvantaged labor market outsiders, i.e., youth, while keeping the rights of the labor market insiders almost untouched (Barbieri & Scherer, 2009; Blossfeld et al., 2005, 2011).

Finally, it is important to underline the highly-skilled mismatching. The number of unemployed 15–34 years old people with a university degree rose from 127,000 in 2007 to 209,000 in 2017: an increase of 65% (Istat) possibly suggesting that high-skilled labor is misallocated.

2. DEMOGRAPHIC TRENDS RELEVANT TO FAMILY FORMATION

In a comparative perspective, Italy is a declining demographic context characterized by a growing population aging trend and by low fertility and birth rates.[4]

With 7.6 births per 1,000 people (together with Japan and after Puerto Rico and the Republic of Korea) Italy was the country with the lowest natality in the world in 2017.[5] In the same year, the average number of children born per woman over a lifetime (fertility rate) was 1.32 (in 2019 it was even lower: 1.29), which is lower than a decade ago when it was 1.37.

The number of deaths exceeded the number of births for many years because of the huge increase of the death rate over time. The natural population change, i.e., the difference between the number of live births and deaths during a given time period, was in 2017–190,910, almost 50,000 deaths more than in the year before (2016)[6] and about sixteen times higher than that of 2011 (–12,020).

The drop in (birth and) fertility rate is a phenomenon that certainly "comes from far away" (Briulotta, 2009) but has become more pronounced over the last decades. For example, in 1970, the fertility rate in Italy was 2.4 children born per

---

[3] 43.0% among young women in the South, 17.5% among those residing in the North.

[4] Fertility rate refers to the number of births per woman; birth rate to the number of births per 1,000 people.

[5] The World Bank Data, https://data.worldbank.org/indicator/SP.DYN.CBRT.IN?most_recent_year_desc=true

[6] Source: http://demo.istat.it/

86 • ROSY MUSUMECI

woman, double compared to today. Anyway, the figure of 2017 (1.32) is not the lowest figure registered in Italy since the minimum was recorded in 1995, when the average number of children born per woman was even lower (1.19). The slight increase in the average fertility rate registered in Italy after that time was in great part due to the growing presence of immigrants, who have more children than the Italians: in 2017, the Italian women's fertility rate was 1.24, whereas that of non-Italian citizens was 1.98.[7] However, for both Italians and immigrants, this demographic indicator is decreasing over time. The reduction of the fertility rate is stronger for immigrants, decreasing from 2.80 in 2007 to 1.98 in 2017, while among Italian women it decreased from 1.30 to 1.24 in the same decade. Why this reduction in the immigrants' fertility rate occurred, in particular whether the reason was an imitation effect or a different composition of the immigrant population with a decrease of the groups who have more children and an increase of those with the same reproductive behaviors of the Italians (for example immigrants from Eastern Europe), we cannot say on the basis of our data.

Another important variable to consider with respect to birth and fertility rate in Italy is the territorial divide. In fact, the demographic structure and procreative behaviors have been historically characterized by an intra-national differentiation, with the Northern Italy having fertility rates and the percentage of children and young people in the total population lower than in the Southern. But, interestingly, this gap has narrowed in recent decades and, in the most recent years, the fertility rate in the Southern Italy (1.29 in 2017) was even lower than in the Northern Italy (1.38) (Istat)[8], probably due to the lower presence of immigrants who have on average higher fertility rates than the Italians.

However, the expected/ideal number of children remains unchanged:[9] two in 2012, the same as in 2005 (Istat, 2017a), with no significant differences according to gender or age (OECD).[10] The analysis of the reasons given for the desire not to plan further children expressed in interviews with women having only one child, shows that the economic or age-related reasons are the two reasons most frequently reported by the interviewees for their choice to have a one child family; only in the third place did the interviewed women state that they have already reached the ideal number of children.

Italy is also the country with the highest mother's age at first childbirth in Europe, with the postponing of reproductive choices increasing in recent years: 31.89 years for women, 35.45 for men. Moreover, motherhood (and fatherhood) is becoming an increasingly rare phenomenon: the percentage of women having

---

[7] Istat, http://dati.istat.it/Index.aspx?DataSetCode=DCIS_INDDEMOG1; in 2019, it was 1.18 for Italian women, 1.98 for foreign women (total 1.27).

[8] Source: Istat, URL: http://dati.istat.it/Index.aspx?DataSetCode=DCIS_FECONDITA1

[9] It refers to the number of children a couple decides to keep having, and then stop.

[10] Source: OECD family database, ChartSF2.2.A. http://www.oecd.org/els/family/database.htm#structure

no children in 2017 was 22.0 among women aged 40 years old (born in 1977) and 11.1 among those aged 67 years old (born in 1950).[11]

One of the reasons why in Italy we observe a strong reduction in fertility rate over time is the increasing mean age of marriage and, therefore, of mothers' and fathers' age at first childbirth. In fact, in Italy, the majority of births happen inside marriage, births outside marriage are few compared to those observed in other developed countries, although they show a growing trend.[12] Moreover, a high age to the first child for women implies that the first child is in many cases also the only child (Saraceno & Naldini, 2013). As we will better see in section 6, another important reason is related to women's (and men's) difficulties in reconciling work and family responsibilities due to low availability of part-time jobs in the labor market, underdeveloped public and workplace reconciliation policies, as well as scarce availability of (affordable) childcare services.

Moving from births and fertility to the average size of households, in 2015, in Italy, the mean average number of people per household in all household types was 2.3 (OECD-34 average was 2.46) (OECD)[13], 3.7 considering only couple households with children. The total number of households in Italy is 25,981,996.

Speaking of household types, those with two partnered adults, either married or in civil or registered partnership, or cohabiting (that is "couple households") represented 54.6% of the total household types in 2017, –5.5 percentage points compared to eight years earlier. In particular, the incidence of couple households with children decreased over time, from 39.0% in 2009 to 34.05 in 2017. The second most common type of household in Italy is the "single person household," i.e., household with a single adult living alone. It is a growing type of household (+3.8 percentage points) mainly due to the growing aging population. 10% of the all households in Italy are households with only a single adult and at least one child ('single parent households'). The rest of households are 'other' household types, including 'extended families', such as those with three generations living in the same household (parents, children, and grandparents).

Regarding marriage, as one of the ways to start a family, the crude marriage[14] rate (marriages per 1,000 people) is very low in a comparative perspective, being fewer than 3.2 marriages per 1,000 people in 2017, while the OECD average stands at 4.8 with most countries having a crude marriage rate between 4 and 5.5 marriages per 1,000. The Italian figure of 2017 was lower in comparison to the decade before by –1.1 and by –4.5 percentage points in comparison to 1960.

---

[11] Source: Istat, URL: https://www.istat.it/it/archivio/224393

[12] The proportion of all live births where the mother's legal marital status at the time of birth is other than married ('births outside marriage') has constantly grown since the 1960s—from 2.4% in 1960 to 30.9 in 2017; in the decade 2007–2017, the proportion of births outside marriage has increased by 12.7 percentage points. This is in part linked to the increasing number of couples choosing cohabitation and not marriage as a way to start a family.

[13] Source: OECD family database, Chart SF1.1.A. Average size of households by household type, 2015a. http://www.oecd.org/els/family/database.htm

[14] The figures refer to heterosexual couples since same-sex marriage is not allowed in Italy.

88 • ROSY MUSUMECI

Regarding the distribution of marrying persons by previous marital status (previously 'single never married', 'divorced', or 'widowed'), the share of spouses who both have been married in the past ('divorced') has almost doubled over time from 2.8% in 2007 to 5.2 % in 2017; the share of spouses who both have not been married in the past ('single never married') decreased in the decade 2007–2017 by –7.1 percentage points; while the share of widowers is constant over the period (0.2% every year).

Over the decades, marriage underwent a process of secularization: from a situation in the past where religious marriages were the majority, Italy arrived to a situation, in 2017, where the share of religious and civil marriages (considering all the marriages, not only first marriages) is almost the same, with religious marriages being the majority only by one percentage point compared to civil ones (50.5% versus 49.5%); in the year after, 2018, the share of civil marriages surpassed that of religious marriages, becoming the majority of the overall marriages celebrated, although by a few percentage points (50.1% versus 49.9%). If we only consider who got married for the first time, the proportion of civil marriages in 2017 was 30.9%.

There are marked territorial differences: in Northern and Central Italy, civil marriages are the majority of the overall marriages for a long time now, whereas in Southern Italy, in 2018, couples continued to greatly prefer religious marriage to civil: they chose religious marriage in 69.6% of cases versus 30.4%, while in Northern Italy, in the same year, the share of religious marriages was 36.1% and in Central Italy 40.5%.

The mean age of marrying persons at the time of first marriage, in 2017, was 35 for men and 32.2 for women, with an increasing trend in the decade 2007–2017; if we go even further back, in 1990, these figures were –6.1 and –6.3 years respectively for men and women.

As by gender, the mean age of marrying persons varies by the territory where people live. In the South of Italy, people on average get married earlier than in Central or Northern Italy: in 2017, 31.1 years *versus* 33.3, respectively, and 32.6 for women and 34.2 years *versus* 36.5 and 35.9 for men.

In 2018,[15] two thirds (64%) of persons married in religious ceremony were aged 18–34 with a concentration in the age group 30–34 (38.8%), about 1/5 were 35–39 years old, 14.3% were 40 or over. People married in civil ceremony are on average older than the spouses in religious marriage: the great part of them (52.9%) are in fact 40 years old or over; moreover, the proportion of 60 years old spouses is over 10 times higher than among people marrying in religious ceremony (11.5% *versus* 0.5%).

Regarding the educational level, in the same year, the majority of persons getting married in religious ceremony had secondary education (Isced 3) (46.4%), one third (32.9%) primary education (Isced 1–2) and 20.6% tertiary education. Among

---

[15] The data for 2017 are incomplete.

Trends and Challenges in Family Formation in Italy • **89**

people choosing civil marriage ceremony, the share of those with tertiary education is quite similar (20.9%), while the share with primary education is higher (37.4%) and that of spouses with secondary education degree is lower (41.7%). Therefore, among spouses choosing civil marriage, there is a lower proportion of medium to higher educated persons than among those choosing religious marriage.

Marriage is not the only way to live as a couple. According to OECD, in 2011, the share of cohabiting households in Italy was 8.92% of the overall partnership households, 4.50% without children, 4.43% with children.[16] The share of 20+-year-olds living with a partner was 5.17%, the share of 20–34-year-olds was 6.88%.

With respect to demographic trends, some information about the main characteristics of the recent migration process in Italy are presented in Table 6.1.

According to the Italian Statistics Institute (Istat, 2017b), during 2016, the immigration flow was equal to nearly 301,000 (+7% compared to 2015), immigrants with a foreign citizenship were the majority by far (263,000, equal to 87%). The largest number of immigrants recorded were Romanians (45,000), followed by Pakistanis (15,000), Nigerians (15,000), and Moroccans (15,000). Compared to 2015, the immigration of Cingalese (–18%), Chinese (–17%), and Bengalis (–14%) to Italy was decreasing. In relative terms, African immigrants showed the highest increases: Guinean citizens (+161%), Ivorians (+73%), Nigerians (+66%), and Ghanaians (+37%). Emigration continued to grow and during 2016 it was equal to 157,000 (+7% compared to 2015).

The increase in emigration was only due to the rise in the number of national emigrants (from 102,000 in 2015 to 115,000 in 2016). The largest share of emigrants chose the United Kingdom (21.6%), Germany (16.5%), Switzerland (9.9%), and France (9.5%). Among the nationals, 25,000 emigrants older than 24 held a university degree. This percentage showed a considerable increase compared to 2015 (+9%). Emigrants with a medium or low educational level increased as well (+11%).

Regarding internal migration, during 2016, 1 million and 331,000 people changed residence among Italian Municipalities (+4% compared to 2015). The large majority of residence changes (1,006,000) took place within the same region, while 324,000 people chose a different region of residence. The number of foreign citizens that migrated within the country is 230,000, +27,000 compared to 2015.

3. SOCIO-ECONOMIC CONDITIONS

According to Istat,[17] in 2017, the family annual net income in Italy was on average 34,450 euro when the main earner was a man, 26,324 (about –23%) in case of a

---

[16] Source: OECD online database, URL: http://www.oecd.org/els/family/database.htm Table SF3.3.A. Partnerships and cohabitation, 2011a

[17] Source: author's calculations based on Istat data "Condizioni economiche delle famiglie e disuguaglianze" available at URL: http://dati.istat.it/

TABLE 6.1. Main Demographic Indicators, Italy, 2007–2017

	2007	2008	2009	2010	2011	2012	2013	2014	2015	2016	2017
Fertility rate (Italian + Immigrants)	1.40	1.45	1.45	1.46	1.44	1.42	1.39	1.37	1.35	1.34	1.32
Fertility rate (Italian)	1.30	1.34	1.33	1.34	1.32	1.29	1.29	1.29	1.27	1.26	1.24
Fertility rate (Immigrants)	2.80	2.65	2.55	2.43	2.36	2.37	2.10	1.97	1.94	1.97	1.98
Mean age of mother at the birth of the first child	31.03	31.08	31.15	31.26	31.36	31.39	31.49	31.55	31.67	31.78	31.89
Mean age of father at the birth of the first child	34.80	34.82	34.89	34.95	35.02	35.08	35.12	35.16	35.26	35.34	35.45
Births outside marriage	18.20	19.70	20.50	21.96	24.50	24.80	25.95	27.60	28.70	29.90	30.90
Household Types											
Single person households	—	—	28.1	28.4	29.4	30.1	30.1	30.6	31.1	31.6	31.9
Couple households without children	—	—	21.1	21.4	20.9	20.4	20.4	20.6	20.5	20.4	20.6
Couple households with children	—	—	39.0	38.2	37.2	36.2	36.2	36.1	35.4	34.7	34.0
Single parent households	—	—	8.7	8.9	9.3	10.0	9.7	9.4	9.7	9.7	10.0

Family Size

1	—	—	28.1	28.4	29.4	30.1	30.1	30.6	31.1	31.6	31.9
2	—	—	27.3	27.6	27.5	27.4	27.3	27.1	27.1	27.3	27.5
3	—	—	20.8	20.9	20.4	20.2	20.2	20.0	20.1	19.8	19.6
4	—	—	17.8	17.4	17.1	16.5	16.7	16.9	16.2	16.0	15.7
5	—	—	4.7	4.5	4.3	4.5	4.3	4.1	4.2	4.2	4.1
at least 6	—	—	1.2	1.3	1.3	1.3	1.3	1.3	1.2	1.2	1.2
Marriage Rates	4.3	4.2	3.9	3.7	3.4	3.5	3.2	3.1	3.2	3.4	3.2
Male Mean Age at First Marriage	32.6	32.8	33.0	33.2	33.5	..	34.0	34.2	..	34.7	35.0
Female Mean Age at First Marriage	29.6	29.8	30.0	30.3	30.5	..	31.1	31.3	..	31.9	32.2
Share of religious marriage											50.5
Share of civil marriage											49.5

Note: Sources: Istat online database, URL: http://dati.istat.it/ and (for*) OECD online family database, URL: http://www.oecd.org/els/family/database.htm (—) indicates no data available.

woman. Compared to the decade before (2007), it increased by 4.9% in the first case, and 10.5% in the second. As expected, the higher net income is observed among families where the main earner has tertiary education, since higher levels of education allow for more qualified and better paid jobs than lower educational levels. In 2017, the annual net income was 46,152 euro for families whose main earner is a university graduate, +70% compared to families where the main earner is junior high school licensed (Isced 2), +37% when he/she completed secondary education (Isced 3). In the same year, the net income of family with a main earner aged 35 or less was 26,254 euro, –48.5% compared to 55–64 years old main earner families. The annual income varies also according to the number of children in the household: when there is one child, it is +18% compared to situations with no children in the household.

The highest incidence of families in absolute and relative poverty is observed when the person of reference is aged 18–34, respectively 9.6% and 16.3% (i.e., +5 and +6.3 percentage points compared to the incidence of families in absolute and relative poverty when the person of reference is older, aged 65 and over). Compared to a decade before, in 2017, these figures increased by +7.7 and +8.5 percentage points. Therefore, it seems that poverty has grown among young families. At the individual level, the highest incidence of absolute and relative poverty of the total number of residents is that of youth aged 17 or less (respectively 12.1% and 21.5%) followed by those aged 18–34 (10.4% and 19%). In both cases, these are growing figures in comparison to 2007 (+ 9 and 10.3 percentage points among youth not older than 17, +7.7 and 8.8 among people aged 18–34).

The share of early school leavers aged 18–24 in 2017, in Italy, was 14%, –5.5 percentage points than a decade before. The incidence of early school leavers is higher among boys (16.6% vs 11.2% among girls). In the South of Italy, the incidence of early school leavers is higher than in the North or Central Italy (18.5% vs 11.3 and 10.7), especially for men (among them the percentage is even higher, 21.5%).

Regarding housing, in 2017, 20.1% of people lived in a rented house, 79.9% in their own property house. The proportion of people in the second housing condition (property) has slightly decreased over the decade. The presence of children in the household seems to lower the probability to be a homeowner: among persons not having children, the percentage of home owners is 81.4%, among persons having one or two children, the percentage is about 76%, and with three or more children, it is 67%. The percentage of homeowners grows with the level of education: it is maximum among those with tertiary education (86.5%) and minimum among the low educated (72.1%). If we consider the professional status, we see a polarization between the retired persons (presumably mostly elderly) and the unemployed (presumably mostly young): the homeowners are 90.3% among the former, 65.9% among the latter. This is consistent with the fact that among youth aged 35 or less, the percentage of persons living in an owned property home is 60.6%, while among persons aged at least 65, it is much higher, 89.6%. Moreover, this figure decreased very much over the decade for youth up to 35 years (–13.6 percentage points).

Below are some figures on the labor market position of families in Italy from the OECD[18] and Istat[19] databases. In 2017, according to the distribution (as %) of children aged 0–14 in one-couple households by employment status of adults in the household, the great part of children (37.8%) in Italy live in families where there is only one adult working full time and one adult not working. The proportion of children living in families with two adults working full time is much lower compared to the EU average (30.8% *vs* near half), although it slightly increased in comparison to 2007 (+ 1.6 percentage points).

This distribution reflects, in part, that of couples according to their occupational condition. In Italy, in 2017, in 43.9% of total couples, with female partner aged 25–64, both partners were employed (mainly in the North of Italy). Among these, the so-called *dual earner family model*, where both partners work full time, amounts to near two thirds (62.3%), whereas *one and a half model*, where the male partner works full time while the female partner works part-time amounts 32.1% of couples with both partners employed. In 39.4% of cases, only one partner is employed and in 16.7% both are not employed. Among the 25–34 years old youth, the incidence of full time dual earner couples is lower in comparison to couples aged 25–64 (–3.2 percentage points), while the incidences of couples where he works full time and she part time (+2.2 percentage points), where both work part time (+0.5 percentage points), or where she works full time and he part time are higher.

4. NORMATIVE FRAMEWORK

In Italy, family and children are a value in itself. Regarding the parental roles, despite the changes in contemporary fatherhood ideals and practices, which see men more involved in the care of their children than in the past, the mother is considered the main person responsible for childcare (Naldini, 2015). An indicator of the traditional behaviors regarding gender and parental roles and childcare is the facultative parental leave taking. Parental leave is used more by mothers than by fathers. Between 2015 and 2019, on average, around 320,000 employees in the private and agricultural sectors benefited from parental leave. Of these, on average, 82 percent were women. However, there was an improvement during the period: the percentage of men out of the total beneficiaries increased from 15% in 2015 to 21% in 2019 (Casamonti, 2021). The gender divide in the use of parental leave has major implications not only for gender equality as such, but also for the social reproduction of gendered experiences of parenthood and parenting behavior (Bertolini et al., 2019).

---

[18] Source: http://www.oecd.org/social/family/database.htm
[19] Source: "Famiglie e mercato del lavoro" at URL: http://dati.istat.it/

94 • ROSY MUSUMECI

Regarding social norms, attitudes and behaviors related to youth autonomy, Italy is a country where young people tend to postpone leaving their parents' home. On average, the transition to housing autonomy takes place around age 30, generally after having celebrated a wedding or deciding to live with one's partner.

Among the factors that discourage leaving the parental home in Italy there are undoubtedly structural and institutional elements, such as the lengthening of the educational path, difficulties in entering the job market, as well as the absence of housing policies to support young people, the weakness of policies to support the family, the absence of generalized income protection measures (Blossfeld et al., 2005; Naldini & Saraceno, 2011). However, cultural factors also play a role (Giuliano, 2007). In Italy, there are in fact cultural and educational models which still do not favor the acquisition of autonomy by children (Bainotti & Torrioni, 2017; Bertolini & Torrioni, 2012; Cavalli, 2007; Ricucci & Torrioni, 2006; Torrioni, 2013) and above all encourage the traditional models in gender relations and family-making (Naldini & Saraceno, 2011). Despite this fact, we have to say that a long stay in the family is not a new phenomenon in Italy (Barbagli & Kertzer, 2005). It is not entirely true, for example, that in the past younger generations left the parental home earlier. According to a study conducted by Barbagli et al. (2003), at the beginning of the twentieth century, men and women left the family when they were about thirty years old, slightly younger than is the case today.

5. INSTITUTIONAL FRAMEWORK

Policy-makers in Italy have traditionally considered that family and related issues, such as partnering and childbirth, belong to the private sphere (Saraceno & Naldini, 2013).

Italy is described as a 'familialistic welfare state', specifically, it is described as a state of 'familialism by default' (or unsupported familialism) which occurs when there are few or no publicly provided alternatives to family care and/or financial support for needy family members, which also translates into defamilialization through the market when individuals and families use their own private resources to buy market care or education services that are not provided through public policies (Saraceno, 2016).

Partially, this happened due to the fact that after the fall of the fascist regime in World War II, there was the will to remove the model of the fascist period (1922–1943), characterized by a very strong political interference in the family. Thus, the Italian family policies are often not explicit and suffer from the lack of any unitary formulation (Bertolini et al., 2018). Rather, they are fragmented, exhibiting one of lowest levels of generosity in Europe, reflected in high rates of child poverty (in 2017, 32.1% of children aged 0–17 in Italy were at risk of poverty or social exclusion,[20] the EU-28 average is 24.9%), as well as a low level of

---

[20] Source: Eurostat, URL: https://ec.europa.eu/eurostat/databrowser/view/tespm040/default/table?lang=en

public support for working parents (Naldini, 2015). In recent years, a reduction in funding for the National Fund for Social Policies occurred, the main financial source for social policies that finance social services and transfers to families. Therefore, municipalities increasingly fall back on their own resources and ask the beneficiary families to share some portion of the costs (Eurofound, 2015).

In the period considered in this chapter (2007 onwards), some policy developments have been implemented in the Italian context.

The Bonus Bebè program was introduced by the 2015 Budget Law and it consists of a one-off allowance of €960 per year for each child born or adopted from 1 January 2015 until 31 December 2017, and is provided to households with an ISEE (the national index used to measure the economic status of Italian families) not exceeding €25,000. The benefit is doubled if the indicator is below €7,000. The aim of the measure is to raise the birth rate (ibid.).

As for same-sex couples, the so-called 'Cirinnà Law' was introduced in 2016. In Italy, same-sex couples' marriage is not allowed, but with this law (no. 76/2016), in 2016, Italy became the 27th country in Europe to legally recognize civil unions of same-sex couples. Under this law, partners in same-sex civil union are required to provide mutual moral and material assistance and to contribute to common needs; moreover, inheritance rights equal to that of married spouses are envisaged. However, partners in same-sex civil unions are not permitted to adopt their partner's children. This law addresses only same-sex couples; therefore, it is not possible for heterosexual couples to enter a civil union. In 2017, the total number of same-sex civil unions was 4,376, of which 2/3 were among men.

Another novelty was the Fornero Law (92/2012) whose goal was to promote "a culture of greater sharing of childcare tasks within the couple, to encourage reconciliation of life and work times" and it introduced one day of compulsory paid paternity leave that can be taken only by the father within five months of the birth of the child; over time, the days of compulsory paid paternity leave have been gradually increased to ten of nowadays. A voucher for baby-sitting or nursery was introduced by the same Law for working mothers with children, in the period of 11 months after the end of compulsory maternity leave. In 2014, the value of the voucher was raised from the initial €300 to €600 per month. The aim of this temporary measure is to incentivize mothers to work (Eurofound, 2015).

In the considered period, self-employed workers and those in non-standard employment were legally entitled to compulsory period of maternity leave (five months) (*congedo di maternità*). In addition, self-employed parents, as well as the majority of working parents on temporary contracts, were legally entitled to three months of paid optional parental leave (*congedo parentale*) during the first year of the child's life. Workers with non-standard contracts that have accumulated insufficient social security funds (i.e. less than the minimum three months of contributions during the last 12 months) are not entitled to this optional leave. The social protection system in Italy is linked to having a permanent contract and workers with fragmented careers are at risk of lacking social protection (Ferrera, 2019).

Working parents with permanent contracts, in contrast, are entitled to six months of parental leave with an allowance of 30% of the monthly income if the leave is taken no later than 6 years as of the birth of the child; it can be used before age 12 of the child but in this case, it is not paid.

Regarding the work-family reconciliation law and policies in Italy, on June 2020, the Italian Minister for Equal Opportunities and Family (Elena Bonetti) and the Minister of Labor and Social Policies (Nunzia Catalfo), in concert with the Minister of Economy and Finance (Roberto Gualtieri), presented a draft law, the so called "Family Act" (DDL n. 2561), "*Deleghe al Governo per il sostegno e la valorizzazione della famiglia*" ("Delegations to the Government for the support and enhancement of the family"). The starting idea is that family policies are social investment policies; in this frame, children are considered the center around which to build all measures for families with children since they—as the Draft Law reads—represent a value and should be considered an enrichment both for the family in which they were born and, above all, for the society that has to share the difficult task of caring for and protecting children from birth with their parents (p. 1).

The Draft Law aims at promoting participation and employment of women in the labor market and gender equality, fighting poverty (including infancy poverty), encouraging sharing of domestic workload, valuing educational and social function of families, and favoring family life-work reconciliation. Among the main objectives and interventions are: to support families through contributions intended to cover—even in the entire amount—the cost related to attendance of educational services for infants and preschoolers, as well as through the introduction of support services in homes for families with children under the age of six, to reorganize and harmonize regulations on parental leaves—one goal is to introduce flexible methods in their management—and mandatory paternity leave for fathers lasting at least ten working days in the first months after the birth of the child (in reality, starting from 2021, paternity leave duration is already ten days). Among the measures aimed at encouraging female work, the Draft Law includes those aimed at encouraging female work especially in the southern regions and those to support female entrepreneurship in the first two years of business launch.

One of the key interventions of this Draft Law is, in particular, the introduction (from July 2021) of the "*Assegno unico universale per i figli*"—a universal financial support which aims at eliminating the sectoral and fragmented nature of the economic measures envisaged by the current legislation, by rationalizing and unifying them into a single universal instrument, strengthened and modulated on the basis of the concrete needs of families. The "*Assegno unico universale per i figli*" is determined on the basis of the economic condition of the household and—at the time of writing (2022)—ranges from a minimum of 50 euros to a maximum of 175 euros for each child (therefore less than the 200-250 euros for each child originally expected by the Draft Law)[21]. A universal part is envisaged, the same for everyone,

---

[21] Source: https://www.inps.it/prestazioni-servizi/assegno-unico-e-universale-per-i-figli-a-carico

Trends and Challenges in Family Formation in Italy • 97

and there is a part that will be added progressively based on family income, number of children (increasing after third child) and presence of disabled children (in this case, the economic support would be increased by 30–50% without age limit).

6. COUNTRY-SPECIFIC CHALLENGES TO FAMILY FORMATION

The younger Italian generations tend to prolong the stay in the family of origin and by that also the process of their own family formation, even after leaving the education system and entering the world of work.

According to Eurostat,[22] the proportion of young people aged between 18 and 34 living with their parents in 2016 was 65.8%; this is a much higher figure than that observed in other European countries, for example, Germany (41.9%). The estimated average age of young people leaving their parents' home is 31.3 years.

In Italy, housing autonomy seems to expose young people to the risk of poverty more than in other countries: the rate of young people at risk of poverty aged 16–29 who do not live with their parents is 31.7%, the share of young people at risk of poverty aged 16–29 living with their parents of origin is 23.5%.[23]

One of the reasons for a slow transition to adult and autonomous life is job insecurity and high level of unemployment among young generations in Italy.

The diffusion of temporary labor contracts and unemployment among youth in the Italian context makes the transition to autonomy, adulthood and family formation problematic. The 2008 crisis has worsened this scenario. According to Eurostat,[24] in 2018, the 15–29 years old temporary employees in Italy comprised 50.6% of the total number of employees (the highest figure in Europe after Spain and Portugal[25]), with a strong increasing trend over the decade (+19 percentage points compared to 2007).

The Italian labor market is characterized by a series of structural imbalances regarding age, gender, territorial divide, type of labor contract, and level of education.[26] They are summarized below. First of all, youth has higher unemployment rates than adults. In 2018, the youth unemployment rate (aged 15–29) was 24.8%. Due to the economic crisis, it increased from 14.5% in 2007 to 31.6% in 2014.

In 2016, the proportion of temporary employees aged 15–29 out of the total number of the employed in that age group was 42.5% in Italy, with an increasing trend in recent years (in 2018, compared to 2016, + 8.1 percentage points). The level of youth unemployment (15–29 years) in 2016 was 28.4%. As for gender differences, young women have higher unemployment rates (+ 3.7 percentage

---

[22] Source: Eurostat [ilc_lvps08] and [yth_demo_030].
[23] Author's calculation based on Eurostat: https://ec.europa.eu/eurostat/data/database
[24] Source: https://appsso.eurostat.ec.europa.eu/nui/show.do?dataset=yth_empl_050&lang=en
[25] Young temporary employees comprise 56.1% of the total number of employees in Spain and 51.6% in Portugal.
[26] The source for the figures presented here is Istat http://dati.istat.it/.

98 • ROSY MUSUMECI

points) compared to their male peers and are also more exposed to fixed-term work than their peers (+ 5.4 percentage points in Italy).[27]

The diffusion of temporary contracts and unemployment can make the assumption of parental responsibilities problematic, discouraging them to the extent that they risk making maternity and paternity unsustainable both from an economic point of view (due to income discontinuity) and in terms of family and work reconciliation (given that many of these contracts do not provide for maternity and parental leave and/or involve working hours difficult for family and work reconciliation).

Having children and becoming parents is one of the aspects of family formation. As we have seen, in Italy, these have become more and more rare experiences in women's and men's life courses.

There is no doubt that greater availability of contraceptive methods has played a crucial role over time, however, one has to explore the interweaving of economic, social and cultural factors (Saraceno & Naldini, 2013). A vast literature describes the Italian context as a discouraging one to the choices of maternity and paternity from different points of view (Sabbadini, 2005).

One of these views related to the extent to which and the way in which contemporary societies support the growing presence of women in the labor market (Saraceno & Naldini, 2013). The rates of women's activity and employment, i.e., their propensity to work in a more or less continuous manner during their life course, have grown over the last three or four decades, driven by their rising education levels and the tertiarization process of the economy (Reyneri, 2011); however, this growth clashes with a series of obstacles linked with family and work reconciliation and responsibilities, and in countries such as Italy, where there are no adequate policies to support the 'double presence' of mothers (Balbo, 1978), the recurrent conciliation strategy, especially for women who are more 'attached' to work, would consist of the reduction in the care workload and, ultimately, the number of children. That children, in Italy, still represent a barrier for women to access and, above all, to maintain work is clear, for example, from the substantial invariability between different age cohorts of the share of mothers who leave work (at least temporarily) for the birth of children (Saraceno, 2003). Children are an obstacle to accessing and maintaining work for women, as the social and institutional contexts do not provide the conditions for them to be able to enter the labor market and to stay there continuously (Bradshaw & Ditch 1993; Gauthier 1996; Gonzàlez et al., 2000; Plantenga & Remery 2009).

Public and social policies, in particular, can encourage procreative choices in various ways: by providing adequate interventions to support parenting, for example, in the form of monetary payments to support the economic-financial cost of children (family allowances, family, maternity allowances, baby bonuses etc.),

---

[27] Source: Author's elaboration based on Eurostat data available at the URL: https://ec.europa.eu/eurostat/data/database

Trends and Challenges in Family Formation in Italy • **99**

but, above all, the leave (i.e., compulsory or optional leave from work for employed parents) and childcare services, the availability of which has been shown to have positive, 'virtuous' effects (Esping-Andersen, 2009) on gender equality and women's labor market participation (female employment rates in Europe are higher and even more children are born in countries where the diffusion of public services for children is greater) (Plantenga & Remery, 2009) or, again, by promoting greater flexibility of working hours and city services (Saraceno & Naldini, 2013). In 2015, Italy spent an average of 2.49% more of GDP on family benefits than in 2009 (1.99) and compared to the OECD average (2.40), but less than many European countries (France: 3.68, Sweden: 3.54, Hungary: 3.53, Denmark: 3.44, Iceland: 3.40, Norway: 3.38, Luxembourg: 3.37, Belgium: 3.24, Finland: 3.11, Germany: 3.06, Estonia: 2.96, Czech Republic: 2.91)[28].

A great part of this spending is in cash (1.29%). Only about 0.66% of total spending was for services in 2015, with a lower proportion in 2009 when it was over 1/3 of the overall spending on family. In 2005, the share of public spending in cash was higher (about + 10%) compared to 2009.

The average coverage rates of public nursery schools in Italy, although in (slight) growth over the last few years, continue to be among the lowest in Europe and abysmally far from the targets set for 2010 by the 2002 Barcelona Summit. The inadequacy of the Italian network of public services (of which nursery schools represent only one category) to satisfy the growing demand for services in support of childcare, explains, in part, the conspicuous recourse by Italian parents to the informal help network, help which, however, even when available, does not always turn out to be able to withstand the overload of care that emerges from the increase in the care needs of elderly parents: the children of female workers, between one and two years of age, continue to be entrusted mainly to grandparents when the mother is at work; however, over a three-year period, there has been an increase in the use of public nurseries (+1.4%) and above all private ones (+4%). The greater increase in the use of private nests compared to public ones is, in our opinion, an indicator, on the one hand, of the fact that, although growing, the supply of public services for early childhood in Italy is still largely insufficient in comparison to the demand and, on the other hand, of the growing development of a private offer market (although often in agreement with local authorities) (Sabbadini et al., 2010), which, especially in the South, where public services are less common, often represents the only strategy to face the needs of reconciling care and work times for families who cannot or do not want to entrust their children to the care of their families of origin.

These data must be interpreted, in addition to referring to the undoubted scarce supply of services for children, also in the light of perceptions, norms and cultural models about children's needs, how they should be looked after and by whom: in this regard, recent studies (Plantenga & Remery, 2009) state that more or less tra-

---

[28] Source: OECD Social Expenditure Database, http://www.oecd.org/social/expenditure.htm

ditional cultural norms can influence, in fact, the demand by families for childcare services and that, in Italy, the widespread attitude among parents is that children should not attend custody facilities until they are at least 2 or even 3 years old.

Attitudes like these are widespread especially in those social contexts, such as the Italian, where family plays a crucial role and where the division of gender roles within it is more rigid and asymmetrical. In Italy, despite the growing inclusion of women in the labor market, the division of domestic work and care between men and women living as couples is still rigid and asymmetrical. Considering the population aged 15 years or more and the average weekly day, in 2013–2014, women spent 4 hours and 33 minutes for unpaid domestic and care work, men 1 and 46; the gender gap between the proportion of women and men declaring to have devoted time for unpaid family work is 19.1 percentage points. Moreover, in the same years, among the couples with both the partners employed full fime and with children, the proportion of couples where the male partner does more family work than his female partner is only 15,0% (Istat, 2019).

In terms of the labor market and company policies, the (un)friendly organization of working times and hours with respect to those with family responsibilities represents a further step that makes up the (un)favorable social and institutional framework for the parental responsibility (Manzi & Mazzucchelli, 2020; Naldini, 2006). Greater availability of part-time jobs (less common than in the rest of Europe and compared to potential internal demand) and, in general, flexible working hours would facilitate family-work reconciliation and lead to an increase in female employment rates; not surprisingly, these rates are higher in countries where part time is more widespread (Reyneri, 2011).

Although quantity and quality of public interventions in support of family and work reconciliation and the characteristics and organization of the labor market can encourage or discourage procreative choices, on a cultural level, the decline in fertility is affected by individuals' and couples' attitudes toward sexuality, which is increasingly perceived and experienced as a dimension in its own right, separate from procreation. On the other hand, such a decline is affected by the emergence of a different meaning, value and place assigned to children in the personal and family life cycle (i.e., children as "resources" in the past societies have now become an "investment" in contemporary ones); these attitudes have led to the downsizing of the ideal family model (Saraceno & Naldini, 2013).

7. CONCLUSION

This chapter analyzed the main trends and challenges in family formation in Italy. Firstly, it described the main characteristics of the national context by illustrating the main social, historical, political, and economic developments. Secondly, focusing especially on the pre-Covid pandemic situation and precisely on the decade 2007–2017 (but also providing more recent data, when available), the chapter illustrated the main demographic trends relevant to family formation: household types, marriage rates, mean age of marriage, fertility rates, age of mother at first childbirth, births outside marriage, general migration trends—inward and outward. Since family formation dynamics are influenced by the normative framework—intended from a sociological perspective—section three was about socio-economic conditions of families with particular regard to the labor market, housing, poverty, and social exclusion. Section four provided a short description of the prevailing attitudes toward gender and parental roles in Italy, the family itself, and the main social and cultural norms around family life. Section five describes the Italian institutional framework, i.e., the main recent key family policies and legislative developments. The last section of the chapter discussed the peculiarities of the challenges to family formation in Italy.

REFERENCES

Bainotti, L., & Torrioni, P. M. (2017). Che genere di socializzazione? Crescere in famiglia: percorsi di costruzione delle identità femminili e maschili [What kind of socialization? Growing up in the family: paths for the construction of female and male identities]. *AG-About Gender, 6*(12), 190–217.

Balbo, L., (1978) La doppia presenza [The double presence]. *Inchiesta, 32*, 3–6.

Barbagli, M., Castigioni, M., & Della Zuanna, G. (2003). *Fare famiglia in Italia* [Making family in Italy]. il Mulino.

Barbagli M., & Kertzer D. (2005). *La storia della famiglia in Europa. Il Novecento* [The history of the family in Europe. The twentieth century.]. Laterza.

Barbieri, P., & Scherer, S. (2009). Labour market flexibilization and its consequences in Italy. *European Sociological Review, 80*, 1–16.

Bertolini, S., Moiso, V., & Musumeci, R. (Eds.). (2018). *Young adults in insecure labour market positions in Italy—The results from a qualitative study*. EXCEPT Working Papers, WP No 18. Tallinn University, Tallinn. http://www.except-project.eu/working-papers/

Bertolini, S., Musumeci, R., Naldini, M., & Torrioni, P. M. (2019). Italian couples with non-normative work-care plans and practices. In D. Grunow, & M. Evertsson (Eds.), *New parents in Europe: Work-care practices, gender norms and family policies, USA-UK* (pp. 148–168). Edward Elgar Publishing.

Bertolini, S., & Torrioni, P. M. (2012). Giovani-adulti flessibili? Le ripercussioni del lavoro atipico sulle strategie di uscita dalla famiglia di origine in Italia e Francia [Flexible young-adults? The repercussions of the atypical work on the strategies of exit from the family of origin in Italy and France]. In S. Cordella, & G. Masi, (Eds.), *Condizione giovanile e nuovi rischi sociali. Quali politiche?* [Condition of youth and new social risks. What policies?]. (pp. 83–104). Carocci.

Blossfeld, H. P., Hofäcker, D., & Bertolini, S. (Eds.). (2011). *Youth on globalised labour market. rising uncertainty and its effects on early employment and family lives in Europe*. Barbara Budrich Publishers.

Blossfeld, H. P., Klijzing, E., Mills, M., & Kurz, K. (Eds.). (2005). *Globalization, uncertainty and youth in society*. Routledge.

Bosoni, M. L. (2011). Uomini, paternità e lavoro: la questione della conciliazione dal punto di vista maschile [Men, fatherhood and work: Issue of reconciliation from the male point of view]. *Sociologia e politiche sociali. 14*(3). 63–86.

102 • ROSY MUSUMECI

Bradshaw, J., & Ditch, J. (1993). *Support for children. A comparison of arrangements in fifteen countries* (Research Report 21). HMSO.

Briulotta, T. (2009). Atipici in famiglia. La vita a due nell'incertezza lavorativa [Atypical workers in the family. The life as couple in the job insecurity]. In R. Palidda (Ed.), *Vite flessibili. Lavori, famiglie e stili di vita di giovani coppie meridionali* [Flexible lives. Jobs, families and lifestyles of young southern couples]. FrancoAngeli.

Casamonti, M. (2021). *Congedi parentali e di maternità/paternità: chi si prende cura dei minori?* [Parental and maternity/paternity leave: who takes care of minors]. In OCPI (Osservatorio sui conti pubblici italiani). https://osservatoriocpi.unicatt.it/cpi-Congedi.pdf

Cavalli, A. (2007). *Giovani non protagonisti.*[Young people not protagonists]. il Mulino-Rivista Web, 3.

Dadush, U. (2013). *Is the Italian economy on the mend?* Carnegie Europe. URL: https://carnegieeurope.eu/publications/?fa=50565&reloadFlag=1

Dermott, E. (2008). *Intimate fatherhood. A sociological analysis*. Routledge.

Esping-Andersen, G. (2009). *The incomplete revolution. Adapting to women's new roles*. Polity Press.

Eurofound. (2015). *Families in the economic crisis: Changes in policy measures in the EU.* Publications Office of the European Union.

Ferrera, M. (Ed.). (2019). *Le politiche sociali* [The social policies]. Il Mulino.

Gauthier, A. H. (1996). *The state and the family. A comparative analysis of family policies in industrialised countries*. University Press.

Giuliano, P. (2007). Living arrangements in Western Europe: Does cultural origin matter? In *Journal of the European Economic Association, 5*, 927–952.

Gonzàlez, M. J., Jurado, T., & Naldini, M. (Eds.). (2000). *Gender inequalities in southern Europe. Women, work and welfare in the 1990s*, Frank Cass.

Istat. (2017a). *La salute riproduttiva della donna* [Women's reproductive health.]. Author. https://www.istat.it/it/files//2018/03/La-salute-riproduttiva-della-donna-1.pdf

Istat. (2017b). *International and internal migration year 2016* (pp. 1–9). Author. https://www.istat.it/it/files//2017/11/EN-trasferimenti-di-residenza.pdf

Istat. (2019). *I tempi della vita quotidiana. Lavoro, conciliazione, parità di genere e benessere soggettivo* [The times of everyday life. Work, reconciliation, gender parity and subjective well-being]. https://www.istat.it/it/files//2019/05/ebook-I-tempi-della-vita-quotidiana.pdf

Lucidi, F., & Raitano, M. (2009). Molto flessibili, poco sicuri: Lavoro atipico e disuguaglianze nel mercato del lavoro italiano [Very flexible, not very secure: atypical work and inequalities in the Italian labor market]. *Economia e Lavoro, 2*, 99–115.

Magaraggia, S. (2015). *Essere giovani e diventare genitori. Esperienze a confronto* [Being young and becoming parents. Comparing experiences]. Carocci.

Manzi, C., & Mazzucchelli, S. (Eds.). (2020). *Famiglia e lavoro: Intrecci possibili* [Family and work: Possible connections]. Vita & Pensiero.

Martin Prosperity Institute. (2011). *Creativity and prosperity: The global creativity index*. http://martinprosperity.org/media/GCI%20Report%20Sep%202011.pdf

Naldini, M. (2006). *Le politiche sociali in Europa* [Social policies in Europe]. Carocci.

Naldini, M. (Ed.). (2015). *La transizione alla genitorialità. Da coppie moderne a famiglie tradizionali* [The transition to parenthood. From modern couples to traditional families]. Il Mulino.

Naldini, M., & Saraceno, C. (2011). *Conciliare famiglia e lavoro. Vecchi e nuovi patti tra sessi e generazioni* [Reconciling family and work. Old and new pacts between genders and generations]. Il Mulino.

Plantenga, J., & Remery, C. (2009) *The provision of childcare services. A comparative review of thirty European countries.* European Commission, Directorate-General for Employment, Social Affairs and Equal opportunities G1 Unit.

Reyneri, E. (2011). *Sociologia del mercato del lavoro* [Sociology of the labor market]. Il Mulino.

Ricucci, R., & Torrioni, P. M. (2006). Da una generazione all'altra: una famiglia pacificata? [From one generation to the next: A peaceful family?] In F. Garelli, A. Palmonari, & L. Sciolla. *La socializzazione flessibile. Identità e trasmissione dei valori tra i giovani* [Flexible socialization. Identity and transmission of values among young people]. (pp. 25–64). Il Mulino.

Rosina, A., & Fraboni, R. (2004). Is marriage losing its centrality in Italy? *Demographic Research. 11,* 149–172.

Sabbadini, L. L. (2005). *Conciliazione dei tempi di vita e denatalità* [Reconciliation of life times and denatality]. Relazione alla Camera dei deputati, Roma, 13 dicembre.

Sabbadini, L. L., & Cappadozzi, T. (2011). *Essere padri: tempi di cura e organizzazione di vita* [Being fathers: Time for care and organization of life]. [Paper] Men, fathers and work from different perspective. Milan (Italy), 2 February 2011.

Sabbadini, L. L., Romano, M. C., & Crialesi, R. (2010) *Famiglie in cifre* [Families in figures] (dossier), Conferenza nazionale della famiglia. Famiglia: storia e futuro di tutti, 8–10 Novembre 2010, Milano. Dipartimento per le politiche della famiglia, Istat.

Saraceno, C. (2003). La conciliazione di responsabilità familiari e attività lavorative in Italia. Paradossi e equilibri imperfetti [The conciliation of family responsibilities and work activities in Italy. Paradoxes and imperfect balances]. *Polis, 17*(2), 199–228.

Saraceno, C. (2016). Varieties of familialism: Comparing four southern European and East Asian welfare regimes. *Journal of European Social Policy, 26*(4), 314–326.

Saraceno, C., & Naldini, M. (2013). *Sociologia della famiglia* [Sociology of family]. Il Mulino.

Sensenbrenner, F., & Arcelli, A. F. (2013). Italy's economy is much stronger than it seems. *The Huffington Post.* https://www.huffpost.com/entry/italy-economy_b_3401988?guccounter=1&guce_referrer=aHR0cHM6Ly9lbi53aWtpcGVkaWEub 3JnLw&guce_referrer_sig=AQAAAEdEZTXeyDCUvZ1JdeW8hw91iig2wFg_ wxIM8yNWc55ng5AOQdlAK4TFQ0uiNKoXlTpTMkeSfzDUi-A3T9VA9zck- 4wjIhBTlTiXqKs5k7CoekwVLENm_dPSrxUUUR-jGBW_sYhc9TX4LkkXZlE- 1pdSNC9w7wCyVxSwEve7PqrC9

Torrioni, P. M. (2013). Diventare autonomi, dimostrarsi responsabili [Become autonomous, prove responsible]. In G. Maggioni, P. Ronfani, M. C. Belloni, V. Belotti (Eds), *Bambini e Genitori. Norme, pratiche e rappresentazioni della responsabilità* [Children and Parents. Norms, practices and representations of responsibility] (pp. 115–128). Donzelli Editore.

World Bank. (2019). *Gross domestic product (2017). The World Bank: World Development Indicators database.* https://web.archive.org/web/20190228214812/https:// databank.worldbank.org/data/download/GDP.pdf

CHAPTER 7

SOCIAL AND ECONOMIC CHALLENGES AND OPPORTUNITIES IN FAMILY FORMATION IN LATVIA

Līva Griņeviča and Dina Bite

Latvia University of Life Sciences and Technologies

Anna Broka

Tallinn University

1. NATIONAL CONTEXT

Latvia is one of the so-called post-communist countries where the soviet heritage both in economic and social structures confronts the Western ideas of democracy and free market system. The restoration of the state's independence in 1990 caused wide rearrangements in political, economic and social spheres. On the one hand, people in Latvia have to cope with a set of situations and problems that are common to other post-communist countries. According to international research about post-communist countries, family deinstitutionalization and destabilization processes lead to the weakening of family bonds, diversification of family life

---

Family Formation Among Youth in Europe: Coping With Socio-Economic Disadvantages,
pages 105–122.
Copyright © 2022 by Information Age Publishing
www.infoagepub.com
All rights of reproduction in any form reserved.

forms, and decreased fertility, the last of which gives rise to problems with simple generation substitution. Young people face changes in cultural models of sexuality, high valuing of freedom and individuality in connection with new challenges and problems (Szafraniec et al., 2018). However, on the other hand, there are some specifics in terms of the cultural background, ethnic discourse, labor market situation etc.

Issues of depopulation, territorial polarization and shrinking processes of population and infrastructure have been present in the recent 30 years and have accompanied important transitions in economy and social life (Bite, 2016). The inhabitants of Latvia, as a post-communist country, face various, often contradictory, factors that influence their choices regarding family formation. Taking into account the depopulation tendencies—low fertility, rather high mortality and emigration—the age structure of the population and the family forms in the society have changed significantly.

After the 2008 economic recession, family formation was affected by two main push-pull factors—1) labor migration and 2) regional economic disparities. Family institutional settings were organized via extended networks and with new mobility solutions. While national level policies were addressing re-emigration, improvement in education, reforming health and developing social services at the local level, local municipalities addressed the infrastructure attractive for investments and employees, tried to deal with housing shortages, supported early childhood education and schools, as well as provided support for families with more than three children, etc.

In 2020, the national economic instability was linked with the unexpected Covid-19 pandemic affecting various areas of the family life (i.e., economic situation, increasing unemployment and worsening of general socioeconomic conditions).

Latvia has large regional disparities—the Riga region produces more than half of the Latvian GDP and has twice the level of GDP per capita, while other regions remain below this level with a decreasing tendency (OECD, 2018). Along with regional inequalities, the welfare of the population is higher in Riga and Pieriga regions, with comparatively higher labor market demand and availability of services for families. The substantial government spending on education and development of innovative entrepreneurship in the regions are the most effective tools to ensure regional economic development. Still, new social risk factors appear due to family re-(e)migration, rather flexible conditions of the labor market, and comparatively low social protection requiring political decision-makers to be both responsive and effective at the same time (Hiļkevičs & Štefenberga, 2013; Lulle et al., 2019; Rajevska & Rajevska, 2020).

A considerable rapid demographic downturn transition accounts for 1.92 million people at the beginning of 2019. In early 2019, there were 122,271 young people living in Latvia, aged 18–24, which is almost two times less than in 2009 when there were 238,000 young people living in Latvia (Central Statistical Bureau of Latvia, 2019g). In addition, the share of children is 359 000 or 18.7% of

Social and Economic Challenges and Opportunities in Latvia • **107**

the total population, with an increasing pattern of 1.4 percentage points compared to 2014 (17.3%). Increasing birth rates in the period from 2013 to 2016 can be explained by rather expansive family policies and social assistance (increased amounts and duration of universal and family benefits, gradually raised income tax exemptions for families with children under 15 (or 24, if the child is in education), student support and increased amounts of subsistence guarantee for single-parent families) (Rajevska & Rajevska, 2020). The brain-drain contributes to skill shortages, decreasing economic growth and increasing pressure on pension and health care systems. While Latvia has taken action to tackle these challenges by reforming its education system and promoting active labor market policies, the identified demographic challenges have not been addressed by any long-term family and social policy design.

2. DEMOGRAPHIC TRENDS RELEVANT TO FAMILY FORMATION (BY AGE GROUPS, GENDER AND ETHNICITY)

According to the Study of Young People in Latvia, the majority of young people display a normal path in life transitions: finishing school, starting work, leaving the parental home, getting married and giving birth to the first child (Gūtmane, 2020). However, referring to OECD, young people in Latvia prioritize higher level of education and a successful career over family formation. Latvia is ranking among top OECD countries in secondary educational attainment and has a rather high level of tertiary education (OECD, 2019). Already in the 1990s, the average maternal age for childbirth increased by several years. Women in Latvia are more likely than men to experience the expected decrease in the number of intended children as education levels increase (Eglīte et al., 2002). It is positive that young people choose to acquire high level of education in order to become more competitive in the labor market and to raise the level of welfare. On the other hand, there is low support for families with children and the most recent family policies do not result in substantially increased birth rates. Population continues to decrease and, in comparison to the same period in 2019, it has decreased by 15400 (Central Statistical Bureau of Latvia, 2019b,e,h).

At the beginning of 2019, the largest share of children and young people (aged 0–18) was recorded in Pierīga (21.2%) and the smallest in Latgale (16.5%) region. The shares recorded in municipalities varied between 13% in Nereta municipality and 31% in Mārupe municipality. Latvians accounted for 69% and Russians for 15% of children. In 2018, 2.4 thousand children emigrated from Latvia (15% of the total number of emigrants), while 1.4 thousand children immigrated to the country (13% of immigrants). In 2018, 40 children were seeking asylum in Latvia, and 10 children were granted alternative status. According to the previous Latvian National Development Plan (2014–2020), several family support and social assistance measures have been introduced: labor market participation measures, parental leave, measures that encourage women to return to the labor market, etc.

Housing and environment. In Latvia, most young people live in their parents' or other family members' houses until they have enough personal income to move to their own home or apartment. Only very few of them live in their own home (3% acquired by their parents, 3% by themselves, 7% paid by themselves—rented). The reason for this situation is financial, so living with parents or other family members is most often explained by saving financial resources (Gūtmane, 2020).

Marriage rates. In Latvia, the number of marriages increased in recent years—the number per 1 000 population increased from 4.4 marriages in 2010 to 6.8 in 2018. In 2018, there were 5 697 divorces, which is 21% more than in 2010 when it was not possible to divorce a marriage by a notary. A marriage is regarded divorced when the court ruling becomes legally effective. Since 1 February 2011, marriage in Latvia may be divorced also by a sworn notary—which is the main reason for higher divorce rates (Central Statistical Bureau of Latvia, 2018).

Mean age of marriage. According to statistical data of the Central Statistical Bureau of Latvia, as of 2017, 45% of males and 59% of females at first marriage were aged 29 years or less. Average age for males at first marriage was 32 years, and for females 30 years (Central Statistical Bureau of Latvia, 2019).

Fertility rates. In 2018, fertility rate was 1.61 in Latvia (in 2017 it was 1.70), which still is far from the desired number of children needed for a change of generation: 2.1–2.2. For a normal change of generation, fertility must increase much faster. Last time the total fertility rate of 2.2 was observed in Latvia was in 1986–1987 when 42 thousand children a year were born—the largest number of births since 1946 (Central Statistical Bureau of Latvia, 2019d).

Age of first-time mothers. Average age of women at childbirth in 2018 was 30.5 years (since 2000, average age of women at childbirth has increased by almost four years), at first time childbirth—28 years (Central Statistical Bureau of Latvia, 2019a). Latvia has one of the most advantageous maternity leaves for mothers (94 weeks) (Central Statistical Bureau of Latvia, 2019i).

Births outside marriage. Data of the Central Statistical Bureau show that in 2018, a total of 19.3 thousand children were born in Latvia, 7.6 thousand or 39.4% of which were extra-marital births. A total of 11.7 thousand or 60.6% of children were born in registered marriages. In 2018, a larger number of extra-marital births were registered among women aged 25–29, when the first baby is born usually (Central Statistical Bureau of Latvia, 2019c).

General migration trends—inward and outward. Since 1990, as the result of migration, the population of Latvia was reduced by almost half a million (457 thousand). As the result of international long-term migration, the population in the period 2010–2018 dropped by 126.1 thousand. In 2018, 10.9 thousand persons arrived in Latvia for permanent stay (a period of time equal to one year or more) (9.1% more than in 2017), while 15.8 thousand persons left—12.1% less than in the previous year (Central Statistical Bureau of Latvia, 2019f).

Social and Economic Challenges and Opportunities in Latvia • 109

3. NORMATIVE FRAMEWORK

Social norms dominating in the Latvian society still reveal that family is a crucial factor of people's wellbeing. Research of the aspect of trust reveals that family and closest friends are still the most common persons of trust among young people. There is a marked difference between trusting family and friends and various formal organizations (including government, churches and political parties). According to an international study, young people in Latvia realize their civic activity among their closest acquaintances ("civic privatism") or relate to the public issues helplessly (Muranyi, 2015). In the most recent study about the values in action, the family was mentioned as an important resource for long-term development by 64.5% respondents. While 49.9% of respondents turned to their family in order to receive substantial support within 6-month period (Mihailova & Broka, 2020).

Both national and international studies show that family is one of the most important values among young people. According to the research Young People Situation from Employment Perspective: International Study (2020), studies today indicate that young people's attitudes towards family values are positive, as young people see the family model as a value to them (Gūtmane & Griņeviča, 2020). Articles and research emphasize the importance of family both in society as a whole and in the life of each individual. In society, the family is interpreted as one of the essential contributors to the solidarity of the nation (especially in the aspects of family welfare, respect for family values, family as a place of safety) (Priedola, 2018). Young people associate family with a place where one obtains support and help. Young people aged 18–24 are generally more satisfied with their family life than young people on average in the EU and note that they fully or greatly influence the family decision-making. However, not all young people (25%) are satisfied with the opportunities to spend time with their family (Agency for International Programs for Youth, 2019).

Young people associate family not so much with formal marriage as with partners' informal cohabitation. 61% of young people aged 18–24 consider marriage to be an outdated institution. Although women are slightly less likely than men to agree with this statement, there are also differences between urban and rural areas ((Interdepartmental Coordination Center, 2019). Young people nowadays make the decision to start a family much later than, for instance, their parents, and most children (63.5% in 2018) are born out of wedlock (Central Statistical Bureau of Latvia, 2019g). Among the family values, cozy apartment, house (94%), happy cohabitation with a partner (92%) and ability to ensure a safe future for their children (92%) are highly valued. Values such as children (77%) and family formation (84%) were seen as relatively less significant (Ministry of Education and Science of the Republic of Latvia, 2013), reflecting the known manifestations of consumerism and individualism.

Young people's choices with regard to family formation and different forms of family are realized within the general regulatory framework of society. According to the authors of a generational study conducted in 2019, the importance of traditional values has been declining in the Latvian society, especially with the emergence of more liberal views among the younger population. More often than in the older generations, unregistered cohabitation is accepted among young people, there is a greater desire to support legitimization of homosexual relationships, and rarely a woman or a man need children to find fulfilment. Young people's reproductive behavior is mainly determined by employment status and financial means. Overall, there is a clear trend towards gender equality in the understanding of gender roles (Priedola, 2018).

4. SOCIO-ECONOMIC CONDITIONS

Young people have been defined as one of the important target groups in the main policy documents (National Development Plan of Latvia for 2014–2020, 2012; Youth Law, 2008) operating in such areas as education/vocational training, active labor market policy (ALMPs), poverty reduction and social exclusion. The main activities of these policies are aimed to reduce youth unemployment and promote social inclusion of young people into the labor market, as well as increase young people's social protection and equality. It is also important to provide high quality of education and up-skilling of young people.

According to the research Young People Situation from Employment Perspective: International Study (2020), one of the foundations of a good youth employment policy is to improve the education system and adapt it to the requirements of the modern economy labor market. It is important to take actions on reducing the risk of youth poverty in any country. In reducing the risk of youth poverty, it is important to understand that this is not a short-term but a long-term benefit for the development of each society and economy as a whole. The risk of youth poverty is higher in families where young people are raised only by one parent, so national social protection policies must be focused on serious measures to preserve families and strengthen family values (Gūtmane & Griņeviča, 2020).

Latvia has rather equal and high access to general public funded education (level 0–3). The vast majority of youth at the age of 15 are enrolled in lower secondary education (ISCED level 2) and/or obtain upper secondary education (ISCED level 3) between ages 16 and 18. Higher level of education (level 6) is obtained in the age 20–24 and is rather high, while enrolment in post-secondary non-tertiary education and short-cycle tertiary education is very low (Eurostat, 2020a). Latvia can be characterized as a rather flexible and non-selective education system both in terms of the early childhood education, general education and vocational education and training (Eurydice, 2019). Unfortunately, Latvia did not launch free-of-charge full-time studies in tertiary education (in reference to the Bologna process), in comparison with Estonia (launched in 2013). The payment of studies is shared between state funding and private funding. Differentiated measures are available on the local level for youth experiencing disadvantages, e.g., individual career counselling, free school lunch, support for school equipment, support for families in need, social pedagogy, psychology at school etc. (Eurydice, 2019). The level of public expenditures in education remain rather low and similar pre- and after economic recession (Toots & Lauri, 2017). The major concern today evolves around the ability to respond to the labor market needs, ensure quality of education, equal opportunities, and increase participation.

In 2019, employment rate among men was 5.8 percentage points higher than that among women—68.1% and 62.3%, respectively. The EU average indicator is higher among men as well. The employment rate among women in Latvia was 6.7 percentage points and among men 1.7 percentage points higher than the EU average. Regardless of the fact that Latvian legislation enhances gender equality in the labor market, e.g., by ensuring paid childcare leave, the greatest gender gap in employment may be observed among population aged 25–34 (8.4 percentage points), which is related to the fact that people tend to build families at this age, and household and care duties are distributed unequally. In 2018, employment rate of women in households (consisting of population aged 25–49) having at least one child aged under six was 18.1 percentage points lower than that of men (Central Statistical Bureau of Latvia, 2020).

According to the labor statistics, youth employment is low while they are in education (aged 15–19), but substantially increases from 20 to 29 years of age to 51.9%. Youth unemployment is rather low (9.3%) in the age group from 15 to 29 (Eurostat, 2019, 2019b). Young people are considered rather independent and can assure their living from a rather early stage (starting at age 18–20), i.e., they are enrolled in further education, combining education with work, or simply starting their own family life. Income insecurity or poverty remains to be an important hindering factor for early transition to adulthood.

The Baltic countries, in respect to poverty reduction and application of youth orientated ALMPs, are valued as being most decisive (Tosun et al., 2017). Since 2016, at-risk-of-poverty remains at approx. 16%, which is comparatively lower than the situation during recession (Eurostat, 2019a). Dependency on family income in the age group between 15–19 years is closely interrelated with education, while other subsistence is closely related to family benefits and social assistance for families in need on local level.

One of the concerns challenging both education/ VET system and labor market is the state of the youth not being in education and training (NEET) and their ability to re-enter. Early leavers from education and training or the NEET rate increase with age is evident in higher level of education (starting with upper secondary education) (see Figure 7.1. Eurostat, 2019, 2019b,c).

Social assistance, adequacy and coverage of social protection for different groups of young people across regions vary. In general terms, youth (from 18 to 20 or, if studying, to 24 years) can apply for all types of social benefits, such as unemployment or family benefits if they are living with their parents or if they have children. In addition, there is housing and social assistance or additional social assistance for single parenthood or disability (Council of Europe, 2020).

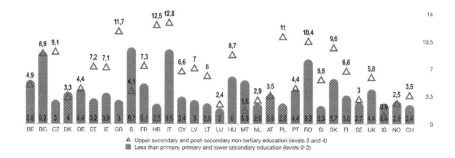

FIGURE 7.1. Youth NEET Rate (%) With Less Than Primary, Primary and Lower Secondary Education (Levels 0–2) and Upper Secondary and Post-Secondary Non-Tertiary Education (Levels 3 and 4), Age Group 15–29. Data source: Authors, using data from Eurostat.

The ALMPs play the most crucial role in the poverty reduction strategy among youth, especially the NEETs. Traditional vocational education programs (VET) were supplemented by work-based learning (WBL) programs, "Youth Guarantee" since 2013 and "Upskilling Pathways" since 2016—partly EU co-funded programs directly oriented at youth, especially the NEET youth inclusion in the labor market. Free training and career opportunities were assured until 2018 for more than 6500 young people (Council of Europe, 2020). In 2013–2014, Latvia adopted as many as seven youth-oriented reforms and spent the largest share of expenditures (% of GDP) on training and incentives, but less for job creation and start-ups (Tosun et al., 2017). Still, Latvia has difficulties in integrating youth into the labor market, which may bring about other disadvantages besides unemployment and poverty risk. Early leavers from education and training are among the highest in Latvia (8.7% in age group 18–24). Employment among youth is rather high (51.9% in age group 20–29) (Eurostat, 2019, 2019b). Positive results can be explained with available public funded education, ALMPs as part of education/training and public work initiatives, as well as the ability to combine work with education. Even though social welfare services are not analyzed in detail here, some positive effects of the expansion of social policies are evident. Differentiated and flexible education and employment arrangements, social entitlements and supplementary support measures (ALMPs) at the state and municipal levels in Latvia encourage young people to become more self-sufficient, independent and establish families earlier.

5. INSTITUTIONAL FRAMEWORK

Similar to other EU countries, Latvia follows competitive knowledge economy and productiveness as part of the EU development strategy, with the commitment to invest in children and families (Esping-Andersen, 2002). According to the welfare regime typology (Esping-Andersen, 1990), the Baltic countries are considered to represent a post-communist version of the Anglo-Saxon world with an important role of the market and family in welfare provision (Aidukaite, 2009; Toots & Backmann, 2010). A more specific family policy entails a conservative-corporatist regime with modest child benefits and a heavy reliance on social insurance programs based on employment (Aidukaite, 2019). The Latvian family policy, specifically analyzing social security policies during the period from 2007–2019, can be characterized by expansion of the general social services and increased support for poor families and families in need of differentiated services (care for children with disabilities, foster care etc.). Changes in family policy can be divided into three main periods: severity of economic crisis (2008–2012), expansion and reconstruction of social policy areas after the crisis (2013–2017) (Rajevska & Rajevska, 2020), and initial shift towards universality and progressivity. The economic crisis is considered an austerity period in different policy areas, especially those affecting families with children and the elderly. Compared with other Baltic States, support for families with children was most significantly reduced during the crisis. During the recovery phase, it took the direction towards an effective state in economic dimension, while family policies and social assistance were shifting in between continuity, predictability and flexibility (Āboliņa, 2016). The simplified taxation regime that was introduced (in 2010), i.e., the micro-tax, self-employment, part-time, revealed during the Covid-19 pandemic that approx. 150 000 people are not socially insured. This was an important push for the state to introduce new initiatives for families in need (Mihailova & Broka, 2020). The existing Latvian pension scheme is sustained by taxpayers with minimized responsibility of the state and pension fund managers. In the absence of a social safety net, Latvian pensioners are among the poorest in the EU (Rajevska & Rajevska, 2020).

Although the population increase as the main priority of family policy and social security policies was acknowledged, birth rates increased only partially in line with increasing birth allowances and maternity/paternity leave schemes, extra support for larger families and income tax deduction equivalent for every child. The most important shortage is the lack of cross-sectoral coordination and intensified social investment policy measures, especially targeting single-parent families and parenthood in general. Availability of early-childhood education is diversified between the regions, while family support and social assistance are increasingly marketized. The increasing flexible forms of work (teleworking), distance-work or other flexible work arrangements are at the edge of precarious employment and social insecurity. While flexible labor market conditions are assured, family support measures are still not sufficient and do not significantly improve the financial situation of large families with children and the elderly.

The core of family support policy in Latvia is based on three key elements: financial support for families, support in the form of services or in-kind support, and other family-oriented activities. Family protection and support by the State is defined in the Constitution (Section 110), whereas marriage is strongly supported between man and woman as a family. Ten types of in-cash universal state social allowances paid on regular basis and three types of lump-sum allowances (Law on State Social Allowance, Section 3) are encompassing the rights of parents and the child, special support for disabled children, children left without parental care or suffering from violence. More than 18 amendments with three Constitutional Court decisions (on Sections 4 and 20) and four Supreme Court decisions (on Section 3, 6, 9 and 10) were made in regard to different types of family allowances between 2007 and 2019. The universal family allowance (11.38 euros) is granted for all children aged 1–15 years, or 20 years if the person is studying[1]. Considerable welfare redistribution changes were made to support large families with increased allowance[2] (entered into force 1 January 2018). Since 2013, childcare benefit increased to 171 euros and is granted until age of 1,5 years, and 42.69 euros until age 2 for every next child. Special support measures were implemented for families taking care of children with disabilities and severe disabilities[3] (Cabinet of Ministers, 2009; State Social Insurance Agency of the Republic of Latvia, 2020). Following the deinstitutionalization process (2009–2017), several additional allowances were introduced for guardians, foster families and child adoption. The deinstitutionalization process is in mid-term implementation stage, but it is promising a continuity of supportive arrangements both for children out of family care and for children with disabilities (Broka et al., 2017, 2018).

Another objective of family policy development in Latvia relates to employment enhancement—labor market accessibility for families with children: part-time job opportunities or flexible working time arrangements and day-care facilities for working parents. Working time regulations is a matter of an individual agreement and evolves around regular daily working hours (40 hours weekly) of a five-day working week, overtime and part-time work in Latvia (Labour Law, 2001). During the economic recession (2008–2012), part-time work increased from 7% to 11% and can be explained by shorter working hours adopted to minimize employment cuts (European Institute for Gender Equality, 2014). Even though the law prohibits discrimination, the gender pay gap can be identified in lower paid jobs where women are employed (health care, education etc.). From 2012–2018, the share of part time workers (from 8.8% to 7%) and involuntary part-time[4] work decreased especially among women (from 42.5% in 2012 to 29.6% in 2018). Possible explanation might be scarce availability of paid jobs, disproportion of the high qualification of workforce and labor demand for low qualified workers (Eurofound, 2018). Employment flexibility can be characterized by different types of agreements and contracts, but only a part of those agreements stipulate the obligation to pay social insurance tax (32.15%).

---

[1] Not receiving scholarship, except EU funded, and not married.

[2] For the second child (22.76 euros), the third (34.14) and for more than four children (50.07 euros) and extra payment (summing up for two children—10 euros, three—60, and next—50 euros).

[3] Since 2009, the allowance increased from 71.14 euros to 106.72 euros; additional childcare benefit for children with severe disability increased from 106.72 euros to 313.43 euros per month in 2019.

[4] Part-time working because they could not find full-time.

Different types of child-care facilities are available and provided, e.g., by municipalities, at educational institutions or by families (receiving methodological support) or other private sector providers. In 2013, the Ministry of Welfare adopted new regulations supporting diversified child-care services (Cabinet of Ministers, 2013). Diversified options resulted in an increased formal childcare provision both in the group under three years, from 15% in 2007 to 25.8% in 2018 (for 30 hours a week), and from three to compulsory school age from 51% to 84.8% (Eurostat, 2020). Shortages of public childcare are evident in the larger cities and the capital Riga, while less evident in smaller cities and rural areas. The use of formal childcare starts from approx. 1.5 years of age—which corresponds to the end of the maternity leave. The development and play centers established by private entities as alternative pre-school educational institutions are eligible to receive public funding (Mihailova & Broka, 2020). The development of a comprehensive social care and other services for families and children depend on the common understanding of family needs in the context of their activities in the labor market.

6. COUNTRY-SPECIFIC CHALLENGES TO FAMILY FORMATION

In the context of family deinstitutionalization and destabilization, the coexistence of extremely different forms of family in Latvian society should be emphasized. For example, in rural areas of Latvia, there are often families where parents have gone abroad to make money, leaving their children with grandparents or other relatives (presence of extended families). Occasionally, municipalities and schools are not only bearing the function of educators, but are the important social agents in childcare and upbringing in the families experiencing difficulties in fulfilling family functions. With the high proportion of divorced families and so-called post-nuclear families in Latvia, the boundaries between traditional family members and one or the other family are not strictly defined and supported. The unmarried couples' law has been initiated several times (most recent debate in 2019 was abolished) and did not get support in government due to the elaborated formulation in the Constitution arguing that the state primary supports the family of a mother and a father being married (Constitutional Assembly, Article 110, Amendments of 2005, entry into force 7 November 1922), religious arguments and tradition. The further debate about cohabiting partnership relations and non-traditional forms are still hardly accepted in the society.

After divorce, children usually remain in the care of their mother, which is not usually a subject of dispute. The results of an intergenerational study show that the understanding of gender roles is gradually changing according to the principles of gender equality; the care of young children is the only area that women and men still consider predominantly a "woman's territory" (Interdepartmental Coordination Center, 2019). At the same time, there are initiatives in Latvia that highlight the role of the father in the family, stimulating discussions about the care provided by both genders during cohabitation and after divorce (Family Support Association "Fathers", 2017).

Another aspect of family formation is marked by the policies of the state institutions to increase birth rate and strengthen the marriage institute. Increasing birth rate is seen as a prerequisite for the future existence of the Latvian nation. In its planning documents, the state supports the formation of families and their stability, supports parents in crisis situations, promotes birth, strengthens marriage and increases the value of marriage in society (Āboliņa et al., 2019). In addition to monetary and material benefits, there is also an ideological orientation in favor of marriage. Traditionally, pre-marriage courses are offered by various religious organizations, but in 2015, the Ministry of Justice of the Republic of Latvia also developed and implemented a pilot project on the economic, social and legal aspects of marriage (Ministry of Justice of the Republic of Latvia, 2016). The pilot project was unsuccessful due to the low level of responsiveness of the population, which also points to the gap between the actual behavior of the population towards family formation and the efforts of public authorities to improve the demographic situation. As the anthropologists' research revealed in 2008, the existence of the traditional ideal family model is often problematic in real life, and a large number of "diverse" families remain outside the family boundaries of state support policies (Putniņa, Zīverte, 2008). On the one hand, it can be seen that the conservative and traditional perceptions of the family and the importance of the reproductive function influence young people's choices about starting a family in Latvia. At the same time, young people face the challenges of the consumer society, which, first of all, makes them think about economic security. Since in the post-communist countries of Europe, the young are living below the standards determined in the EU policy in respect to all the indicators: the area and standard of utilized flats, the numbers of rooms per person or household operating costs (Backmann & Gieseke, 2018), it is more difficult to meet the demands of the consumer society for certain goods and lifestyles, so family formation is postponed. As a result, partnerships are maintained "on a temporary basis", with a more rational approach than in previous generations. A study on intergenerational differences in Latvia reveals that family formation among respondents is mainly related to positive feelings—it is expected to increase the joy of life and satisfaction with life, the opportunity to achieve other goals in life. In turn, one in five respondents is concerned about the loss of independence (Interdepartmental Coordination Center, 2019).

Relocation of young families with children from the cities to the countryside and, in some cases, the formation of communities, is a relatively new phenomenon in Latvian society (Idū, 2019). Here, the marriage institute and gender roles are being reconstructed, which testifies to the coexistence of diverse family forms in the Latvian society and among young people.

7. CONCLUSION

The demographic situation in Latvia is closely connected with the effect of the human capital, which affects the development of the national economy. In general, the society's ageing and the relatively low birth rate has a negative impact on

Latvia's economic situation and well-being. Low incomes and benefits, as well as unemployment, contribute to emigration, thereby decreasing the number of economically active population and worsening the demographic situation in Latvia. The society's ageing contributes to changes in the structure of the labor market. As the population shrinks, it is essential to boost economic productivity and development. This means effective use of resources by producing high value-added goods and services for foreign markets.

Education quality and availability for Latvia's inhabitants and foreigners are significant challenges for the development of human capital and population growth in Latvia. From a long-term prospective, changes in the labor market and the ability to prepare the young generation for innovative labor market requirements are challenges to be addressed.

In Latvia, it is still rather difficult to assess social investments in terms of affordability and quality of pre-school education due to the provision of diversified services. Generous parental leave benefits are supporting parents with small children, yet the benefits are rather based on the entire system of benefits. Although parental benefits are raised, the birth rate has not increased. During the economic downturn, the social policy response to reducing unemployment and poverty, and beyond, was initially successful, yet at the same time there was a lack of clear evidence to support the social investment strategy. Job security and retraining after returning from parental/ maternity leave is also not clearly evident. There is a need to continue with supportive measures not as part of the poverty reduction or population growth strategy but as part of reconciliation of family and work life duties, taking the gender pay gap seriously into consideration.

In Latvia, there is a tendency to think about family formation when the young people have reached their career goals. As mentioned previously, the support for families with children is low and there is a need for improvements in the long term.

ACKNOWLEDGEMENTS

The research task performed by the author Anna Broka was partly financed by the project "Values in Action: Promotion of responsible, secure and educated civil society in Latvia through research and model development" (project Nr.VPP-IZM-2018/1-0013). It is implemented within the National Research Program "Latvian heritage and future challenges for the country's sustainability."

REFERENCES

Āboliņa, L., Mežs, I., & Mileiko, I. (2019). Demogrāfiskās politikas izaicinājumi un pasākumi dzimstības veicināšanai [Demographic policy challenges and measures to promote birth rates]. In *Tautas ataudze Latvijā un sabiedrības atjaunošanas izaicinājumi* [Generation of the people in Latvia and the challenges of social renewal. University of Latvia]. Latvijas Universitāte. Scribbr. http://doi.org/10.22364/talsai

Āboliņa, L. (2016). *Ģimene un tās atbalsta politikas attīstība Latvijā (1990–2015)*. Promocijas darbs [Development of the family and its support policy in Latvia (1990–

118 • LĪVA GRIŅEVIČA, DINA BITE, & ANNA BROKA

2015). Doctoral dissertation]. Latvijas Universitāte. Scribbr. https://dspace.lu.lv/dspace/handle/7/31863

Agency for International Programs for Youth/Jaunatnes starptautisko programmu aģentūra. (2019). *Jauniešu labbūtība Baltijas valstīs: pētījuma ziņojums* [Youth welfare in the Baltic States]. SIA "Excolo Latvia". Scribbr. https://youthpitstop.com/app/up-loads/2019/02/Well-being-of-Young-People-in-the-Baltic-States_2018_LATVIA.pdf

Aidukaite, J. (2009). Old welfare state theories and new welfare regimes in Eastern Europe: Challenges and implications. *Communist and Post-Communist Studies, 42* (1), 23–39.

Aidukaite, J. (2019). The welfare systems of the Baltic States following the recent financial crisis of 2008–2010: Expansion or retrenchment? *Journal of Baltic Studies, 50*(1), 39–58, DOI: 10.1080/01629778.2019.1570957

Backmann, K., & Gieseke, J. (2016). *The silent majority in communist and post-communist states. opinion polling in eastern and south-eastern Europe* (p. 238, Edited Collection). Peter Lang Edition.

Bite, D. (2016, May 12–14). Social practices of rural population for renewal of society. In L. E. Bite, & D. Z. Kruzmetra (Eds.), Z. *International conference "New challenges of economic and business development—2016: society, innovations and collaborative economy": Proceedings* (pp. 113–124). University of Latvia.

Broka A., Mihailova A., & Demme-Vimba D. (27–28 April 2017). Meaningful employment of young adults with intellectual disabilities in Latvia. *Proceedings of 18th Annual international scientific conference Economic science for rural development* (pp. 38–47). Jelgava.

Broka, A., Mihailova, & H., Demme-Vimba, D. (2018). Atbalsta sistēmas analīze sociāli mazaizsargāto jauniešu spējināšanā/ spēcināšanā lauku apvidos vidzemes reģionā [Support system analysis strengthening socially vulnerable young people in rural areas in Vidzeme region]. In Rajevska, F. (Ed.), *Sociālās politikas transformācijas līkloči* [The turns of social policy transformation] (pp. 141–178). Zelta Rudens Printing.

Cabinet of Ministers. (2013). *Cabinet regulation No. 404, Requirements for providers of child supervision services and procedures for registration of providers of child supervision services.* Scribbr. https://likumi.lv/ta/en/en/id/258873

Cabinet of Ministers No. 1607. (2009). *Ministru kabineta noteikumi Nr. 1607 "Noteikumi par bērna invalīda kopšanas pabalstu."* Scribbr. https://likumi.lv/ta/id/202852

Central Statistical Bureau of Latvia. (2018). *Number of marriages and divorces.* Scribbr. https://www.csb.gov.lv/en/statistics/statistics-by-theme/population/marriages/key-indicator/number-marriages-and-divorces

Central Statistical Bureau of Latvia. (2019). *Average age at first marriage.* Scribbr. https://www.csb.gov.lv/en/statistics/statistics-by-theme/population/marriages/key-indica-tor/average-age-first-marriage

Central Statistical Bureau of Latvia. (2019a). *Average age of women at childbirth.* Scribbr. https://www.csb.gov.lv/en/statistics/statistics-by-theme/population/fertility/key-indicator/average-age-women-childbirth

Central Statistical Bureau of Latvia. (2019b). *Bezdarba līmenis otrajā ceturksnī Latvijā bija 6,4%* [Unemployment rate in the second quarter in Latvia was 6.4%]. Scribbr.

Social and Economic Challenges and Opportunities in Latvia • **119**

https://www.csb.gov.lv/lv/statistika/statistikas-temas/socialie-procesi/nodarbina-tiba/meklet-tema/2589-bezdarbs-2019-gada-2-ceturksni

Central Statistical Bureau of Latvia. (2019c). *Dzīvi dzimušie laulībā un ārpus laulības pēc mātes vecuma* [Live births in marriage and outside marriage by maternal age]. Scribbr. https://data1.csb.gov.lv/pxweb/lv/iedz/iedz__dzimst/IDG060.px

Central Statistical Bureau of Latvia. (2019d). *Fertility rates.* https://www.csb.gov.lv/en/statistics/statistics-by- Scribbr. theme/population/fertility/key-indicator/fertility-rates

Central Statistical Bureau of Latvia. (2019e). Iedzīvotāju skaits republikas pilsētās. novadu pilsētās un novados [Population in the cities of the republic.county cities and counties]. Scribbr. https://www.csb.gov.lv/lv/statistika/statistikas-temas/iedzivotaji/iedzivotaju-skaits/galvenie-raditaji/iedzivotaju-skaits-republikas-pilsetas

Central Statistical Bureau of Latvia. (2019f). *Immigration, emigration and net migration.* Scribbr. https://www.csb.gov.lv/en/statistics/statistics-by-theme/population/migra-tion/key-indicator/immigration-emmigration-and-net-migration

Central Statistical Bureau of Latvia. (2019g. October 9). *Jaunieši Latvijā* [Youth in Lat-via]. Scribbr. https://www.csb.gov.lv/lv/statistika/statistikas-temas/iedzivotaji/iedzivotaju-raditaji/meklet-tema/394-jauniesi-latvija-2019

Central Statistical Bureau of Latvia. (2019h. October 9). *10 gadu laikā jauniešu skaits Latvijā sarucis gandrīz divas reizes* [Number of young people in 10 years has shrunk almost twice in Latvia]. Scribbr. https://www.csb.gov.lv/lv/statistika/statisti-kas-temas/iedzivotaji/meklet-tema/2793-jauniesi-latvija

Central Statistical Bureau of Latvia. (2019i). *Last year 53% of the first-born children were born outside marriage.* Scribbr. https://www.csb.gov.lv/en/statistics/statistics-by-theme/population/number-and-change/search-in-theme/1643-born-children-out-side-marriage-2013

Central Statistical Bureau of Latvia. (2020). *Employment Rate.* Scribbr. https://www.csb.gov.lv/en/gender-equality-indicators/Employment-and-Earnings

Constitutional Assembly. (1922.). *The constitution of The Republic of Latvia.* Latvijas Vēstnesis 43. 01.07.1993.

Constitutional Court decision No 2019/99.8. (2019). *On the Compliance with Articles 91 and 109 of the Satversme of the Republic of Latvia on the Compliance of Section 4, Paragraph one and Section 20, Paragraph one, Clause 2 of the State Social Benefits Law. Constitutional Court. Type: judgment.* Accepted: 16.05.2019. Scribbr. https://www.vestnesis.lv/op/2019/99.8

Constitutional Court decision No 209. (2005). *On the Compliance of Section 4, Paragraph five, Clause 2 of the State Social Benefits Law "and have lived in the Republic of Latvia for a total of not less than 60 months, of which the last 12 months have been continuous" with Article 110 of the Satversme of the Republic of Latvia. Publisher: Constitutional Court. Type: judgment. Adopted: 22.12.2005.* Scribbr. https://www.vestnesis.lv/ta/id/124748-par-valsts-socialo-pabalstu-likuma-4-panta-piektas-dalas-2-punkta-vardu-un-latvijas-republika-nodzivojis-kopuma-ne-mazak-ka-60-...

Constitutional Court decision No 98. (2012). *On the Compliance of Section 20, Paragraph one, Clause 1 of the State Social Benefits Law with Articles 91 and 109 of the Sat-versme of the Republic of Latvia. Publisher: Constitutional Court. Type: judgment. Accepted: 21.06.2012.* Scribbr. https://www.vestnesis.lv/ta/id/249490-par-valsts-

120 • LĪVA GRIŅEVIČA, DINA BITE, & ANNA BROKA

socialo-pabalstu-likuma-20-panta-pirmas-dalas-1-punkta-atbilstibu-latvijas-republikas-satversmes-91-un-109-pantam

Council of Europe. (2020). *MISSCEO Comperative tables*. Scribbr. https://www.coe.int/en/web/european-social-charter/missceo-comparative-tables

Cross-Sectoral Coordination Centre (CCSC). (2012.). *Constitutional Court decisions on Law on State Social Allowances*.

Eglīte P., Markusa I. M., Pavliņa I., Gņedovska I., Ivbulis B., & Brants M. (2002). Apcerējums par Latvijas iedzīvotājiem, Nr.9, Ģimeņu veidošanās un valsts atbalsts 'fimenēm atjaunotajā Latvijas Republikā [Reflection on the Population of Latvia, No.9, Family formation and state support for families in the restored Republic of Latvia] (p. 116). BO SIA LZA Ekonomikas institūts.

Esping-Andersen, G. (1990). *The three worlds of welfare capitalism*. Polity Press.

Esping-Andersen, G. (2002). A child-cantered social investment strategy. In G. Esping-Andersen, D. Gallie, A. Hemerijck, & J. Myles, (Eds.), *Why we need a new welfare state*. Oxford University Press.

Eurofound. (2019.). *Living and working in Latvia*. Scribbr. https://www.eurofound.europa.eu/country/latvia#working-life

Eurofound. (2018). *Living and working in Latvia*. Scribbr. Accessed 20.10.2019 from: https://www.eurofound.europa.eu/country/latvia

European Institute for Gender Equality (EIGE). (2014). *Gender equality and economic independence: part-time work and self-employment*. Review of the Implementation of the Beijing Platform for Action in the EU Member States. European Institute for Gender Equality. Scribbr. https://eige.europa.eu/publications/gender-equality-and-economic-independence-part-time-work-and-self-employment-report

European Union. (2018). *Living conditions in Europe, 2018 edition. Statistical Books, Eurostat*. Publications Office of the European Union. Scribbr. https://ec.europa.eu/eurostat/documents/3217494/9079352/KS-DZ-18-001-EN-N.pdf/884f6fec-2450-430a-b68d-f12c3012f4d0

Eurostat. (2019). *Youth employment by age and educational attainment level (aged 20–29)*. Scribbr. https://ec.europa.eu/eurostat/en/web/products-datasets/-/YTH_EMPL_010

Eurostat. (2019a). *At risk of poverty rate (cut-off point: 60% of median equalized income after social transfers)*. Scribbr. https://ec.europa.eu/eurostat/statistics-explained/index.php?title=Income_poverty_statistics&oldid=440992

Eurostat (2019b). *Youth employment by sex, age and educational attainment level (all ISCED 2011 levels)*. Scribbr. https://data.europa.eu/euodp/data/dataset/O7XkB-8W0TcCuQMC3uxbiA

Eurostat (2019c). *NEET rates*. Scribbr. https://ec.europa.eu/eurostat/statistics-explained/index.php/Statistics_on_young_people_neither_in_employment_nor_in_education_or_training

Eurostat. (2020). *Children in formal childcare or education by age group and duration—% over the population of each age group*. Scribbr. http://appsso.eurostat.ec.europa.eu/nui/show.do?dataset=ilc_caindformal

Eurostat. (2020a). *Pupils and students enrolled by education level, sex and age*. Scribbr. https://ec.europa.eu/eurostat/web/products-datasets/product?code=educ_uoe_enra02

Social and Economic Challenges and Opportunities in Latvia • **121**

Eurostat Database. (2020). *Pupils and students enrolled by education level, sex and age.* Scribbr. https://ec.europa.eu/eurostat/web/products-datasets/product?code=educ_uoe_enra02

Eurydice. (2019). *National education systems. Estonia, Latvia, Lithuania, Denmark, Sweden, Finland and Norway.* Scribbr. https://eacea.ec.europa.eu/national-policies/eurydice/national-description_en

Family Support Association "Fathers." (2017). *Dad to 13%.* Scribbr. http://tevi.lv/lv/tetis-uz-13-procentiem/

Gūtmane. S. (2020). *Study of young people in Latvia* (pp. 27). Latvian Cristian Academy.

Gūtmane. S., & Griņeviča. L. (2020). *Young people situation from employment perspective: International study.* Scribbr. http://kra.lv/wp-content/uploads/2020/10/ZR6-2020-13_Gutmane3Grinevica_145-175.pdf

Hiļķevičs. S., & Štefenberga D. (2013). Problems of Latvia's regional economic development and innovative entrepreneurship. *Regional Review, Research Papers, 9,* 16–24.

Idū. K. (13.11.2019.). *Izkāpt no burbuļa? Jaunu ideju pārnese laukos* [Get out of the bubble? Transfer of new ideas to the countryside]. Scribbr. https://ir.lv/2019/11/13/izkapt-no-burbula-jaunu-ideju-parnese-laukos/

Interdepartmental Coordination Center, Institute of Philosophy and Sociology, University of Latvia. (2019). *Latvijas ģimenes paaudzēs 2018: analītisks ziņojums* [Latvian Families in generations 2018: Analytical Report (2019)]. DOI: 10.5281/zenodo.2587219

Labour Law. (2001). *Latvian Journal No. 105, July 6, 2001; Reporter of the Saeima and the Cabinet of Ministers of the Republic of Latvia No. 15, 09.08.2001.* Scribbr. https://likumi.lv/ta/id/26019

Law on State Social Allowances. (2002). *Latvian Journal No. 168, 19.11.2002; Reporter of the Saeima and the Cabinet of Ministers of the Republic of Latvia No. 23, 12.12.2002.* Scribbr. https://likumi.lv/ta/id/68483

Lulle, A., Janta, H., & Emilsson, H. (2019). Introduction to the special issue: European youth migration: human capital outcomes, skills and competences. *Journal of Ethnic and Migration Studies. 47*(8).1725–1739.

Mihailova, H., & Broka, A. (2020). *The social investment in childhood: Is inclusive early childcare and education (ECE) valued in Latvia?* Paper prepared within the National Research Program research project "Values in Action: promotion of responsible, secure and educated civil society in Latvia through research and model development" (No. *VPP-IZM-2018/1-0013) and* presented on 15th International Scientific Conference "Social Sciences for Regional Development", Daugavpils University

Ministry of Education and Science of the Republic of Latvia/ Izglītības un zinātnes ministrija. (2013). *Jauniešu iespēju, attieksmju un vērtību pētījums* [Study on youth opportunities, attitudes and values]. IZM. SIA "Excolo Latvia". Scribbr. https://www.izm.gov.lv/images/statistika/petijumi/23.pdf

Ministry of Justice of the Republic of Latvia/ LR Tieslietu Ministrija. (2016, October 26). *Pirmslaulību mācību programma* [Premartial counselling curriculum]. Scribbr. https://www.tm.gov.lv/lv/cits/pirmslaulibu-macibu-programma

Muranyi. I. (Ed.) (2015). *Eternal return? The specter of radicalism among young people in Europe and Hungary* (p. 224). L'Harmattan.

National Development Plan of Latvia for 2014–2020. (2012). *Approved by a Decision of the Saeima on 20 December 2012. Cross-Sectoral Coordination Centre (CCSC).*

122 • LĪVA GRIŅEVIČA, DINA BITE, & ANNA BROKA

Scribbr. https://www.pkc.gov.lv/images/NAP2020%20dokumenti/NDP2020_English_Final.pdf

OECD. (2018). Regions and cities at a Glance 2018 – Latvia. Scribbr. https://www.oecd.org/cfe/LATVIA-Regions-and-Cities-2018.pdf

OECD. (2019). *Economic surveys, Latvia. Overview.* Scribbr. https://www.oecd.org/economy/surveys/Latvia-2019-OECD-economic-survey-overview.pdf

Priedola, I. (2018). *Latvijas iedzīvotāju noskaņojums un vērtības* [Mood and values of the Latvian population]. KANTAR TNS. Scribbr. https://www.kantar.lv/wp-content/uploads/2018/05/Kantar-TNS_Iedzivotaju-Vertibas-Noskanojums_Prezentacija-MK_08.05.2018.pdf

Putniņa, A., & Zīverte, L. (2008). *"Neredzamās" viena dzimuma partneru ģimenes Latvijā* ["Invisible" single-dimensional partner families in Latvia]. Scribbr. http://providus.lv/article_files/1634/original/neredzamas_viena_dzimuma_gimenes.pdf?1332318075

Rajevska, F., & Rajevska, O. (2020). Social policy reforms in Latvia. Shift towards individual responsibility of welfare. In S. Blum, J. Kuhlmann, & K. Schubert (Eds.), *Routledge handbook of European welfare systems* (2nd ed., Ch. 20, pp. 348–366). Routledge..

State Social Insurance Agency of the Republic of Latvia (2020). *Official statistics..* Scribbr. https://www.vsaa.gov.lv/budzets-un-statistika/statistika/

Supreme Court Decisions on Law on State Social Allowance. (2017). *Decision No. SKA-811/2017* (A420215715)

Supreme Court Decisions on Law on State Social Allowance (2019). *No SKA-77/2019* (A430338514)

Supreme Court Decisions on Law on State Social Allowance. (2019). *Decision No SKA-77/2019* (A420228514)

Szafraniec, K., Domalewski, J., Wasielewski, K., Szymborski, P., & Wernerowicz, M. (2018). *The me-generation in a post-collectivist space: Dilemmas in a time of transition.* eter Lang Gmbh.

Toots, A., & Bachmann, J. (2010). Contemporary welfare regimes in Baltic states: Adapting post-communist conditions to post-modern challenges. *Studies of Transition States and Societies, 2*(2), 31–44.

Toots, A., & Lauri, T. (2017). Varieties of social investment policies on two sides of the Baltic Sea: Explaining routes to endurance. *Social Policy& Administration, 51*(4), 550–576.

Tosun, J., Unt, M., & Wadensjö, E. (2017). Youth-oriented active labour market policies: Explaining policy effort in the Nordic and the Baltic states. *Social Policy & Administration, 51*(4), 598–616.

Youth Law. (2008). *Latvian Journal No. 82, 28.05.2008; Reporter of the Saeima and the Cabinet of Ministers of the Republic of Latvia No.13, 10.07.2008.* Scribbr. https://likumi.lv/ta/id/175920

CHAPTER 8

CHANGES IN FAMILY FORMATION

The Case of Lithuania

Edita Štuopytė

Kaunas University of Technology (Lithuania)

1. NATIONAL CONTEXT

Since 1989, Eastern and Central European countries underwent a "triple" transition: from communist dictatorship to pluralist democracy, from being centrally administered to market economy, and from Soviet imperialist hegemony to fully independent statehood (Bideleux & Jeffries, 1998; Norkus, 2008; Tonkūnaitė-Theimann, 2013). Lithuania restored its independence and statehood in 1990 after 50 years of Soviet occupation. Over the last three decades, the demographic characteristics of the Lithuanian family have changed dramatically, which resulted in the weakening traits of the traditional family and the domination of the modern family features such as: decline in marriages, marriages being postponed, cohabitation, predomination of families with few children, voluntary childlessness, etc. (Vyšniauskienė & Brazienė, 2017). As the result of the changes in economic, social and political structures in the country, which affect all spheres of public life,

Family Formation Among Youth in Europe: Coping With Socio-Economic Disadvantages,
pages 123–138.
Copyright © 2022 by Information Age Publishing
www.infoagepub.com
All rights of reproduction in any form reserved.

including the family, the ongoing changes in the families are inevitably closely related to the overall changes in the country (Vyšniauskienė & Brazienė, 2017).

In Lithuania, the changes in the family first started to manifest as the decrease in the number of marriages. After Lithuania regained its independence in 1990, the total number of marriages (number of marriages per 1000 population) was 9.8, but a decade later, in 2000, this rate was only 4.8. During the next two decades, the number of marriages has been changing and the accumulated total number of marriages has increased. In 2018, 19,700 marriages were registered, i.e., 1,500 less than in 2017 and the total number of marriages decreased from 7.5 in 2017 to 7 in 2018. Even though the number of marriages decreased by 4% during the decade, the total number of marriages increased from 6.5 in 2009 to 7 in 2018 (Official site of statistics, 2020).

Another change is that marriages are postponed and are "aging". The research by Stankūnienė et al. (2003) shows that the spread of a new marital relationship—cohabitation—starts in Lithuania with the generation born between 1970–1975. This generation reached the marital age in the early 1990s, at the time when socio-economic transformation of the country was beginning to affect the family. This corelates with the study by Vyšniauskienė and Brazienė (2017), mentioned above—the overall changes in the country have a direct impact on the changes in family formation.

The factors influencing family change in Lithuania vary in origin, duration, potency and, according to Stankūnienė et al. (2003), Vaitiekūnas and Raudeliūnienė (2006), Kanopienė (2012), and Česnuitytė (2015), some factors are specific and specific only to the countries transitioning from a centralized management system to the market economy. The effects of old and new conditions in demographic, matrimonial and procreative behavior overlap.

Some of the factors are long-lasting, inherited from the past decades, and they continue to manifest through mentality, attitudes and effects of the society during the period of fundamental change. These are specific factors typical to postcommunist countries that are transitioning to market economy and are governed by liberal principles of democratic society. First of all, it is the feeling of social deprivation, when the loss of employment or the guaranteed minimum wage, the loss of the centrally regulated housing system, etc., become quite decisive for the major part of society (Stankūnienė et al., 2003).

Other factors have started to emerge in recent decades. These factors force the more inactive members of the society to adapt to the new conditions (work, housing, market relations) and the more active ones to reveal the muted opportunities for self-realization that transcend the family (e.g., career orientation, meeting cultural, recreational needs, etc.) (Stankūnienė et al., 2003).

The third group of factors are short-term and contribute above all to the fluctuations in demographic trends and to the impetus for long-term family change. According to Stankūnienė et al. (2003) and Galdauskaitė (2016), these factors were the result of economic losses at the beginning of the transformation and the consequences of the declining family standard of living during the deep economic crisis of the early 1990s. Becker and Barro (1987), in their research of economic theory of the rational behavior, stated that the consequence of economic difficulties is the decline in the birth rate. As Lithuania underwent significant economic and political changes during 1990–2000, an intensive and fundamental transformation of society began, which affected the marital and procreative behavior of the population, as well as the decline in the birth rate. After the year of 2000, new factors affecting the family institute began to emerge. Rising unemployment in the country in 2004 and the accession to the international labor market after joining the European Union have created huge flows of work-related, short-term and long-term emigration, mainly involving young people. Young people seeking livelihoods outside the country are less likely to start families and give birth to children (Stankūnienė et al., 2003).

According to Stankūnienė et al. (2003) and Galdauskaitė (2016), two groups of Lithuanian family transformation factors can be distinguished. The first group includes specific factors: economic and social transformations (transition to market conditions: instability/crises in economic development, the declining standard of living in the first phase of transformations and during crises, income differentiation, the spread of poverty, unemployment, mass legal/illegal and short/long-term emigration) and social losses (deprivations of post-communist society, the loss of certain social guarantees: employment, education, minimum income, housing, etc.) (Galdauskaitė, 2016). The second group of factors are the fundamental ones: individualization, emancipation, individual freedom, technical advances in medicine (e.g., modern contraception). According to Galdauskaitė (2016), the increase in income and improved social care conditions enabled people to become freer, less dependent on family members and their economic resources. The expansion of education system which provided broader educational opportunities, self-learning and better prospects for skills development, stimulated women's emancipation. Women started to pay attention to self-education, emancipation prompted more intense participation in the labor market (Galdauskaitė, 2016). According to D. Van de Kaa (2010), as cited in Galdauskaitė (2016), the acknowledgement and acceptance of modern contraception became the main means of individual birth control. According to Galdauskaitė (2016), due to this contraception, there has been a decrease in shotgun marriages and, overall, marriage was postponed for later life stages. The new contraception means provided more freedom to individuals, especially those who got married at a young age or wanted to avoid pregnancy as a result of an extramarital affair (Galdauskaitė, 2016). All these factors discussed above have an impact on family as an institution.

According to research by Vaitekūnas and Raudeliūnienė (2006), Česnuitytė, (2015), Galdauskaitė (2016), and Maslauskaitė and Baublytė (2018), the national revival and the consolidation of the statehood of the country promoted the preservation of ethno-cultural identity and traditions, the liberalization of the country's environment, whereas the opportunities to join the human community of the

126 • EDITA ŠTUOPYTĖ

world have become a powerful stimulus in the family life to adopt the lifestyle, norms, attitudes, values of other countries, often without regard to their potentially destructive effects. These family changes affect the youth and their standpoint and attitude towards the family.

2. DEMOGRAPHIC TRENDS
RELEVANT TO FAMILY FORMATION

Young people, as an age category, are enshrined in the Republic of Lithuania Framework Law on Youth Policy, which defines a young person as a person between the ages of 14 and 29 (Seimas of the Republic of Lithuania, 2018).

The analysis of the latest demographic trends in Lithuania shows that the number of young people is constantly decreasing. According to Eurostat data (European Union statistics on income and living conditions (EU-SILC), 2016), in 2004, Lithuania was one of the demographically youngest countries, but over the period of more than ten years, Lithuania moved closer to the demographically oldest countries in the European Union. Analyzing the data provided by the Department of Statistics of Lithuania on the number of young people aged from 15 to 29, we can conclude that the general tendency is that the number of young people is decreasing proportionally in all age groups, but mostly in the age group of 15–19. In the last decade, since 2008, the number of young people in the 15–19 age group decreased from 241,968 to 153,051, in the 20–24 age group from 237,438 to 182,556 and in the 25–29 age group from 206,221 to 193,381 (Lithuanian Department of Statistics, 2019). Looking deeper into the life of young families in Lithuania, it is purposeful to discuss the concept of household in details.

A household refers to cohabiting persons who lead a common household. The concepts of family and household are different, though sometimes interchangeable. A family is a group of two or more people who are related by marriage, kinship or adoption and who live together. Household information provides a more complete picture of Lithuanian families. The results of the 2011 Population and Housing Census of the Republic of Lithuania showed that the number of households in Lithuania was 1 million 267 thousand (to compare:1 million 357 thousand in 2001). 3 million 19 thousand people (99.2% of all residents) lived in households, (to compare: 3 million 460 thousand people in 2001, or 99.3% of residents). There were 870,400 (68.7%) households in urban areas, 397,300 (31.3%) in rural areas. A total of 31.7% households consisted of one person, 62% of two, three or four. Households of five or more persons made up 6.3% of all households (Lithuanian Department of Statistics, 2019).

Population by marital status in the household. Marital status of households in 2011 was as follows: spouses made up 38.9% (1 million 176 thousand), children 18.4% (554.9 thousand), persons living alone 13.3% (401.4 thousand), cohabitants 5% (150.5 thousand), single (unmarried) parents with children 3.6% (107.7 thousand); single mothers and single fathers made up 84.2% (90.7 thousand) and

Changes in Family Formation • **127**

15.8% (17 thousand), respectively, of all single parents with children of all households (Lithuanian Department of Statistics, 2019).

Population by marital status. At the time of the census, persons aged 15 and over were asked what their marital status was: whether they were married, divorced, widowed or never married. Over the last decade (since 2001), the proportion of people who have never been married has increased: men from 28.3% in 2001 to 32.2% in 2011, the corresponding figure for women was from 21.2% to 23.5% (Table 8.1). The proportion of married men and women decreased. In 2011, married men accounted for 54.9% of all men and married women accounted for 45.9% of all women (respectively 60.7% and 51.6% in 2001). The share of divorced persons (0.5% men, 1.2% women) and widows (1.5% men, 2.2% women) has increased over the decade. In 2011, the number of divorced women was 1.6 times higher, and that of widowed women 6 times higher than that of men (Lithuanian Department of Statistics, 2019).

Population by age and marital status. 1 million 293 thousand of population, i.e., every second resident of Lithuania aged 15 and over was married. Married men accounted for 54.9% of all men aged 15 and over, married women for 45.9% of all women aged 15 and over (Table 8.1). The relative share of married men in both urban and rural areas was higher than that of married women. In urban areas, 56.5% of men were married, in rural areas 51.8%, while married women accounted for 45.3% and 47.1%, respectively. According to the 2011 census, the youth (aged 15–29) in Lithuania comprised of 624,718 persons, of whom 103,964 were married, 8,937 divorced, 351 widows, 511,466 never married (Lithuanian Department of Statistics, 2019).

Variety of family forms. Acienė and Čepienė (2013) state that the family institute in Lithuania balances between the traditional marriage-based family model and partnership as a new form of cohabitation. The National Family Policy Concept (2008), adopted in Lithuania, states that the family is a group based on registered marriage between a man and a woman and their biological or adopted children (State Concept of Family Policy, 2008). The Concept embodies only the concept of a marriage-based family. This has led to a great deal of public debate, since some laws currently in force, directly or indirectly, also include the concept of family, and it is inherent in the legal regulation of family and its relationships that family is understood in broader sense than just a marriage-based family, i.e., legislation introduces a broader concept of family composition, different from the one embodied in the Concept (State Concept of Family Policy, 2008). The State Concept of Family Policy (2008) does not include unregistered marriages, single mothers with children, divorced persons with children and so on. The document states that persons related by kinship, mutual assistance or joint economic activity are the groups of society that the state should protect, such as motherhood, fatherhood, childhood, but not as family (State Concept of Family Policy, 2008). However, statistical and sociological research data (Lithuanian Department of

128 • EDITA ŠTUOPYTĖ

Statistics, 2019) show that these groups of society have become an integral part of everyday life and social norm.

In Lithuania, only a partnership between a man and a woman is legalized by law, other partnerships are not officially recognized. Partnership as a form of relationship is preferable to the younger generation, because the approach to the traditional family and its values has changed in this social group and it is not related to the priorities of family formation (State Concept of Family Policy, 2008). It is related to professional career aspirations, self-establishment in the labor market, independence and material stability.

The studies by Maslauskaitė (2009, 2010), Maslauskaitė and Baublytė (2012), Jasilionienė et al. (2013), Česnuitytė (2015), Vyšniauskienė and Brazienė (2017), and Maslauskaitė and Dirsytė (2020) show an increase in tolerance towards alternative forms of family in Lithuania: cohabitation, childbirth while unmarried, increase in the number of the divorced and incomplete families. Thus, research uncovers the discrepancies between the collective image of the family and the new structure of the family institute that emerged over the last two decades. Growing cohabitation (Maslauskaitė, 2009, 2010, 2012; Maslauskaitė & Dirsytė, 2020) links partners on other grounds: common accommodation, emotional and ongoing sexual relationship without legal marriage. The transition from cohabitation to marriage between younger partners takes longer; about one-third of cohabiting couples for whom cohabitation is their first partnership raise children. This shows that cohabitation in Lithuania is not only showing signs of a trial marriage, but also of an alternative to marriage. In parallel with this type of cohabitation, another type of cohabitation is also on the rise, after a previous marriage or death of a spouse: about 30% of all cohabiting partners have been married or widowed before (Maslauskaitė, 2012; Maslauskaitė & Dirsytė, 2020)

Marriage and divorce. The number of marriages and divorces in Lithuania during the last five years is presented in Table 8.1. After the decade of decline (1991–2001) the number of marriages began to increase. In 2006, 21.2 thousand couples married (1.3 thousand more than in 2005), and in 2014, this number was 22.1 thousand. After five years, this figure dropped to 19.7 thousand couples. Nowadays, an increasing number of older people decide to marry in Lithuania. For example, in 1989, the average age of first-time married women was 22.5 and that of men 24. In 2006, it was 26 for women and 27 for men. The average age of married women was 28 and of men 30 and over, after more than a decade (2018). In 2018, the highest number of divorces was among people aged 35–39 (Lithuanian Department of Statistics, 2019).

The department of statistics estimates that in 2017 the average duration of former marriage was 13 years. Almost one fifth (18%) of married people divorced after being married for nearly 10 years, 11.7% in the second decade of married life, and almost 5% have been married for more than 25 years. On average, about 10,000 children are left without a parent (usually without a father) a year after the divorce. More and more couples are living together without registering their

Changes in Family Formation • **129**

TABLE 8.1. Marriage and Divorce in Lithuania 2014–2018 (Lithuanian Department of Statistics, www.stat.gov.lt)

Year	Total number	Urban	Rural
Number of Marriages in Lithuania in the Last 5 Years			
2018	19,734	13,530	6,204
2017	21,186	14,684	6,502
2016	21,347	14,914	6,433
2015	21,987	15,219	6,768
2014	22,142	15,250	6,892
Gross Divorce Rate for 1000 Inhabitants in Lithuania			
2018	3.1	3.1	3.0
2017	3.0	3.1	2.8
2016	3.1	3.1	3.0
2015	3.2	3.3	3.1
2014	3.3	3.5	3.1

marriage. According to the data of the Lithuanian Department of Statistics (2007), almost half (44%) of respondents aged 18–24 agree to live unmarried.

According to the studies by Jasilionienė et al. (2013), the higher risk of divorce is concentrated in lower socio-economic groups in Lithuania and this especially applies to the male subpopulation. Lower education and economic inactivity, due to multiple reasons (unemployment, disability, etc.), the expected number of children per woman related to the higher risk of divorce within the male subpopulation. Among the women, only low education impacts the risk of divorce, while the economic inactivity does not affect the divorce rate. According to Jasilionienė et al. (2013), in Lithuania, as in many Western industrial societies, the relationship between divorce and social class has reversed, where the decrease of social and legal barriers to divorce led to an increase of divorces among the poor and disadvantaged structures of society who are exposed to a higher stress of structural disadvantages.

Birth rate. In Lithuania, the total birth rate, which indicates the expected number of children per woman, increased from 1.55 (2011) to 1.7 (2015), while the overall birth rate (the number of births per 1000 population) rose from 10.2 (2012) to 10.9 (2016), but births still do not ensure natural population change. Over the last five years, the birth rate in Lithuania has decreased by 1,673 (in 2014, 30,369 babies were born, in 2015–31,475, in 2016–30,623, in 2017–28,696, in 2018–28,149).

As discussed above, the first decade after the restoration of independence in Lithuania was characterized by intense economic and political changes that led to a fundamental transformation of the society, which had an impact on its marital

TABLE 8.2. Birth Rates in Lithuania (2014–2018) (Lithuanian Department of Statistics, www.stat.gov.lt)

Number of Children Born to Young Mothers per 1 Thousand Women of Appropriate Age

Village and City Together	Mother's Age	2014	2015	2016	2017	2018
	15–17	5.9	6.0	6.4	5.4	4.6
	15–19	13.6	14.1	13.3	12.2	11.2
	18–19	24.1	25.1	22.8	21.3	19.9

Births Without Marriage to Parents/Persons

Village and City Together	2014	2015	2016	2017	2018
Total by age	8,809	8,719	8,383	7,701	7,434
Under,16	38	27	32	25	17
16–19	831	802	743	634	561
20–24	2,574	2,436	2,141	1,875	1,639
25–29	2,324	2,458	2,477	2,236	2,151

Birth Rate by Maternal Age

	Mother's Age	2014	2015	2016	2017	2018
Village and city together	15–17	6.1	6.1	6.3	5.3	4.6
	18–19	24.0	25.1	22.7	21.3	19.9
	20–24	53.3	53.2	50.2	46.4	43.8
	25–29	113.4	117.6	115.8	109.9	106.1

and procreative behavior, as well as on the decline in birth rates. According to Ralys (2016) and Maslauskaitė and Dirsytė (2020), the changes in family relationships manifested in rapid, large-scale shifts that also reflected in birth rates. The former birth rate model, which was dominated by children born in marriage and birth of the first child at a younger age, ensuring generational change, was replaced by a new model characterized by an increase in the number of children born to unmarried couples, childbirth postponed for later in life and low birth rate which does not ensure generational change (Ralys, 2016).

3. NORMATIVE FRAMEWORK

Sociological research confirms that family remains the most important value in Lithuania (Maslauskaitė & Dirsytė, 2020; Mitrikas, 2007; Ralys, 2016), although society's tolerance for alternative forms of family life is increasing. Increasing divorce rates, remarriage, post-divorce families, single mother and father families, unmarried couples, abortions, gay and lesbian partnerships all contribute to the diversity of forms of the so-called "postmodern family" that undermine traditional family values. Despite the growing diversity of family and partnership forms, it would be wrong to assume that the main traditional homogeneous family is disappearing. It exists and thrives as an ideal, a symbol, as a powerful myth of collective imagination (Stankūnienė et al., 2017).

A study by Acienė and Čepienė (2013) on the attitudes of young people to family showed that the main purpose of the family is to have children, that is, to extend the family and raise their descendants as honest citizens. For young people, the form of partnership is more acceptable, because the value changes in the attitude towards the traditional family in this social group are not related to family priorities, but to professional career aspirations projected to enter the labor market for the purpose of independence and material stability (Acienė & Čepienė, 2013).

Studies by Acienė and Čepienė (2013) and Maslauskaitė and Dirsytė (2020) showed that the Lithuanian social policy does not meet the expectations of young people in terms of family design. Unemployment affects the material stability of the family and, at the same time, encourages labor migration, while the inflexibility of education system reforms and the problem of access to healthcare and childcare facilities do not create a family-friendly environment. The study by Acienė and Čepienė (2013) assessed family through extended family relationship resources. The accumulated data allows a belief in the vitality of young people's traditional attitudes towards the family and the perspective of intergenerational solidarity. The positive experience of relationships at the genetic family is an important normative guideline in making the most important decisions about the family model, family continuity and in planning one's life aspirations, including close relationships with the parents' family (Acienė & Čepienė, 2013).

4. SOCIO-ECONOMIC CONDITIONS

Lithuania, like other EU countries, faces many challenges in integrating young people into the education system and the labor market (Frejka, & Gietel-Basten, 2016). According to the 2016 data, the overall unemployment rate was 17.7%, i.e., 22.8 thousand young people under the age of 29 in Lithuania do not work or cannot find a job (Lithuanian Department of Statistics, 2019). Compared to 2014, youth unemployment rate decreased by 6 thousand young people in two years. According to the indicator about young unemployed people, young women make up 50.1% of the unemployed, while young men make up 49.9%. While the society is still under-exploiting the potential of young people, another major problem is the withdrawal of young people from the labor market, with huge negative consequences for each young person individually. Looking at the level of education of young unemployed people, 30.1% have higher education, 48.2% have high (secondary) education, 14.6%—basic education, 7%—primary education, and 0.1%—no education at all. Of all the unemployed young people under 29, unskilled people make up 37.4% and unemployed people make up 34.6% (Lithuanian Department of Statistics, 2019). According to Pocius and Okunevičiūtė-Neverauskienė (2015), unsuccessful integration into the labor market and the

132 • EDITA ŠTUOPYTĖ

lack of employment are among the most important negative factors that influence many other problems of the youth, for example, they increase social exclusion and encourage the spread of addictive behavior. The at-risk, non-educated and not-in-training youth group (NEET) in Lithuania includes those aged 15–29, and they can be characterized according to how a young person looks for a job—actively or not. Young people are pushed by family environment factors and low educational attainment to fall into the at-risk, unemployed and inactive population. In Lithuania, the problem is emerging as to how the resolve the situation of these young people—there is no specialized database measuring the number of young inactive people living in the country (Pocius, & Okunevičiūtė-Neverauskienė, 2015). Youth unemployment is closely linked to the concept of social exclusion, and NEET youth can be considered as one of the groups experiencing social exclusion in society. Age and employment status factors, which can lead to the experience of social exclusion, are particularly important for this target group (Pocius & Okunevičiūtė-Neverauskienė, 2015).

Accommodation. The study by Brazienė et al. (2018) revealed that in the context of housing provision, young people in Lithuania face increasing risks and diminishing opportunities to provide themselves housing and to achieve residency autonomy. In this context, social, economic and demographic factors are of paramount importance. The majority of the housing sector in Lithuania consists of private housing, and young people often have to live with their parents or rent from private owners due to the lack of financial resources. Lithuania can be described as a country with a neoliberal housing policy, where social housing is accessible only to the most vulnerable population groups. The current situation leaves young people with no alternative to safe residency unless they have the opportunity to become homeowners (Brazienė et al., 2018). Young people in Lithuania start living independently from their parents at the average age of 26; for comparison sake, this age is 20 in Sweden and 30 in Italy, which makes a difference of about ten years. In addition, when analyzing the share of young people who live with their parents by gender, in the age groups of 20–24 and 25–29, there is a tendency for men of all youth age groups to live relatively longer with their parents (Brazienė et al., 2018). It is noteworthy that nearly a quarter of men in the 25–34 age group and only one fifth of women live with their parents (Brazienė et al., 2018). Parental residence is associated with young people who are not married and do not have a partner. However, as many as one-seventh of young households are sharing their parents' housing with their own children and this indicates that some young households are experiencing housing deprivation and limited self-sufficiency. Both rented and youth-owned housing is associated with a self-contained extended household. It is an essential feature of family creation (as partnership or marriage status) and procreative or child socialization (as having children) behavior (Brazienė et al., 2018).

5. INSTITUTIONAL FRAMEWORK

The family is not only socially constructed at the individual level, the society also creates the family construct that includes knowing who can/should belong to the family, live together, have an intimate relationship, what is decent and indecent for family members, etc. The model of the modern autonomous nuclear family proposed by Parsons (1955a) (as cited in Česnuitytė, 2015) is a typical social construct of the family at the society level. Being a family member is associated with certain rights and duties that conform to formal and informal values and norms, and is, therefore, also referred to as "institutionalized family" or "normative family". The problems in the functioning of the family institute are inseparable from social, economic and political changes in the society. The importance of the family institute in Lithuania is revealed by the fierce discussions led over the last two decades between politicians, professionals, scientists, organizations representing family interests and individual members of society regarding the family concept (Česnuitytė, 2015). One of the last waves of debates referred to the adoption of the new Civil Code (Civil Code of the Republic of Lithuania, 2000), which legalized unregistered marriage (partnership), but the State Concept of Family Policy (2008) discussed in the second part of this article aroused the same level of discussions, if not higher. The legal notion of the family becomes relevant in this discussion. According to Vaišvila (2012), the Constitution of the Republic of Lithuania regards family as the basis of the state and society, therefore, family can only be considered an interpersonal relation, which in principle guarantees physical continuity of the society, and a legal relationship (public state registration). For this reason, a same-sex relationship cannot be considered family where the continuity of society is concerned and, in principle, it constitutes a dead relationship. Vaišvila (2012) states that partnership should be considered family and should have a separate, independent legal basis for its existence. It should retain family's inherent ability to guarantee the physical continuity (heterogeneity) of society and have formal legal status (registration by law). Such an approach to family institution is followed in Lithuanian legal/normative documents but, according to Česnuitytė (2015), when following only the institutionalized (normative) concept of family, there are difficulties in defining kinship and identifying family boundaries. Thus, looking at the evolution of the structure of the family institute, it is clear that cohabitation marks a fundamental change in the process of family institutionalization. The marital creation of a "normal family" characteristic of the first modernity is no longer central. The diffusion of new family forms and types brings the structure of the Lithuanian family institute closer to that of the second modernity.

Lithuania has been implementing the Youth Guarantee Initiative since 2014 to reduce the number of unemployed and uneducated young people. Within the framework of Youth Guarantee Projects, young people can find many activities to help them adapt to the labor market and give them the opportunity to try out volunteering or start their own businesses. The main problem is that unemployed and uneducated young people tend to have a lack of motivation—they are inactive and avoid involvement in the labor market (Pocius & Okunevičiūtė-Neverauskienė, 2015). Work-family or family-work conflict in young families occurs rather often when there is a mismatch between work and family needs or family and work needs. The study by Tandzegolskienė et al. (2016) revealed that the innate position of a young family in Lithuania is becoming weaker. They talk about acquired positions that depend on actions and desires of an individual. Despite challenges and contradictions, young parents in families seek to reconcile parenting and career or career and parenting needs, listen to the wishes of the child or spouse, discuss the situation with the employer, get help from relatives or seek social support and, in any case, adapt to the current situation, learn from the current situation, update the existing roles and create new ones (Tandzegolskienė et al., 2016).

6. COUNTRY-SPECIFIC CHALLENGES TO FAMILY FORMATION

The dynamism of postmodern society development processes influences the change of attitudes towards family in Lithuania. Maslauskaitė (2010, 2012) and Maslauskaitė and Dirsytė (2020) identify the reasons for changing family attitudes in a very broad discourse on globalization ("unfriendly" environment created by the market economy, women's employment in the labor market, aspects of consumer culture in family communication, devalued marriage institute, birth, divorce and cohabitation issues, etc.) and look for evidence on how to stabilize the transformation of family life through family support policy. The research by Česnuitytė (2015) showed that the majority of Lithuanian population firstly consider nuclear family members as their family members, but about one-third of the population associate family with the extended family and one-tenth with the boyfriend/girlfriend/cohabitant/spouse or ex-boyfriend/ex-girlfriend/ex-cohabitant. These and other research results suggest that the concept of family, which is typical of the postmodern society, is getting formed in the consciousness of the country's population. It is worth mentioning that the concept of family is dominated by the maternal lineage. This partly reflects the distribution of male and female roles within the family, which is typical of the postmodern family.

Dissertation research entitled Lithuanian Family: Concepts and Practices (Česnuitytė, 2015) revealed that marriage is not a sufficient criterion for identifying family relationships. For example, relatives in marriage—spouse's parents, even when involved in various family events/celebrations, are likely to be named non-family members. The study of Česnuitytė (2015) shows that in real life family can be identified by various criteria: self-help/support, emotional closeness, attachment, joint activities, common interests, living under one roof, short distance between places of residence, formal affiliation or the informal community and other criteria through which investments in interpersonal relationship are made. These criteria may result in distant relatives or even persons not in formal family relationship becoming family members. This study (Česnuitytė, 2015) highlighted that non-marital pregnancy is an incentive for the Lithuanian population to start a family. In the case of non-marital pregnancy, the study finds that the family is formed earlier, especially in the form of unregistered marriage. However, it is statistically significant that the duration of cohabitation in the family based on pregnancy is shorter than when the pregnancy was not the cause of marriage (here we can state only unregistered marriages) (Česnuitytė, 2015). These named facts imply that family is increasingly associated with real life practices in public policy rather than structure and function.

7. CONCLUSION

As Lithuania underwent significant economic and political changes, an intensive and fundamental transformation of society began, which affected the family institute (marital and procreative behavior of the population, as well as declining birth rates). All EU countries claim to have family policies. The Lithuanian state also speaks about this, about family diversity, but at the same time there is a lack of political will to define the family model which would be morally and materially supported. Because of this, the family today has no real support, therefore, in Lithuania, the number of marriages is decreasing and the number of births is lower than the number of deaths.

The factors influencing family change in Lithuania vary in origin, duration, and severity. Among the specific factors, the economic, social transformations and social losses are very important. Individualization, emancipation, individual freedom, technical advance in medicine (e.g., modern contraception) are some of the fundamental factors. All these factors affect young people and young families. Currently, the dominant features of the modern family are gaining ground in Lithuania: declining marriages, postponing marriages to older age, cohabitation, predominant families with few children, voluntary childlessness, etc.

Recent research has highlighted the increasing public tolerance in Lithuania for alternative forms of family life: unmarried cohabitation, childbirth outside marriage, etc. New structures of the family institute emerged. Going deeper into the evolution of the structure of the family institute, it can be seen that cohabitation marks a fundamental change in the process of institutional individualization of the family. The marital creation of a "normal family", characteristic of the first modernity, is no longer central. The diffusion of new family forms and types approximates the structure of the Lithuanian family institute to that of the postmodern family.

REFERENCES

Acienė. E.. & Čepienė. R. (2013). Jaunimo požiūris į šeimą kaip kartų solidarumo prielaida [The attitude of young people towards the family as a precondition for intergenerational solidarity]. *Socialinis darbas. Patirtis ir metodai, 12*(2). 109–122.

Becker. G. S.. & Barro. R. S. (1987). Altruism and the economic theory of fertility. In K. Davis. M. S. Bernstam. & Ricardo-Campbell (Eds.). *Below-replacement fertil-*

136 • EDITA ŠTUOPYTĖ

ity in industrial societies: Causes, consequences, policies (pp. 69–76). Cambridge University Press.

Bideleux, R., & Jeffries, I. (1998). *A History of Eastern Europe. Crisis and change*. New York/UK, Routlege.

Brazienė, R., Žilys, A., Indriliūnaitė, R., & Mikutavičienė, I. (2018). *Jaunimas ir būstas Lietuvoje: skirtingos galimybės, trajektorijos ir iššūkiai: monografija* [Youth and housing in Lithuania: Different opportunities, trajectories and challenges: A Monograph]. Kaunas: Vytauto Didžiojo universitetas.

Česnuitytė, V. (2015). *Lietuvos šeima: sampratos ir praktikos: daktaro disertacija* [Lithuanian family: Concepts and practices: Doctoral theses]. Mykolo Romerio universitetas. Vilnius: Mykolo Romerio universitetas.

Frejka, T., & Gietel-Basten, S. (2016). Fertility and Family Policies in Central and Eastern Europe after 1990. *Comparative Population Studies, 41*(1), 3–56.

Galdauskaitė, D. (2016). Posūkis link naujo šeimos ir gimstamumo modelio. [A shift towards a new family and birth rate model]. *Kultūra ir visuomenė. Socialinių tyrimų žurnalas, 7*(1), 53–77. Retrieved December 15, 2019, from: http://dx.doi.org/10.7220/2335-8777.7.1.3

Jasilionienė, A., Jasilionis, D., Stankūnienė, V., & Maslauskaitė, A. (2013). Skyrybos ir sutuoktinių socialiniai ekonominiai ištekliai [Socio-economic resources for divorce and marriage]. *Filosofija. Sociologija, 24*(4), 237–245.

Kanopienė, V. (2012). Intergenerational communication in Lithuanian families. *Socialinis darbas, 11*(2), 245–256.

Lietuvos Respublikos Seimas (Seimas of the Republic of Lithuania). (2018). *Lietuvos Respublikos Jaunimo politikos pagrindų įstatymo Nr.IX-1871 pakeitimo įstatymas* [Law of the Republic of Lithuania Amending the Law on the Framework of Youth Policy No. IX-1871] (2018m. 2018 m. gegužės 31 d. Nr. XIII-1224). Retrieved December 15, 2019, from: https://e-seimas.lrs.lt/portal/legalAct/lt/TAD/96665ec26a1c11e8b7d2b2d2ca774092

Lietuvos statistikos departamentas (Lithuanian Department of Statistics). (2007). *Lietuvos šeima šiandien (2007 05 11)* [Lithuanian family today (2007 05 11)]. Retrieved September 28, 2008, from: http://www.stat.gov.lt/lt/news/view/?id=1110

Lietuvos statistikos departamentas (Lithuanian Department of Statistics). (2019). *Namų ūkiai ir šeimos, jų sudėtis ir dydis (2013)* [Households and families, their composition and size (2013)]. Retrieved December 10, 2019, from: https://osp.stat.gov.lt/gyventoju-ir-bustu-surasymai1

Maslauskaitė, A. (2009). Kohabitacija Lietuvoje: šeimos formavimo etapas ar „nauja šeima"? [Cohabitation in Lithuania: The stage of family formation or a "new family"?]. In V. Stankūnienė, A. & Maslauskaitė (Eds.), *Lietuvos šeima: tarp tradicijos ir naujos realybės* [Lithuanian family: between tradition and new reality] (pp. 37–98). STI.

Maslauskaitė, A. (2010). Lietuvos šeima ir modernybės projektas: prieštaros bei teorizavimo galimybės [Lithuanian Family and the project of Modernity: Contradictions and possibilities of theorizing]. *Filosofija. Sociologija, 21*(4), 310–319.

Maslauskaitė, A. (2012). Kohabitacijos raida Lietuvoje [Development of cohabitation in Lithuania]. *Lietuvos socialinė raida, 1,* 102–120.

Changes in Family Formation • **137**

Maslauskaitė, A., & Baublytė, M. (2012). *Skyrybų visuomenė. Ištuokų raida, veiksniai, pasekmės* [Divorce society. Development of divorce, factors, consequences]. Lietuvos socialinių tyrimų centras.

Maslauskaitė, A., & Baublytė, M. (2018). Vyrų pakartotinos partnerystės: individualūs ir ankstesnės partnerystės veiksniai [Men ´s re-partnerships: individual and factors of the previous partnership]. *Kultūra ir visuomenė. Socialinių tyrimų žurnalas, 9*(2), 13–35. https://doi.org/10.7220/2335-8777.9.2.1

Maslauskaitė, A., & Dirsytė, I. (2020). Šeiminio gyvenimo kelio trajektorijos: sekų analizės rezultatai [Family life path trajectories: Results of sequence analysis]. *Filosofija. Sociologija, 2,* 139–147.

Mitrikas, A. A. (2007). Lietuvos šeima: vertybiniai pokyčiai 1990–2005 metais. [Lithuanian family: Value changes in 1990–2005]. In R. Žiliukaitė (Ed.), *Dabartinės Lietuvos kultūros raidos tendencijos. Vertybiniai tyrimai* [Current tendencies of Lithuanian culture development. Value research] (pp. 70–88). Kultūros, filosofijos ir meno institutas.

Norkus, Z. (2008). *Kokia demokratija, koks kapitalizmas? Pokomunistinė transformacija Lietuvoje lyginamosios istorinės sociologijos požiūriu* [What is democracy, what is capitalism? Post-communist transformation in Lithuania from the point of view of comparative historical sociology]. Vilniaus Universitetas.

Parsons, T. (1955a). The American family: Its relations to personality and social structure. In T. Parsons, & R. F. Bales (Eds.), *Family socialization and interaction process* (pp. 3–33). Free Press.

Pocius, A., & Okunevičiūtė-Neverauskienė, L. (2015). Tikslinių grupių integracijos į darbo rinką galimybių vertinimas. In *Lietuvos socialinė raida* [Social development of Lithuania]. (pp. 38–59). Lietuvos socialinių tyrimų centras.

Ralys, K. (2016). Family relations and values views: Social changes in Lithuania. *Socialinis ugdymas/Social Education, 43*(2), 19–28.

Stankūnienė, V., Baublytė, M., Žibas, K., & Stumbrys, D. (2017). *Lietuvos demografinė kaita: ką atskleidžia gyventojų surašymai: mokslo studija* [Demographic change in Lithuania: What the censuses reveal: A study of science]. Vytauto Didžiojo universitetas.

Stankūnienė, V., Jonkarytė, A., & Mitrikas, A. A. (2003). Šeimos transformacija Lietuvoje: požymiai ir veiksniai [Family transformation in Lithuania: Features and factors]. *Filosofija. Sociologija, 2,* 51–58.

Tandzegolskienė, I., Tamoliūnė, G., & Bortkevičienė, V. (2016). Jaunų šeimų tėvystės ir karjeros projektavimo patirtys Lietuvoje [Parenting and career planning experiences of young families in Lithuania]. *Holistinis mokymas/Holistic Learning, 2,* 87–103.

Tonkūnaitė-Thiemann, A. (2013). *Socialinės nelygybės profiliai rytų ir vidurio Europos valstybėse: daktaro disertacija* [Profiles of social inequality in Eastern and Central Europe States: Doctoral theses]. Vilniaus universitetas. Vilnius: Vilniaus Universitetas.

Vaišvila, A. (2012). Kitos šeimos formos", arba bandymas priderinti šeimos sąvoką prie atskiro asmens subjektyvumo ["Other forms of family," or an attempt to adapt the concept of family to the subjectivity of the individual]. *Socialinių mokslų studijos* [Societal Studies]. *4*(3), 953–972.

138 • EDITA ŠTUOPYTĖ

Vaitekūnas, S., & Raudeliūnienė, I. (2006). Šeima ir jos transformacija XXI amžiaus pradžioje [The family and its transformation at the beginning of the 21st century]. *Tiltai, 31,* 8–35.

Valstybinė šeimos politikos koncepcija (State Concept of Family Policy). (2008). *Valstybės žinios,* 69-2624. Retrieved December 15, 2019, from: https://e-seimas.lrs.lt/portal/legalAct/lt/TAD/TAIS.322152?jfwid=cxhrnxr4y

Van de Kaa, D. J. (2010). Demographic transitions. In Y. Zeng (Ed.), *Encyclopedia of life support systems. Demography 1* (pp. 65–104). Oxford University Press.

Vyšniauskienė, S., & Brazienė, R. (2017). Palankios šeimai politikos vertinimas Lietuvoje. [Evaluation of family-friendly policy in Lithuania]. *Viešoji politika ir administravimas, 3,* 455–467.

CHAPTER 9

YOUNG PEOPLE AND FAMILY FORMATION IN MALTA

Sue Vella and Joanne Cassar

University of Malta

This chapter outlines the situation of young people in Malta in recent years with particular emphasis on their transition to family life. The chapter starts with a description of social life in Malta as traditionally Catholic but having rapidly secularized and diversified in recent decades. This is followed by demographic trends in respect of young people, particularly in terms of their household arrangements, marriage and divorce, fertility and migration, subsequently discussed in terms of the normative framework. The socio-economic conditions experienced by young people are presented in terms of labor market and educational outcomes, as well as housing and income. A description of the prevailing institutional framework is then followed by an analysis of the challenges facing young people in forming a family today.

NATIONAL CONTEXT

The islands in the Maltese archipelago make up a microstate in the Mediterranean with a population of just under half a million inhabitants. Malta has been a republic since 1964, acquiring this status after centuries of foreign rule, most recently by the Knights of St John from the early sixteenth century and becoming

Family Formation Among Youth in Europe: Coping With Socio-Economic Disadvantages,
pages 139–157.
Copyright © 2022 by Information Age Publishing
www.infoagepub.com
All rights of reproduction in any form reserved.

139

a British colony in 1813. Efforts to diversify the Maltese economy and align the country with European values led to Malta's accession to the European Union in 2004. Malta currently enjoys among the highest economic and employment growth rates and the lowest unemployment in the EU. Levels of inward migration have accelerated since EU accession and Malta is one of the most densely populated countries in the world.

Malta's geographical location in the Mediterranean, its colonial history and position as the smallest state in the European Union all influence its politics, economy and social structures. The "small scale syndrome" prevalent in small island states such as Malta (Baldacchino, 2012, p. 17) is characterized by heightened familiarity and a diminished sense of privacy among citizens. Close-knit communities in Malta are embedded within social contexts that give space for 'everyone to know everybody'. Similar to other Mediterranean countries, the family is a major institution in Malta, and community life is characterized by strong family ties, reliance upon the extended family and dense support networks. The paramount importance assigned to the family infiltrates public discourse concerning different aspects of life. For example, the *National Minimum Curriculum* installed in schools at the start of the new millennium described the family as a hallmark of the Maltese identity and stipulated that "one of the important aims of education should be the preparation and sound formation for marriage and family life" (Ministry of Education, 1999, p. 18).

NORMATIVE FRAMEWORK

Maltese civil society, politics and the economy have been changing rapidly during the last decade. Similar to other southern European countries, Malta has undergone social transitions and shifts that have affected family lifestyles (Moreno Mínguez & Crespi, 2017). Close-knit family relationships are however still central, since the "dominant culture invests the family with a greater role as a social institution than in other countries" (Moreno Mínguez & Crespi, 2017, p. 391). This is true despite a marked rise in employment among married and single women, especially those with a high level of education, and a corresponding move away from traditional gender roles where mothers were typically homemakers and caregivers while fathers were breadwinners.

Traditionally, Catholic beliefs permeated many of the institutions in Maltese society, including the family (Cassar, 2009). For centuries, religion defined and established value systems surrounding family formation and functions. Malta's long history of adherence to Roman Catholicism shaped the conceptualization of a national identity (Mitchell, 2003), which partly expressed itself through family life. Catholic morality dictated family norms, embedded in the national psyche. For the Church, family decisions over matters such as birth control, family size, gender roles within the family, sexual expression and marital separation were not considered private matters but were regarded as public manifestations of Catholic morality. Heteronormativity and the discouraging of sexual activity outside the heterosexual marriage underlie the Catholic moral code. Until a few decades ago, divergence from the Catholic lifestyle often resulted in shame, blame, victimization and social exclusion (Cassar & Grima Sultana, 2016).

Social change in Malta has given rise to more cultural diversity that led to a gradual but growing detachment from Church teachings. As Malta moves away from a conservative, religious past, the Church's hegemony in Maltese society is becoming weaker, resulting in a more distinct separation between Church and State (Bettetini, 2010). Weekly church attendance has declined from around 80% in 1967 to just over one third by 2017 (Caruana, 2019), particularly among the young. Despite this decline, however, many still profess to hold Catholic beliefs to heart. A self-completing survey among 7,000 households in preparation for the 2015 Extraordinary Family Synod found that 70% of people in Malta still adhere to Church teachings on life and family issues, although 44.3% noted that they often find this difficult (Pontificium Consilium pro Familia, n.d.)

The importance of religion in Malta has been reflected in its social policy, leading Deguara (2019) to state that social policy has "tended to be rather congruent with Church morality, reflecting the Church's political influence" (p. 2). An example of this relationship lies in the fact that Malta was the last Member State in the EU to legislate divorce, and only did so after a consultative referendum in 2011 found 53% to be in favor of such legislation. In recent years, legislation on marriage equality has granted same-sex partners the right to contract marriage or register their civil union; they may also adopt children (House of Representatives, 2014, 2017a). Bilateral agreements have also been established with countries that legally allow same-sex parenting. These grant the possibility for international adoptions by Maltese couples that also include same-sex couples.

More than at any other time in Maltese history, blended families are being established as divorced or separated spouses remarry or cohabit. The Church's approach to blended families has evolved. In 2017, and following the papal apostolic exhortation *Amoris Letitia,* the Catholic bishops in Malta issued 14 recommendations to guide the clergy in accompanying separated and divorced Catholics. These recommendations exhort the clergy to treat each case on its own merits, underscoring the important role of individual conscience, prohibiting the sacramental exclusion of separated or divorced persons who meet certain conditions, and recognizing that it may be 'humanly impossible' to abstain from sex in their new relationships (Caruana, 2017).

In respect of young people, familial support networks in Malta help to lessen some of the burdens that young people face and also help to buffer their anxiety (Visanich, 2017). As explained further below, youth in Malta are far more likely to live with their parents than their European counterparts and in fact, are more likely to do so in 2018 than in 2011 or 2015; this is not for lack of work, for 60.1% of all young adults who continued to live with their parents in Malta were in full-time employment (Eurostat, 2018b, pp. 101–102). Up until two decades ago, 68.3% of marital couples chose to live in the same village of their parents (Tabone, 1995). While this is far less the case today, the Maltese are still very likely to get together with family and relatives frequently; in 2015, 34.6% met them on a daily basis, while 40.5% met them at least once a week (Eurostat, 2018b, p. 129).

Despite Malta's traditional religiosity, sexual behavior among young people has become quite acceptable and frequent. A national survey by the Ministry of Health in 2012 found that 44% of those aged 16 to 18 had already had one sexual partner, with the number of partners increasing among the 19 to 29 cohort and decreasing among those aged 30 to 40. Four in five in the 16 to 18 age cohort believe that one should 'be in love' before engaging in sexual intercourse, with the numbers dropping to two in three of those aged between 19 and 40.

The aspiration of the majority of Maltese adolescents is to have 'a happy marriage' (Inguanez et al., 2012, p. 32). Similarly, 80.5% of young people aged 10–30 years living in Gozo (a sister island in the Maltese archipelago) wish to have a family of their own (Azzopardi, 2011, p. 134). The majority of Maltese young people recognize different forms of families with 76% stating that single parents and their children constitute a family (Inguanez et al., 2012, p. 36). A smaller percentage (57.5%) regard a cohabiting couple as a family, but 38% do not (Inguanez et al., 2012, p. 36). The majority of Maltese citizens (77%) agree that homosexual persons are granted the same legal rights as heterosexual persons (European Commission, 2015, p. 3). Despite the pervasiveness of heterosexism in various institutions in Malta, heteronormativity is gradually being questioned, challenged and disrupted by the young generation but also reproduced (Cassar, 2015). Traditional notions of the family are being questioned in the post-closet age (Seidmann, 2002), due to more social visibility and acceptance of different types of families. Secrecies around sexual orientation and gender identity however are still prevalent among a number of Maltese citizens who fear being stigmatized (Cassar & Grima Sultana, 2017). Maltese families who have LGBTQI members experience different levels of openness within the family about non-heteronormative lifestyles (Cassar & Grima Sultana, 2018).

DEMOGRAPHIC TRENDS RELEVANT TO FAMILY FORMATION

This section provides an overview of demographic trends relevant to family formation, presented in European context for comparative purposes.

Household Size and Types

In 2018, the average household size in Malta was 2.5 persons, down from 3 in 2008. Although this is still above the EU28 average of 2.3, household size in Malta has decreased to the greatest extent in the EU over the past ten years. Correspondingly, the number of private households has increased by just over 40%, the highest growth rate along with Luxembourg. The types of households that have increased pertain to single persons, couples without children and single parents, while couples with children have decreased. Nevertheless, the proportion of

Young People and Family Formation in Malta • 143

households in Malta comprising couples with children still, at 22%, exceeded the
EU average of 19.7% in 2018 (Eurostat, 2019a).

In 2017, while two thirds of youth aged 16 to 29 lived with their parents in the
EU, this was true of four in five of the same cohort in Malta. As in all EU member states, young men in Malta (84.8%) are considerably more likely than young
women (79.1%) to live with their parents (Eurostat, 2019c). Although now somewhat outdated, Census 2011 data illustrates that levels of cohabitation among
young people in Malta are less than a third of those in the EU, standing at 4.16%
of those aged between 20 and 34, compared to an EU average of 14.42% for the
same cohort (OECD, 2016).

Marriage and Divorce

Marriage rates in Malta are still relatively high. After peaking at 8.8 persons in
every 1000 in 1980, the crude marriage rate (CMR) has remained quite stable in
the past twenty years. In 2017, the CMR was 6.3, the fifth highest after Lithuania,
Romania, Cyprus and Latvia (Eurostat, 2019b). There has been some change in
the way in which people contract marriage. In 1980, only 4% of all marriages involved civil ceremonies while the remaining were religious (Central Office of Statistics, 1982). Since then, the proportion of civil marriages has risen significantly.
If one excludes all marriages between foreign nationals, then the civil marriage
proportion of all marriages (between spouses of whom at least one was Maltese)
had risen to 30% of all marriages by 2016 (NSO, 2018). While this reflects the
ongoing secularization of the Maltese society, value is still clearly placed upon the
traditional religious marriage ceremony in Malta.

The crude divorce rate in Malta, standing at 0.7 per 1000 persons in 2017, is
the lowest in the EU and less than half the EU average of 1.9 (Eurostat, 2019b).
Divorce rates in Malta have remained quite constant since divorce legislation was
promulgated in 2011. Still, this represents an increase over previous years; for
instance, in 2007, separations and divorces obtained abroad amounted to 0.2 per
1000 persons (NSO, 2015). Blended families are becoming more common. Traditionally, remarriage was exceedingly rare; for instance, data for 1973 show that
only in 0.8% of marriages had the bride or groom been married before, and all had
been widowed (Central Office of Statistics, 1976). Even by 2000, only 4.5% of all
brides had been married previously; this proportion had risen to 11.7% by 2014.

Social change is also evident in the rising age at which women and men contract their first marriage. In 1990, the mean age for men was 27.2 and for women
24.6; by the 2011 Census, these had risen to 31.6 and 29.2 respectively (Eurostat,
2019d).

Fertility

The fertility rate of 1.26 in Malta in 2017 was the lowest in Europe and well
below the EU average of 1.59, having declined steadily from 1.99 in 1980. Unlike

the EU, where the decline in the average birth rate has slowed, this does not appear to be the case in Malta (Eurostat, 2019e). In 2017, the mean age of the mother at the birth of first child was 29 in Malta, similar to the EU average (Eurostat, 2019e). The proportion of births occurring to girls aged between 10 and 19 has dropped between 2008 and 2017 in both the EU (from 4.1% to 2.6%) and in Malta (from 6.7% to 3.7%) where they remain marginally higher (Eurostat, 2019e).

The share of live births outside marriage has risen over time, from the lowest share in the EU at 0.7% in 1960 to 25.9% of all births in 2013, though still below the EU average of 41.1%. While 40.2% of all births outside marriage in 2000 occurred to girls below the age of 20, this proportion had markedly decreased to 14.9% by 2013. Just under two thirds of births outside marriage occur to women aged between 20 and 29, while the remaining quarter occur among women aged 30 and over (Eurostat, 2019e).

Migration

Similarly to other countries in Southern Europe, Malta has moved from being a country of emigration (in the early to mid-twentieth century) to being one of immigration in the twenty first century. The ten years from 1965, for instance, saw an annual average of just under 4,000 emigrants a year (or around 1.3% of the population), mainly destined for Australia, the UK and Canada (Central Office of Statistics, 1976). By 2017, levels of inward and outward migration of the Maltese were very low, both at less than 0.5% of the 2017 population (NSO, 2019) although of course, this figure does not reflect the number of the Maltese who have, since accession, taken up work and residence in another EU member state.

In respect of inward migration, historically comparable data are not available. In 1975, the non-Maltese population (largely the families of British servicemen) amounted to 6% of the total population (Central Office of Statistics, 1976), declining to 2.5% by 1995 (NSO, 2002). Malta's accession to the EU in 2004 brought about a steady inflow in the number of EU nationals, as well as third country nationals. The year 2018 saw a level of immigration equivalent to one tenth of the 2017 population, with slightly more third country nationals than EU nationals. Emigration of these groups was far lower, at less than 2% of the total population. This has resulted in an unprecedented share of foreign nationals living in Malta in 2019. Based on data by the Electoral Commission and the public employment service, it has been estimated that there are around 100,000 foreign nationals in Malta, making up more than one fifth of the total population of whom four-fifths are believed to be EU nationals (Diacono, 2019).

SOCIOECONOMIC CONDITIONS

This section provides data on young people in Malta—set within European context—in respect of the labor market, education, housing and poverty. Unless oth-

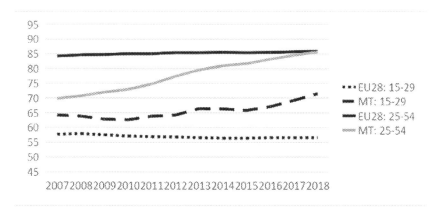

FIGURE 9.1. Activity Rates 2007 to 2018, Malta and EU28 Source: Eurostat (2019f)

erwise specified, all data in this section is derived from the Eurostat database and refers to youth between the ages of 15 and 29.

The Labor Market

By 2018, the activity rate[1] in Malta for those of prime working age had caught up with the EU average. In respect of those aged between 15 and 29, 71.5% were active, having risen from 64.2% in 2007. The youth activity rate is considerably higher than the EU28 average of 56.6% and second only to the Netherlands. Youth activity rates were higher among EU nationals (79.2%) and third country nationals (74.8%) than Maltese youth (70.8%). They were also higher for young men (73.1%) than young women (69.7%).

With respect to youth employment rates, there has been an increase of ten percentage points in Malta from 2007 (57.8%) to 2018 (67.5%), currently above the EU average of 49.8% and second only to the Netherlands. The ten point employment rate disparity between young women and men in 2007 has virtually closed and currently stands at 1.7% in favor of young men. The employment rates are higher for EU youths (75.5%) and third country youth (70.1%) than Maltese youth (66.9%). 13.8% of youth in Malta are employed on a part-time basis, compared to 23.4% in the EU; the rates are higher for EU youth in Malta (19.9%) and for third country youth (15.2% in 2016). Only 10.9% of youth in part-time work are involuntarily so, compared to 27.7% in the EU.

Turning to unemployment, Malta had the third lowest unemployment rate in 2018, standing at 3% for those of prime working age. In respect of youth, the unemployment rate in Malta declined from 9.9% in 2007 to 5.5% in 2018, compared

---

[1] Those in employment plus the unemployed who are available for work.

146 • SUE VELLA & JOANNE CASSAR

to the EU28 rate which has remained at 12 since 2007. As in the EU, the rate is higher among young men (6.6%) than young women (4.4%) in Malta. It is also significantly higher for youth whose educational attainment is at level 2 or below, standing at 19.5% in 2018, and decreasing to 5.6% among those with levels 3 or 4. Unemployment rates for EU youth in Malta are not available; for third country youth, however, unemployment in 2016 stood at 22.8% and marginally exceeded the EU28 average of 22.2%. Long-term unemployment among youth in Malta stood at 1% in 2018.

In respect of young people who are neither in education, employment or training (NEET), the picture in Malta is mixed. Overall, and irrespective of educational attainment, 7.4% of the 15 to 29 age cohort are NEET (almost half the EU28 rate of 12.9%); the rate is considerably higher for young women (9%) than young men (5.9%). However, if one focuses on youth with an educational attainment between ISCED levels 0 and 2 (less than lower secondary), the proportion of NEETS doubles to 15.8% (above the EU average of 15.1%) with a marked gender discrepancy where the NEET rate of young women of low educational attainment (22.5%) is more than double that of their male counterpart (10.9%). In 2016, the NEET rate for third country youth was almost three times the national one at 21.3%, while reliable data for EU youth are not available.

Education

While Malta still has a far larger overall share of the population at ISCED level 0 to 2 (less than lower secondary level), recent years have seen a marked change in educational attainment overall. Since 2007, the share of those with ISCED 0 to 2 has declined by over 20 percentage points, with the ISCED 3 to 4 share rising by 10% and the ISCED 5 to 8 by 12.5%. This change is more marked among young people. The share of tertiary graduates has doubled since 2007 to stand at 27.1% of all youth, having overtaken the EU average of 20.7%. A greater share of young women (30.4%) than young men (24%) now have tertiary education, while a greater share of young men (34.8%) than young women (27.4%) have less than secondary education. Figure 9.2 below depicts the shifting distribution of educational attainment in the EU and Malta.

Despite this remarkable success, however, Malta still has the highest proportion of early school leavers in the EU, amounting to 17.5% of the 18 to 24 age cohort in 2018 compared to the EU average of 10.6%. That said, the rate of early school leavers has almost halved from 2007 when it stood at 30.2%. It is more common among young men (19.4%) than young women (15.5%).

Housing

As already noted in Section 3.1, young people in Malta are much more likely to live with their parents, especially young men, than their European counterparts; they are also less likely to cohabit. In part because of this, young people in Malta

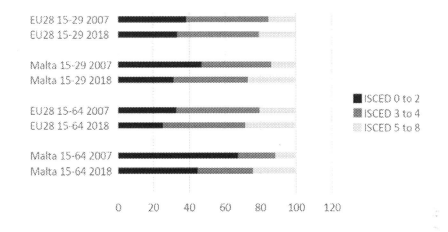

FIGURE 9.2. Educational Attainment by ISCED levels, EU28 and Malta, 2007 and 2018. Source: Eurostat (2019g)

have typically had a far lower housing cost overburden[2] than other young people in Europe, also reflecting Malta's high levels of home ownership (70.9% [NSO 2016]) and rent controls enduring from pre-1995 leases. In 2017, only 1.2% of young people in Malta lived in households with total housing costs exceeding 40% of their disposable income, compared to 11.9% in the EU. Only 2.1% of those aged 16 to 24 faced severe housing deprivation[3] (EU28 6.1%), while less than one fifth of their European counterparts lived in overcrowded dwellings (5.1% compared to 23.8% in EU28) (Eurostat, 2019j).

The housing prospects, however, are very different for youth seeking to enter the property market today. House prices spiked between 2006 and 2008, slowing down thereafter only to start rising again by 2014 and rising annually by over 5% year on year since then (Eurostat, 2019i). In recent years, property market overheating has raised concern among social partners and NGOs. According to the Federation of Estate Agents, the average asking price for a 100sqm two-bedroomed apartment in 2019 was €246,442 (Cilia, 2019), bearing in mind that the median equivalized net income for youth aged 18 to 24 in 2018 was €15,668 per annum. The rise in prices led to the issue of Directive 16 by the Central Bank of Malta on borrower-based measures, establishing maximum loan terms, a maximum loan-to-value ratio and a maximum debt-service-to-income ratio (except where additional security is provided) (Central Bank of Malta, 2019a), as the

---

[2] The percentage of young people living in households where the total housing costs amount to more than 40% of disposable income (both figures net of any housing allowances).

[3] Living in an overcrowded dwelling which also has one of the following features: too dark, leaking roof, no bath/shower or indoor toilet.

Central Bank also warned that loan repayments are becoming larger in relation to income and creating possible vulnerabilities should a downturn occur (Central Bank of Malta, 2019b). At the same time, it is near impossible for young people on average salaries to rent a property as rental values have risen sharply; in a study commissioned to KPMG and presented in 2019, rental values almost doubled over the past six years to range between €814 and €1118 per month in 2016 (Grech, 2017). New rent law reforms are being proposed for 2020 which, while stopping short of rent control, establish minimum rent durations and cap second and subsequent rent increases, also introducing tax credits for landlords offering stable rents.

POVERTY AND SOCIAL EXCLUSION

In 2017, 19.3% of the Maltese were at risk of poverty or social exclusion (AROPE). The risk was lower for those aged between 16 and 29 (14.9%), whose AROPE rate was around half that of their European counterparts (27.9%). This 2017 youth AROPE rate of 14.9% is identical to that for 2007, which rose between 2010 and 2015 and then declined again. As illustrated in Figure 9.3 below, the risk of poverty and social exclusion is higher for young men in Malta than young women. Young people living alone were 5.3% more likely to face this risk in 2016 than those living with their parents. The AROPE rate is also considerably higher for EU youth (42.5%) and non-EU youth (41.5) in Malta.

Turning to monetary poverty alone, this affected 10.8% of young Maltese in 2018 though the rates were higher for other EU youth (14.5%) and non-EU youth

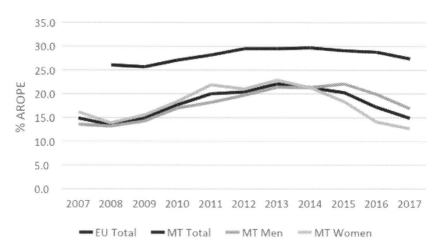

FIGURE 9.3. AROPE 2007 to 2018, Youth in the EU28 and Malta. Source: Eurostat (2019j)

$(15.2\%)^4$. The risk is almost double when considering only those young people not living with their parents (19.3% in 2016), likely due to housing costs. In-work poverty risk is considerably lower in Malta, amounting to 3.6% of employed youth in 2017 (EU 9.9%). In respect of severe material deprivation among Maltese youth, this rose from 4.4% to exceed EU averages between 2013 and 2015 but has since declined markedly to stand at 2.7% in 2017 (EU28 7%). Again, it was higher for other EU youth (5.6%) and non-EU youth (6.4%) in 2017. In respect of very low work intensity, only 5.2% of youth lived in such households in 2017 (amounting to half the rate of youth in Europe) but rising to 8.3% of youth who did not live with their parents. The risk was much higher for young men living alone (12.8%) than young women (5%), and also higher for other EU youth (18.8%) and non-EU youth (17.8%).

INSTITUTIONAL FRAMEWORK

Since 2007, there have been a number of legislative developments to reflect the diversifying nature of family life in Malta. Until 2011, Malta was only one of three states that did not have divorce legislation, the others being the Philippines and the Vatican City. The prospect of divorce generated much controversy at the time, after a Private Member's Bill for the introduction of divorce was tabled in the Maltese parliament. The Parliament resolved that a non-binding referendum should be held on whether or not divorce law should be introduced, and the referendum was held in May 2011. 53% of voters approved, and divorce legislation was promulgated later that year.

Since 2011, there has been a spate of legislation that addresses family diversity. In 2014, the Civil Unions Act granted partners in a civil union the same rights, responsibilities and obligations as married couples, including the right of joint adoption. The Cohabitation Act of 2016 sets out the rights and duties of cohabitants as defined in the Act and set out in a public deed registered with a notary. Also, in 2016, legislation was passed to distinguish between sexual orientation, gender identity and gender expression, and to ban the practice of conversion therapies. In 2017, changes to the Marriage Act removed reference to gender, replacing 'husband' and 'wife' with spouse and thereby removing distinctions between different-sex and same-sex couples before the law. By Legal Notice in 2017, the right was established for persons in civil unions to convert their civil union into marriage. Equal treatment was further extended by Legal Notice in 2017 which extended a provision for leave from work during IVF treatment to all couples irrespective of sexual orientation.

Malta is the only country in the EU where abortion is considered a criminal offence, although in the last 25 years no woman has been imprisoned for having had an abortion (*Times of Malta*, 2021). Medical measures to save a mother's life are

---

[4] Data for other EU and non-EU youth to be treated with caution as Eurostat cites them as having low reliability, likely due to sample size.

150 • SUE VELLA & JOANNE CASSAR

permissible. A number of Maltese women are known to travel to other European countries to undergo abortion (Mifsud et al., 2009). A survey in 2018 found that 95.2% of the Maltese do not agree with abortion in the first twelve weeks (Sansone, 2018). The issue is divisive, with pro-life and pro-choice groups occasionally engaging in fierce debate, and political parties using it as a weapon to attack the other. There do not seem to be any actual measures to legislate for abortion in the foreseeable future.

Concerns over abortion were also raised in 2015 and 2016 in connection with the proposed introduction of the morning-after pill to Malta, with opponents arguing that it was an abortifacient while the pro-choice lobby argued that it was not. The issue also divided opinion in Parliamentary Committees and the Medical Council. In late 2016, the Medicines Authority declared that the pill was to be available over the counter, subject to a few questions by the dispensing pharmacist. While the Chamber of Pharmacists stated that such questions were in line with international standards to protect safety and confidentiality, a women's lobby has claimed that questions often give rise to awkwardness or shame, and should only be raised respectfully and in private, not over the counter (*Times of Malta*, 2019).

In terms of taxation and social security, married couples are treated equally irrespective of sexual orientation. Taxation in Malta is progressive, and couples may opt for individual or joint tax computation, depending on what works best for them. Social security in Malta has two broad pillars—contributory and non-contributory benefits. The first are based on contribution conditions and individualized rights, although married supplements are available for those whose spouse does not have a contributory record. Young people who have made the necessary contributions may benefit in their own right (for instance, to unemployment, sickness or injury benefits). On the other hand, non-contributory benefits ('social assistance') are based on an assessment of means and are payable to the 'head of household', so young people who live with their families would not be entitled, in their own name, to claim social assistance. A lump sum marriage grant is payable to persons who get married, and means-tested children's allowance is also payable to families with dependent children. It is also to be noted that in Malta, tertiary education is free of charge (as is primary and secondary education in public schools) and in addition, a monthly stipend is payable to university students.

COUNTRY-SPECIFIC CHALLENGES TO FAMILY FORMATION

Challenges to family formation stem from social, cultural and personal factors that are linked with each other. The factors outlined in this section interfere with young people's plans to start a family. They demonstrate that vulnerable young people are mostly at risk of facing obstacles when contemplating or planning to have a family of their own.

Meeting the Right Partner

Whereas a number of women opt not to have children, other women and men who wish to start a family might face problems with finding a 'suitable' mate and as they grow older, the options to socialize with potential partners decrease. Intentional single parenthood is still relatively rare in Malta, and very few women who have not met the right partner opt for artificial insemination. It is particularly difficult for persons to form a family if their first marriage dissolves before having children and meeting a second partner with whom to form a family can be a lengthy process.

Disability

Maltese society still perceives a disjuncture between being disabled and being sexual (Azzopardi-Lane & Callus, 2014). Stereotypical assumptions that portray persons with physical and intellectual disability as 'asexual' or 'hyper sexual' might present obstacles to them in starting a family. Maltese mothers with disability are faced with social misconceptions that describe them as incapable or unfit of being mothers (Azzopardi-Lane & Callus, 2016). These stigmatizing labels augment the effects of disability (Azzopardi-Lane & Callus, 2016). Qualitative data with Maltese young persons with disability shows that they were told not to risk getting pregnant because of their hereditary condition. Persons they knew also told them that they did not want to have children with them for the same reason (Debattista, 2015). Young persons with intellectual disability desire more opportunities to engage in sexual relationships (Azzopardi-Lane & Callus, 2014). Financial assistance for people with intellectual disability is not provided by the state to live with a partner (Azzopardi-Lane & Callus, 2014).

Physical and Mental Ill-health

Young people's mental health and general wellbeing directly affects their interpersonal relationships, their functioning at school, work and in society and how they conduct their life. Poor physical and mental health might present numerous challenges to them in starting a family. For example, young people who suffer from chronic depression or personality disorders might withdraw socially. They might lack social skills and this might further contribute to poorer physical and mental health problems. These long-term issues have implications for their ability to fulfil their potential. A minority of Maltese young people (1.8%) stated that they feel a persistent sense of inner void (Inguanez et al., 2012, p. 38). Although the majority of Maltese young people reported having a worthy purpose in life and stated that they are 'happy' (Inguanez et al., 2012), there is a general lack of research on the extent to which their overall psychological functioning hinders or supports them in starting a family.

Low Income

Even if youth poverty rates in Malta remain below those in the EU, especially in view of their longer stay within the parental home, financial commitments such as buying a house, car and other commodities might delay the onset of starting a family. Weddings in Malta tend to be lavish and expensive affairs, further adding to young couples' financial burden. It is, however, housing affordability, whether through rent or mortgage, that currently poses the greatest concern to young people wishing to embark on an independent life of their own.

Access to Sexual and Relationship Education

A national survey in 2012 on sexual knowledge, attitudes and behavior identified a number of important lacunae in sexual education among young people (Directorate for Health Information & Research, 2012). On average, teenagers reported that they were 12 years of age before learning about puberty and reproduction, and were more likely to learn about aspects of sexual behavior from friends than from parents or teachers. While 41% of the 16 to 18 age group said that they have had sex at least once, awareness of contraception and of available genito-urinary services among this cohort was rather limited.

Blended Families

Although social stigma attached to parents of children born outside marriage has been decreasing, even where these parents are teenagers, (Cutajar, 2006), such stigma may still create barriers for the parent concerned—usually the mother—to enter a new long-term relationship, often due to pressures arising from the new partner's family. Similar pressures are faced by separated or divorced parents seeking to enter a new relationship, especially if the partners do not have children of their own. However, blended families are becoming far more common and 'accepted' than they once were, and cohabiting couples who do not marry are now protected under the *Cohabitation Act* (House of Representatives, 2017b). That said, psychosocial support for blended families, especially in respect of the parenting challenges they sometimes pose, is still in its infancy.

Infertility

Infertility poses a heartbreaking challenge to persons who wish to start a family. That said, fertility treatment in Malta is state funded. Amendments to the *Embryo Protection Act* (House of Representatives, 2018) that regulates in vitro fertilization (IVF) allowed for an increase in the number of fertilized eggs and the freezing of embryos; the rate of success for IVF procedures is however still low and stands at 22% (Xuereb, 2019). Persons undergoing IVF procedures are entitled to paid leave from work. This counts for all couples irrespective of their sexual orientation (Legal Notice 156 of 2017).

Traditional Expectations of Care

In some cultures, young women are expected to devote their entire life to their family members and remain single for this purpose; this has also traditionally applied to Malta. Eldest daughters, especially, have been expected to care for the siblings still living in the household, as well as their parents as they age (Gordon, 2003). This caring role is usually assigned from childhood and is rooted in gendered roles and socio-cultural expectations. That this issue is under-researched locally affirms the invisibility of these female caregivers.

CONCLUSION

In general, Maltese young people have various channels of support and social structures that help them to start a family. In addition to family support, young people in Malta today enjoy a low unemployment rate, free higher education and free childcare. They also however face a number of disadvantages in starting a family. A context of rising living costs and housing affordability problems makes it difficult for those on low income to start a family on a sound footing, and the prospects for the sizeable number of youth who leave school without post-secondary qualifications are limited. Other challenges derive from social, cultural and personal factors, which interact and compound each other, such as poor physical and mental health, infertility, stigma and social exclusion.

Recognition of the challenges facing young people has resulted in various policy amendments and implementation of existing measures such as those stipulated by the Action Plan of *The National Youth Policy* which aims at supporting young people in different areas of life (Teuma et al., 2015, pp. 15–20). The analysis of all policies affecting young people from the perspective of a Family Impact Lens, such as that proposed by Bogenschneider et al. (2012), may serve to further support young people in their transition to forming, or indeed re-forming, a family in Malta today.

REFERENCES

Azzopardi, A. (2011). *Young people in Gozo: A Study*. OASI Publications.

Azzopardi-Lane. C.. & Callus. A. M. (2014). Constructing sexual identities: People with intellectual disability talking about sexuality. *British Journal of Learning Disabilities. 43*. 32–37.

Azzopardi-Lane. C.. & Callus. A. M. (2016). Disability and parenting—The experiences of four women with disability. *Considering Disability 1*(3/4). 1–34.

Baldacchino. G. (2012). Islands and Despots. *Commonwealth and Comparative Politics 50*(1). 103–120.

Bettetini. A. (2010). Religion and the secular state in Malta. In J. Martinez-Torron & W. C. Durham (Eds.). *Religion and the secular state* (pp. 493–503). The International Center for Law and Religion Studies. Brigham Young University.

154 • SUE VELLA & JOANNE CASSAR

Bogenschneider, K., Little, O. M., Ooms, T., Benning, S., Cadigan, K., & Corbett, T. (2012). The family impact lens: A family-focused, evidence-informed approach to policy and practice. *Family Relations 61*(3), 514–531.

Caruana, C. (2017, January 14). Divorced, remarried 'at peace with God' may receive Communion. *The Times of Malta.* https://timesofmalta.com/articles/view/divorced-remarried-at-peace-with-god-may-receive-communion-bishops.636462

Caruana, C. (2019, January 27). Mass attendance set to collapse in the years to come. *The Times of Malta.* https://timesofmalta.com/articles/view/mass-attendance-set-to-collapse-in-the-years-to-come.700305

Cassar, J. (2009). Being a lesbian is no sin: Religion, sexuality and education in the lives of female students. *Mediterranean Journal of Educational Studies, 14*(1), 45–67.

Cassar, J. (2015). Sex and secrecies: An exploration of students' conceptualizations of het-eronormativity. *Journal of LGBT Youth, 12*(4), 419–435.

Cassar, J., & Grima Sultana, M. (2016). Sex is a minor thing: Parents of gay sons negotiat-ing the social influences of coming out. *Sexuality & Culture, 20*(4), 987–1002.

Cassar, J., & Grima Sultana, M. (2017). Parents of gay sons redefining masculinity. *Open Journal of Social Sciences, 5*, 170–182.

Cassar, J., & Grima Sultana, M. (2018). No way am I throwing you out! Adjustments in space and time for parents of gay sons. *Journal of Family Studies.* DOI: 10.1080/13229400.2018.1523020

Central Bank of Malta. (2019a). *Borrower-based measures.* https://www.centralbankmalta.org/borrower-based-measures

Central Bank of Malta. (2019b). *Financial stability report 2018.* https://www.centralbank-malta.org/financial-stability-report

Central Office of Statistics. (1976). *Demographic review of the Maltese Islands for the year 1975.* Central Office of Statistics.

Central Office of Statistics. (1982). *Demographic review of the Maltese Islands for the year 1980.* Central Office of Statistics.

Cilia, J. (2019, May 11). *Shocking new breakdown of average apartment cost by local-ity will blow your mind—And your wallet.* LovinMalta. https://lovinmalta.com/lifestyle/living-in-malta/shocking-new-breakdown-of-average-apartment-cost-by-locality-will-blow-your-mind-and-your-wallet/

Cutajar, J. A. (2006). Teenage mothers—The right to work and study. In P. G. Xuereb (Ed.), *The family, law, religion and society in the European Union and Malta. Civil society project report.* European Documentation and Research Centre, University of Malta.

Debattista, M. (2015). *Persons with disability and intimate relationships: Realities in the Maltese context.* Unpublished MA dissertation, University of Malta.

Deguara, A. (2019). Sexual morality and shame among Catholics whose lifestyle does not conform to church teaching. *Sexuality & Culture.* https://doi.org/10.1007/s12119-019-09591-w

Diacono, T. (2019, April 18). Over 100,000 foreigners now living in Malta as island's population just keeps ballooning. *LovinMalta.* https://lovinmalta.com/lifestyle/liv-ing-in-malta/over-100-000-foreigners-now-living-in-malta-as-islands-population-just-keeps-ballooning/

Directorate for Health Information and Research. (2012). *Sexual knowledge, attitudes and behaviour. National Survey.* Malta Ministry for Health.

European Commission. (2015). *Discrimination in the EU in 2015: Eurobarometer 83.4 Results for Malta.*

Eurostat. (2018a). *News release 38/2018: Women in the EU earned on average 16% less than men in 2016.* https://ec.europa.eu/eurostat/documents/2995521/8718272/3-07032018-BP-EN.pdf/fb402341-e7fd-42b8-a7cc-4e33587d79aa

Eurostat. (2018b). *Living conditions in Europe: 2018 Edition.* Publications Office of the European Union.

Eurostat. (2019a). *Household composition statistics.* https://ec.europa.eu/eurostat/statistics-explained/index.php/Household_composition_statistics#Household_size

Eurostat. (2019b). *Marriage and divorce statistics.* https://ec.europa.eu/eurostat/statistics-explained/index.php/Marriage_and_divorce_statistics#Fewer_marriages.2C_more_divorces

Eurostat. (2019c). *Share of young adults aged 18–34 living with their parents by age and sex (ilc_lvps08).* Retrieved 24 August 2019 from: https://ec.europa.eu/eurostat/data/database

Eurostat. (2019d). *Mean age at first marriage (demo-nind).* Retrieved 25 August 2019 from: https://ec.europa.eu/eurostat/data/database

Eurostat. (2019e). *Fertility indicators (demo_fer).* Retrieved 25 August 2019 from: https://ec.europa.eu/eurostat/data/database

Eurostat. (2019f). *Labour market (labour).* Retrieved 26 August 2019 from: https://ec.europa.eu/eurostat/data/database

Eurostat. (2019g). *Youth education and training (yth_educ).* Retrieved 26 August 2019 from: https://ec.europa.eu/eurostat/data/database

Eurostat. (2019h). *Housing conditions (ilv_lvho).* Retrieved 30 August 2019 from: https://ec.europa.eu/eurostat/data/database

Eurostat. (2019i). *House price index (tipsho20).* Retrieved 30 August 2019 from: https://ec.europa.eu/eurostat/data/database

Eurostat. (2019j). *Youth social inclusion (yth_incl).* Retrieved 30 August 2019 from: https://ec.europa.eu/eurostat/web/youth/data/database

Gordon, P. A. (2003). The decision to remain single: Implications for women across Cultures. *Journal of Mental Health Counselling, 25*(1), 33–44.

Grech, H. (2017, November 30). Malta average rental prices increase by 47% between 2013–2016, signs of 'overheating'. *Malta Independent.* https://www.independent.com.mt/articles/2017-11-30/local-news/Malta-average-rental-prices-increase-by-47-between-2013-2016-signs-of-overheating-6736182097

House of Representatives. (2014). *Act IX of 2014—Civil Unions.* http://www.justiceservices.gov.mt/DownloadDocument.aspx?app=lp&itemid=26024&l=1

House of Representatives. (2017a). *Act XXIII of 2017. Marriage Act and Other Laws (Amendment) of 2017.* http://justiceservices.gov.mt/DownloadDocument.aspx?app=lp&itemid=28609&l=1

House of Representatives. (2017b). Act XV of 2017. *An Act to regulate cohabitations and to provide for other matters dealing with them or ancillary to them.* http://www.justiceservices.gov.mt/DownloadDocument.aspx?app=lp&itemid=28387&l=1

House of Representatives. (2018). *An ACT to amend the Embryo Protection Act, Cap. 524.* http://justiceservices.gov.mt/DownloadDocument.aspx?app=lp&itemid=29033&l=1

156 • SUE VELLA & JOANNE CASSAR

Inguanez, J., Gatt, R., & Schembri, S. (2012). *Mirrors and windows: Maltese young people's perception on themselves, their families, communities and society.* Agenzija Zghazagh.

Legal Notice 156. (2017). *Employment and industrial relations act (Cap. 452): Leave for Medically Assisted Procreation National Standard Order, 2017.* https://deputyprimeminister.gov.mt/en/epa/Documents/Act_and_Legal_Notices/LN156_Leave%20for_Medically_Assisted_Procreation_EN.pdf

Mifsud, M., Buttigieg, G. G., Savona Ventura, C., & Delicata, S. (2009). Reproductive health in Malta. *The European Journal of Contraception and Reproductive Health Care, 14*(4), 249–257.

Ministry of Education. (1999). *Creating the future together: National minimum curriculum.* Malta Ministry of Education.

Mitchell, J. P. (2003). Looking forward to the past: National identity and history in Malta. *Identities: Global Studies in Power and Culture, 10*, 377–398.

Moreno Mínguez, A. & Crespi, I. (2017). Future perspectives on work and family dynamics in Southern Europe: the importance of culture and regional contexts. *International Review of Sociology, 27*, 389–393.

NSO. (2002). *Demographic review 2001.* National Statistics Office.

NSO. (2015). *Demographic review 2005–2011.* National Statistics Office. https://nso.gov.mt/en/publicatons/Publications_by_Unit/Documents/C5_Population%20and%20Migration%20Statistics/Demographic_Review_2005_2012.pdf

NSO. (2016). *Housing budgetary survey.* National Statistics Office.

NSO. (2018). *International day of families 2018.* National Statistics Office. https://nso.gov.mt/en/News_Releases/View_by_Unit/Unit_C1/Living_Conditions_and_Culture_Statistics/Documents/2018/News2018_075.pdf

NSO. (2019). *World population day 2019.* National Statistics Office. https://nso.gov.mt/en/News_Releases/View_by_Unit/Unit_C5/Population_and_Migration_Statistics/Documents/2019/News2019_108.pdf

OECD. (2016). *Cohabitation rate and prevalence of other forms of partnership.* Retrieved 25 August 2019 from http://www.oecd.org/els/family/SF_3-3-Cohabitation-forms-partnership.pdf

Pace, R. (2012). Growing secularisation in a Catholic society: The divorce referendum of May 2011 in Malta. *South European Society and Politics, 17*(4), 573–589.

Pontificium Consilium pro Familia. (n.d.). *In Malta the family stands strong.* http://www.familiam.org/pls/pcpf/v3_s2ew_consultazione.mostra_pagina?id_pagina=6577

Sansone, K. (2018, February 4). Malta Today survey: Abortion remains a no-go area for Maltese. *Malta Today.* https://www.maltatoday.com.mt/news/data_and_surveys/84223/maltatoday_survey_abortion_remains_a_nogo_area_for_maltese#.YL5kbL7ivIU

Seidman, S. (2002). *Beyond the closet: The transformations of gay and lesbian life.* Routledge.

Tabone, C. (1995). *Maltese families in transition: A sociological investigation.* Ministry for Social Development.

Teuma, M., Borg, A., Cassar, J., Greenland, C., Micallef, A., Saliba, B., & Zammit, J. (2015). *National youth policy—Towards 2020. A shared vision for the future of young people*. Malta: The Parliamentary Secretariat for Research, Innovation, Youth and Sport.

Times of Malta. (2019, September 11). *Dispensing the morning-after pill*. https://timesof-malta.com/articles/view/dispensing-the-morning-after-pill.734638

Times of Malta. (2021, June 1). *No woman imprisoned for abortion in 25 years.* https://timesofmalta.com/articles/view/no-women-imprisoned-for-abortion-in-25-years.876125

Visanich, V. (2017). Youth in the age of anxiety: The case of a southern European location. *Contemporary Social Science, 12*, 333–346.

Xuereb, M. (2019). *States it is time for further Amendments in IVF Law*. https://www.tvm.com.mt/en/news/jghid-li-wasal-iz-states-it-is-time-for-further-amendments-in-ivf-law-ghal-aktar-emendi-fil-ligi-tal-ivf/

CHAPTER 10

CHALLENGES AND CHANGES IN FAMILY(IES) FORMATION IN PORTUGAL SINCE THE TRANSITION TO DEMOCRACY

Catarina Pinheiro Mota

University of Trás-os-Montes and Alto Douro, University of Porto, Portugal

Helena Carvalho and Paula Mena Matos

University of Porto, Portugal

This chapter aims to report the major challenges and changes in family formation in Portugal, based on an analysis of the social, historical, political and economic context over the past 40 years. There are changes in the roles of young people with the increase of educational levels, their entry into the labor market, and the postponement of family formation. Increased legislation on sexuality and reproduction rights gains prominence, as does the social acceptance of new forms of family. A significant decrease in birth and fertility rates is leading to important demographic losses. The economic crisis that has occurred over the last decade has contributed to the postponement of young people's economic independence. Portugal is currently

---

Family Formation Among Youth in Europe: Coping With Socio-Economic Disadvantages,
pages 159–174.
Copyright © 2022 by Information Age Publishing
www.infoagepub.com
All rights of reproduction in any form reserved.

159

160 • MOTA, CARVALHO, & MATOS

presenting a more favorable scenario with the economic recovery and the encouragement of family support policies.

1. NATIONAL CONTEXT

Social, Historical, Political, Economic

Portugal is one of the oldest nation-states in Europe and has a long and rich social and political history. An enthusiastic Republican period came after the Monarchy in 1910, followed by different governments. In 1933, the Salazar regime was set up with the Constitution defining the New State as a "unitary and corporative republic" approved in a national referendum (Sousa, 1996). This dictatorship government aimed at the construction of a strong republican and corporatist state under the moral principles of the Catholic Church (Baiôa, et al., 2003). Portugal managed to stay neutral during the Second World War and, despite the defeat of the right-wing dictatorships in Europe, Salazar's position had not been seriously damaged. Although the regime survived the war and benefited economically from it, it failed to invest in the modernization of the country: state services were kept to a bare minimum, traditional agricultural structures were not reformed, and no appropriate stimulus was given to the industry (Baiôa, et al., 2003). The country continued to vastly underperform on its potential for growth, while basic political rights such as universal suffrage, free trade unions and freedom of expression continued to be denied. The regime's highly centralized system virtually isolated decision-makers from those who they were theoretically supposed to represent and serve. This "acceptance" was in part due to the people's fear of being punished and, at the same time, due to high rates of illiteracy of the population (Baiôa, et al., 2003).

The Portuguese authoritarian regime, which ruled the country for half a century, was brought to the end by a coup in 1974 led by young officers of the Armed Forces. The April Revolution of 1974 was called the "Carnation Revolution" (Revolução dos Cravos), since during the revolution people offered red carnations to soldiers on the streets who put them in the barrels of their riffles. It became a symbol of a peaceful revolution. The regime's police and para-military forces were eradicated, special courts for political crimes were also eliminated, and political liberties were restored: freedom of expression, association, full participation in political life, etc. (Sousa, 1996). The revolution was an important milestone for women's rights, challenging traditional gender roles. Important changes were observed in the Portuguese society: women's universal voting rights and progressive participation in politics, the abolition of legal permission for honor crimes committed by fathers or husbands, the freedom to leave the country and travel without prior husband's authorization, the freedom of expression granted to women and decision-making power (Aboim, 2010b). Concurrently, the 1976 Constitution decreed important measures having an impact on family formation

Family(ies) Formation in Portugal Since the Transition to Democracy • **161**

and development, namely sexual freedom, reproductive health and family planning, as well as access to education and the labor market (Aboim, 2010b).

The revolutionary period was over in 1976, but democratic stability was still a distant reality. Following the next ten years, until the integration in the European Community in 1986, Portugal entered a period of economic, social and political instability. In just 12 years of democracy, there were 10 constitutional governments. By 1986, internal political life had stabilized considerably. Some political changes were constituted, mainly because the radical parties that emerged after the Revolution had all but disappeared, and two main forces became dominant, both occupying the center of the political spectrum—the Socialist Party and the Social Democrat Party (Sousa, 1996).

The entrance of Portugal into the European Union in 1986 had an important effect on the convergence of national policies and social measures contributing to stable economic growth and development, largely through increased trade ties and an inflow of funds allocated by the European Union to improve the country's infrastructure. At the same time, Portugal was not an industrial society and could not, therefore, be integrated in the designated advanced industrial economies (OECD, 2019a). Even so, in 1999, it continued to enjoy sturdy economic growth and falling rates of unemployment. The country qualified for the Economic and Monetary Union of the European Union (EMU) in 1998 and joined ten other European countries in launching the euro on the 1st January 1999 (OECD, 2019a). Portugal made significant progress in raising its standard of living to that of its EU partners. Gross Domestic Product (GDP) per capita on a purchasing power parity basis rose from 51% of the EU average in 1985 to 78% in early 2002. By 2005, it dropped to 72% (of the average of all of the then 25 EU members, including seven with GDP per capita lower than Portugal) as GDP per capita rose in other EU countries. Unemployment stood at 4.1% at the end of 2001, above the EU average (OECD, 2019a). However, from 2002 to 2007, important changes in Portuguese economic and political panorama were observed. The unemployment rate increased dramatically to 65% (270,500 unemployed citizens in 2002, 448,600 unemployed citizens in 2007) and, from 2007 to 2013, a growing trend in unemployment rates was observed (Figure 10.1). In December 2009, the rating agencies lowered its long-term credit assessment of Portugal from "stable" to "negative", voicing pessimism with respect to the country's structural economic indicators.

Between 2010 to 2013, a financial crisis emerged in Portugal. The global recession resulting from the United States financial crisis had a disastrous impact on the Portuguese economy (Eichenbaum et al., 2016). In addition, the financial collapse of two important banks, the budgetary slippage of "public–private partnership" (PPPs), and swaps contracts that resulted in potential losses higher than 3000 million euros, contributed to the Portuguese highest economy's recessions since 1970 (Wall & Correia, 2014). As a consequence, there has been an increase in unemployment rates, salary cuts, heavier taxation and general disinvestment in

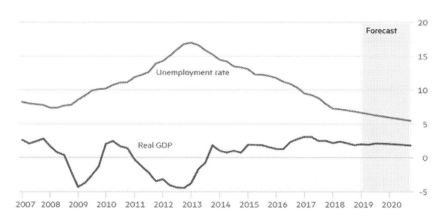

FIGURE 10.1. Portugal Economic Recovery—Real GDP and Unemployment Rates. Source: OECD Economic Outlook: Statistics and Projections (database), November 2019.

family policies. Family and child well-being indicators, such as poverty, material deprivation, work intensity, fertility, school drop-out and expenditure, reveal that the Portuguese family and work conditions have worsen during this period (Wall & Correia, 2014).

In April 2011, Portugal confirmed the receipt of a financial bailout from the IMF and the European Union worth €78 billion. The three-year EU aid program incorporating the €78 billion support package ended in May 2014. The year of 2014 marked the start of the recovery of the Portuguese economy (PEO, 2015). GDP is now back to its pre-crisis level and the unemployment rate has declined by 10 percentage points since 2013 to below 7%, one of the largest reductions in any OECD country over the past decade (Figure 10.1). This decline is not independent from the significant increase in emigration rates, namely of woman and highly qualified young people (Perista & Carrilho, 2015). Legacies of the crisis remain, with the poverty rate of the working age population still high and perceptions of subjective well-being below pre-crisis levels (OECD, 2019a).

Demographic Trends Relevant to Family Formation

In 2018, Portugal's estimated population was 10,276,617, with 14,410 inhabitants less than in the year before. Since 2010, the downward population trend has been increasing, although with important deceleration since 2017. This results from the increase in net migration (from 4,886 in 2017 to 11,570 in 2018) since there was a negative *natural population growth* (from –23,432 in 2017 to –25,980 in 2018). Thus, the rate of net migration showed, in 2018, a positive rate of 0.11%, while on the other side, the rate of natural increase showed a negative rate of 0.25% (INE, 2019a). The number of inhabitants from foreign countries living in Portugal was 480,300, the highest number recorded since 1976 (SEF/GEPF, 2019). The ten most represented countries of origin are Brazil, Cape Verde, Romania, Ukraine, United Kingdom, China, France, Italy, Angola and Guinea-Bissau (SEF/GEPF, 2019).

In 2018, with regard to the structure of the population by age groups, the percentage of young people (aged 0–14) stood at 13.7% of the total resident population, those aged 15–24 represented 10.6%, those aged 25–64 stood at 53.8%, and the percentage of the elderly (aged 65 and over) was 21.8% of the total. This age distribution led to an ageing ratio of 159.4 elderly per 100 young people (i.e., 4.0 p.p. increase vis-à-vis the previous year). The changes in the size and age-sex structure of the resident population in Portugal, in particular due to low birth rates and increased longevity in the last decades, suggest that, aside from the population decrease in the last years, the demographic ageing continued. Life expectancy at birth was estimated at 80.80 years. In 2016–2018, men and women could expect to live up to 77.78 years and 83.43 years, respectively. Within a decade, there was a gain of 2.06 years of life for the total population, 2.29 years for men and 1.62 years for women (INE, 2019a).

With respect to the number of live births of mothers residing in Portugal, in 2018 it was 87,020—an increase of 1.0 % compared to 2017, which translated into a crude birth rate of 8.5 live births per 1,000 inhabitants. There was also a slight recovery of the total fertility rate (TFR) in relation to previous years, which stood at 1.41 children per woman in 2018, compared to 1.37 in 2017 (Figure 10.2). Even so, since the last 30 years, Portugal has shifted from being one of the

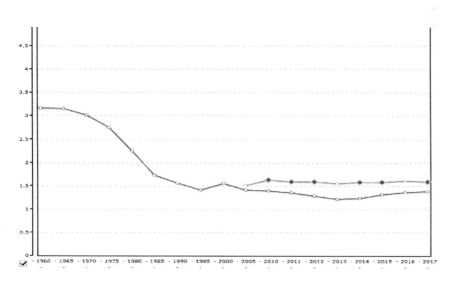

FIGURE 10.2. Synthetic Fertility Rate in Europe (UE28) (yellow line), Evidence in Portugal (green line). Source: PORDATA

high fertility countries in Europe to having the lowest fertility rate. There were 281 deaths in the first year of life in 2018, an increase of 52 cases compared to the previous year.

Also, in 2018, the mean age of women at first childbirth was 29.8 years, 2.1 years more compared to 2008, and the mean age of women at childbirth (regardless of birth order) went up to 31.2 years (PORDATA, 2019a). In the EU, the proportion of live births outside marriage stood at about 43% in 2016, whereas it was 54.9% in Portugal (PORDATA, 2019a). This seem to be more that 15% higher than in 2000, with an increase of 1% each year, that may signal changing patterns of family formation, with births occurring to non-marital relationships, cohabiting couples and single parents (EUROSTAT, 2019).

The number of marriages in Portugal in 2018 was 34,637, with a growth of 3% compared to the previous year, leading to an increase in the gross marriage rate from 3.3 to 3.4 marriages per thousand inhabitants. The data confirmed a trend over the past decade among both men and women to postpone their first marriage, with the average age rising from 33.2 to 33.6 years among men and 31.6 to 32.1 years among women in 2018, compared to 2017 (PORDATA, 2019b). There has been an increase in average age at first marriage of 1.9 years for both sexes over the last six years and an increase in average marriage age of 2.8 years among men and 2.7 years among women. More than half of marriages (68%) were first marriages (between singles), but this proportion dropped slightly compared to 2017 (68.5%). Also, civil marriages (67.1%) are largely more represented, compared with Catholic ones (32.5%)—a consistently increasing trend since 2007 (civil marriages 52.5%, Catholic marriages 47.4%) (PORDATA, 2019b).

Statistics showed that divorce rates in Portugal decreased in line with what has been happening since 2015. In 2018, 20,345 divorces were registered in Portugal, 3,032 less than in 2015. In this sense, the upward trend registered from 1974 (777 divorces) to 2002 (27,708 divorces) has been suffering an inverse path since 2010 (27,556) and more consistently since 2015 (PORDATA, 2019). According to the National Institute of Statistics (INE) (2019c), there was a growth of same-sex marriages from 25 to 75 from 2013 to 2018, given that since 2010 Portugal approves same-sex civil marriage. In 2018, there were in Portugal a total of 4,144,619 private households, 22.7% of which were single individuals, 24.3% couples without children, 34% couples with children, 11.1% single parent families, and 7.9% other types of private households (PORDATA, 2019a).

2. SOCIO-ECONOMIC CONDITIONS

Concerning the labor market, the active population (age 15–64) in Portugal in 2018 ascended to 78.8% (52,326 people) of the working age population, confirming the growth trend since 2013 (76.9%). We also observe a growing trend of educational qualifications of the active population. In 2013, the proportion of population with secondary or higher education was 43.6%, in 2018 it was 54% (PORDATA, 2019b). The unemployed population in 2018 was 7.0%, in contrast to 16.2% in 2013 (PORDATA, 2019b). The youth unemployment rate (population aged 15–24) was 20.3%, contrasting the dramatic proportion of 38.1% in 2013. Among the unemployed population in 2018, 51.1% were looking for a job for one and more years (long-term unemployment), i.e., 6.4% less than in the previous year. In 2017, the average monthly (gross) earnings of employees in Portugal amounted to €1,130.79 (INE, 2019a). This value was higher by €25.22 (2.3%) than in the previous year, representing a real increase (i.e., having in consideration the effect of the change in the consumer price index) of approximately 0.9% (INE, 2019a). The minimum salary in 2020 was fixed to 635 euros, an important increase of 150 euros since 2014 (PORDATA, 2019b).

The number of recipients of unemployment allowances was 406,000, i.e., 12.4% less than in 2016 and 14.7% less in terms of the values managed. The number of recipients of social integration income was 288,000, i.e., 0.2% more than in the previous year. The risk of poverty rate in the 18–64 age group was 16.7%, while in the population over 65 it was 17.7%. Children are the population group most affected by and exposed to poverty, particularly the so-called monetary poverty, i.e., they live in households in which 'per capita' income is below 60% of the median 'per capita' national income (INE, 2019a). Especially with only one active parent, one-parent households are more vulnerable, particularly if the household head is a woman, due to their lower labor force stability and wages (OECD, 2019). Despite increasing one-parent employment rates, poverty rates remain high on average since employment is no longer a guarantee for poverty prevention. Single mothers are often in low-paid jobs or part-time jobs with insufficient in-work benefits to reduce their poverty rates (Pailhé et al., 2014). Additional information about Portugal are the ratings of housing indexes. In Portugal, housing index measures the evolution of housing prices in the residential market. Housing index in Portugal increased to 141.49 index points in the second quarter of 2019 from 137.14 index points in the first quarter of 2019. **Lisbon is the most expensive Portuguese city to buy a house in**, with an average price of 4,263 euro per m². In the second and third place are Porto (2,677 euro/m²) and Faro (1,753 euro/m²). Between 2011 and 2018, the number of inhabitants in Portugal decreased from 10,542,398 to 10,276,617, which represents a rate change of –2.52% (INE, 2019b). Population estimated prevalence has decrease in 274 and increased in 34 of the 308 Portuguese municipalities mainly concentrated in the littoral and in the Lisbon metropolitan area (INE, 2019b).

With respect to educational rates, above 25% of adults (aged 25–64) in Portugal have attained tertiary education. Although this share still falls below the OECD average of nearly 40%, it represents a considerable improvement over the past decades. Among the younger generation (aged 25–34), tertiary education attainment rate in 2018 was 35%, considerably higher than the 14% attainment rate among 55–64-year-olds and 12 percentage points higher than in 2008 (OECD, 2019b). Despite high enrolment rates, tertiary education attainment in Portugal suffers from low completion rates. In Portugal, around 41% of 19–20-year-olds—

166 • MOTA, CARVALHO, & MATOS

the age at which tertiary education begins in most OECD countries—are enrolled in tertiary education, above the OECD average of 37%. Completion of tertiary education, however, remains a challenge. Only 30% of students who enter a bachelor's program graduate within three years—the expected duration of the program (average is 39%). Within six years, completion increases to 65%, which is still below the average of 67% (OECD, 2019b).

3. NORMATIVE FRAMEWORK

Portuguese culture, mostly influenced by values inherent to the Catholic Church/ Christianity, describes family formation in a close relationship with marriage. However, these links have always been gendered. Forty years ago, it was culturally expected that women leave home just to get married and usually start a family. With the end of the dictatorship and the Constitution in 1976, the struggle for women's rights contributed to their decision-making power and increased their personal freedoms, which implied changes in the family formation paradigm, as well as in gender roles. With the increase in education levels and the entry of women into the labor market, the traditional "male breadwinner and housewife" was no longer prevalent as a Portuguese family pattern—now this pattern is often associated with low education levels and lack of employment opportunities (Aboim, 2010a). In fact, in contrast to higher prevalence of women in higher education (58.4%), women seem to have consistently higher rates of analphabetism (2011 data—6.8% women, 3.5% men). Additionally, although Portugal seems to have higher full employment rates than other Southern European countries (Aboim, 2010a), unemployment seems to affect women disproportionally—a growing gap registered since 2014 (2018 data—55.5% 44.5%) (PORDATA, 2019b). Portugal is still far from equality for men and women with regard to family roles, with women assuming most roles related to children and household care (Perista et al., 2016). According to Aboim (2010a), Portuguese gender culture results from the combination of severe domestic inequalities and women's full employment rates. Dual earner couples with young children seem to be a prevailing reality in Portugal, in fact, it is the only country from the 15 countries included in the International Social Survey Programme (ISSP) that showed an increase in dual earners couples with a pre-school child (Aboim, 2010a). Portugal has the second highest rate in dual earner couples with children under the age of 3 in Europe (66%) (Wall & Escobedo, 2013). The necessity of being fully involved in both contexts is in direct clash with women's aspirations of being equally considered in the workplace and, as mentioned, they are highly involved in the labor force, working full-time and with long schedules. Due to this and the extensive labor demands, along with increasing women's expectations to win top positions, the postponement of family formation in Portugal is a reality, particularly among younger cohorts.

The new parenthood protection system, implemented since 2009, was an important turning point in leave policies in Portugal, contributing to gender equality in work-family reconciliation (Cunha et al., 2017). Besides protecting the individual rights of the mother (42 compulsory days after childbirth) and the father (5 compulsory plus 15 optional days), it introduces the possibility of parents sharing an additional 120 to 150 days of bonus leave (ISS, 2020). Since then, we observe a growing trend in shared initial parenting leave, from 12,506 applications in a 6-month period in 2009 to 20,941 applications in 2015 (Cunha et al., 2017). According to the results of the ISSP 2012 Survey, there was a favorable recognition, both by men and women, of the benefits of fathers taking up parental leaves in terms of parental relations, conjugal dynamics and gender equality, individual well-being and women's careers (Cunha et al., 2017).

At the same time, reproductive trajectories of different ages of women (25, 30 and 35) suggest in these three age cohorts that the number of children tends to decrease with the increase of age of first maternity (Cunha et al., 2016). This change in birth rates accompanied the evolution and role of young people in society, opening up the possibility of accessing various reproductive choices. In Portugal, the emergence and affirmation of sexual and reproductive rights contributed significantly to the emancipation of women and the way families developed. Contraceptive methods, initially introduced into the Portuguese National Health System through the concept of Family Planning, initiated birth control. However, from the 1990s onwards, sexual and reproductive health rapidly spread to feminist movements, guaranteeing the right to enjoy the benefits and health care, and the exercise of individual rights (Vilar, 2016).

With respect to freedom of choice, in April 2007, woman's right to interrupt her pregnancy before week 10 was introduced into the abortion law. Abortion at later stages was only allowed for specific reasons, such as risks to woman's health, rape or other sexual crimes, or fetal malformation. In February 2016, the Portuguese Parliament reversed the law imposing mandatory counseling and medical payments for women seeking an abortion through the public health service. The introduction of voluntary interruption of pregnancy was an important moment for women's freedom with regard to their sexual and reproductive health in Portugal, but it does not constitute a reason for the decline in birth rates. The number of legally induced abortions has dropped from 18,607 in 2008 to 15,492 in 2017 (EUROSTAT, 2019).

5. INSTITUTIONAL FRAMEWORK

The dynamics of family formation has changed in contemporary societies. The sequencing of life stages over the course of life is becoming more diverse and more unpredictable. Furthermore, compared to previous decades, Portugal now sees more people cohabit, have children outside marital unions, experience the dissolution of their unions, re-partner, enter stepfamilies, live separately from their children or remain childless. Family life courses have become increasingly diverse as the sequence of events and the pace at which they occur have become less standardized. The postponement of family projects results from sociocultural changes concerning greater investment in education trajectories, professional careers and prevailing individualistic values, together with economic precariousness and job uncertainty (Saraiva & Matos, 2016). Moreover, new types of households, such as single parent families, Living-Apart-Together (LAT) relationships and same sex couples are emerging.

With the decrease in marriage rates and the rise in non-marital births and divorce, the number of single-parent families has increased substantially in the last few decades (Pailhé et al., 2014). On average, across European countries, nearly 15% of all children live with one parent, about 10% in Portugal (OECD, 2019a). Women are over-represented amongst single parents—they represent 85% of single parent families in OECD countries—since women live with children more often than men and they are more often granted physical custody. At the same time, currently in Portugal, couples have further departed from the obligation of marriage and may even take on more or less separate experiences—Living Apart Together (LAT). In this case, LAT relationships can forge a compromise between a job and a relationship with someone who lives and works elsewhere (Pailhé et al., 2014). A structural factor here are the improvements in transportation and communications that increase the livability of LAT relationships. These reasons increase the probability of falling in love with someone who lives far away and make it easier to maintain a relationship over a long distance. Also, we can recognize that the increased emphasis on individualism and self-fulfillment heightens the incidence of LAT relationships. Individuals have more opportunities to create their own life course and pursue their own goals without the approval of the extended family (Pailhé et al., 2014).

Finally, in Portugal, a significant number of LGBT people are starting families. Research has been pointing to similarities between heterosexual and same-sex couples (e.g. Gato, 2016). In fact, Portugal was the first country in Europe and the fourth in the world to prohibit discrimination on the ground of sexual orientation in its Constitution. With regard to LGBT rights, Portugal was ranked 6th on the list of 45 countries in terms of equality policies in 2015 (Gato & Leal, 2019). Some egalitarian laws have allowed for improvements in recent years with regard to same-sex couples' family rights. In 2010, Portugal approved same-sex civil marriage and, in 2016, it approved access to the adoption of children, as well as access to medically assisted reproduction techniques for all women, regardless of their sexual orientation, marital status or fertility status (Gato & Leal, 2019). The number of same-sex marriages in Portugal has increased from 523 in 2017 to 607 in 2018. Between 2013 and 2018, there were 2,515 same-sex marriages, with a higher predominance among men (1,484) (INE, 2019a).

Regardless of family configuration and due to the low levels of births during the last two decades in Portugal, there was a need to implement population reinstatement measures, including incentives for family formation, in order to compensate population's aging. Over the past decade, the Portuguese government has sought to develop social policies to support families. As part of reconciling family and working life, there was a need to support households with children in

Family(ies) Formation in Portugal Since the Transition to Democracy • **169**

their early years, highlighting the government proposal for a Program to Encourage Birth and Partial Employability, which supports the transition to part-time work by parents. Also, the aim was to improve the conditions for balance tasks sharing and responsibilities between women and men, and to carry out national campaigns with businesses and the general public with dissemination in the media, public spaces and other appropriate media (Ferreira, 2016).

The reconciliation of work and family has also been supported through community funding and the still operative Axis 7—Gender Equality—of the Human Potential Operational Program (POPH) of the National Strategic Reference Framework (QREN). The main objectives were: 1) Reduce persistent inequalities between women and men in the labor market, particularly in the salary; 2) Promote female entrepreneurship as an element of women's mobilization for active economic life and disseminate good practices; 3) Encourage the implementation of equality plans in private companies and monitor compliance with the rules regarding the implementation of these plans in the state business sector; 4) Strengthen women's access mechanisms to places of economic decision (Ferreira, 2016).

For this purpose, some programs have been implemented after 2010 for couples with children, namely: 1) *Tax justice* with the reduction of "IRS" (income taxes); reduction of "IMI" (house acquisition state taxes), and benefits in social security state support; 2) *Work–family reconciliation* with one-year part-time parental leave; 100% paid with parent-alternating and flexible and simultaneous sharing of parental leave; and possibility of leave extension; employment incentives for pregnant women, mothers/fathers with children up to 3 years old; 3) *Education, health and social support* with decrease in spending on textbooks; health care during pregnancy and the first six years of life - mandatory family doctor assignment to all pregnant women; broadening medical support in infertility situations; resource condition for medical fees; 4) Local commitment with improvement and certification of "Child-Friendly Organizations", namely household tariffs for water, waste and sanitation; creation and development of "Resource Banks" at the service of children and families; vacation and after school times; reduction on student pass and family pass for public transport (Wall, 2016).

6. COUNTRY-SPECIFIC CHALLENGES TO FAMILY FORMATION

Considering the last three decades, some changes have been reported in the Portuguese society. The entry into the European Union in 1986 had a significant influence on the perspectives of social and economic standards. However, due to the underdeveloped conditions of the state, the change of traditional and conservative ideas from the dictatorial government has been a long process.

The increase in employability and educational levels in the 1980s and 1990s provided a strong incentive for stabilization with regard to family formation. Traditionally in Portugal, leaving home tended to coincide with the possibility of economic stability through permanent employment. Until then, rising schooling has guaranteed a promise of finding a more stable and better paid job. Due to the influence of the Catholic religious' culture, the beginning of family constitution was also related to leaving home at the time of marriage. However, both cultural and socio-economic reasons have brought a significant change in the last two decades. Due to the fragile economic situation in the Portuguese society in 2002, the tendency towards family formation decreased. The main reasons were related to the decrease of economic power, namely the increase of unemployment and precarious work, which led to the difficulty of finding financial autonomy (Cunha et al., 2016). As a result, many young people tended to postpone leaving home and increasingly invested in higher education to achieve a stable future work prospect (e.g., Robette, 2010; Saraiva & Matos, 2016). However, this issue was significantly gendered. These changes were more clearly seen among women, who tended to increase their education levels and seek to invest in their professional careers.

At the same time, a change of paradigm of personal emancipation happened in Portugal, so the process of separation-individuation and the transition to adulthood tended to be significantly delayed (Mendonça & Fontaine, 2013). Although Portugal has a cultural influence aimed at preserving the proximity to the family, particularly in helping with childcare and providing an extent of economic support, this change of paradigm of personal emancipation seems to have delayed the normative course of the constitution of new families. In Portugal, as in many countries on the Mediterranean coast, it has become common for children to stay in their parents' house until older ages (30 years and over) and to be economically dependent on them, as it is difficult to find financial stability to buy or rent a home. As a result, the lack of jobs has led young people to invest more in higher education in Portugal, although it is no guarantee of entry into the labor market (Mendonça & Fontaine, 2013).

In the last decade in Portugal, competition in the labor market has become increasingly aggressive, and the entry of women into work contexts usually connoted by Portuguese culture to men (e.g. construction, business and sports) represent an important aspect of postponing family formation. Some obstacles are still encountered in terms of women's employability, particularly in entities that offer resistance in respect to parity and also as well as employment rights (Cunha et al., 2016). Thus, family formation may be a consequence of women accepting commitments to have no children in the future, in order to ensure levels of attendance and unconditional willingness to perform the tasks at work (Kreyenfeld et al., 2012).

In Portugal, the increasing number of women in management positions in various areas of the economic sector is now a reality, but in many of these cases family formation is postponed or compromised by the short time spent with the family. These data corroborate the fact that the age of maternity is increasingly postponed, so that, although the mean age of women at first childbirth was 29.8 years, it is increasingly common for women to have their first child in their 40s. Given the current socio-economic experience, Portuguese society seems to experience significant cultural changes and it is beginning to accept more openly the

Family(ies) Formation in Portugal Since the Transition to Democracy • **171**

individual choices, in particular the role of women and their free choice regarding family formation or maternity.

As a direct consequence of delaying motherhood, women are facing more difficulties in getting pregnant due to lower levels of fertility, with increased anxiety about the expectation and frustration inherent to the difficulties in becoming pregnant (Cunha et al., 2016). It is noteworthy that in Portugal the age limit for access to assisted reproduction techniques (ART) funded by the Portuguese National Health Service is 42 years, with a legally established upper age limit of 50 years (CNPMA, 2020). As a result, the number of premature births is increasing and complications during pregnancy and childbirth are a reality.

7. CONCLUSION

Portugal is a country with long-term cultural traditions closely related to the Catholic Church. After a dictatorial regime that persisted for 40 years, Portugal's entry into the European Union was an important milestone for the change of the family paradigm. The global financial crisis and the Portuguese recession added additional challenges to youth economic independence and to family formation. Women's emancipation and entry into the labor market, combined with the growing concern about sexual and reproductive health, as well as important human rights achievements, such as the same sex marriage legislation, contributed also to the diversification of family's configurations in Portugal. Currently, Portugal lives a variety of new types of households such as one-parent families, Living-Apart-Together (LAT) relationships and same-sex couples. Over the years, this led to a progressive decrease in the birth rate, but a greater concern for the quality of life. The absence of economic opportunities has created a delay in the separation-individuation process of young people, who decide to continue studies and stay at home with their parents until a late age. In addition, there is the family paradigm shift, which focuses on the personal and professional needs fulfillment that delays or makes family formation unfeasible. Policies to encourage the formation of the family currently seem to be a concern for the Portuguese government entities. The country's economic recovery is now underway and could serve a further revision of family formation.

REFERENCES

Aboim, S. (2010a). Gender cultures and the division of labor in contemporary Europe: A cross-national perspective. *The Sociological Review, 58,* 171–196. doi: 10.1111/j.1467-954X.2010.01899.x

Aboim, S. (2010b). Género, família e mudança em Portugal [Gender, family and change in Portugal]. In K. Wall, S. Aboim, & V. Cunha (Eds.), *A vida familiar no masculino. Negociando velhas e novas masculinidades* [Family in male: Negotiation of old and new masculinities] (pp. 39–66). Lisboa: Comissão Para a Igualdade No Trabalho e No Emprego.

Abortion Legislation. (2016). *Abort report.* https://abort-report.eu/portugal

172 • MOTA, CARVALHO, & MATOS

Baiôa, M., Fernandes, P. J., & Meneses, F. R. (2003). The political history of nineteenth-century Portugal. *e-Journal of Portuguese History, 1*(2), 1–18.

Conselho Nacional de Procriação Medicamente Assistida (CNPMA). (2020). *Declaração Interpretativa sobre o Acesso às Técnicas de PMA e a Entrada em Vigor da Lei* n. 9/2010, de 31 de Maio, 2010 [Interpretative declaration about access to PMA thecnics and current entry law]. http://www.cnpma.org.pt. Consultado em 24 de Janeiro de 2020.

Cunha, V., Vilar, D., Wall, K., Lavinha, J., & Pereira, P. T. (2016). *A(s) problemática(s) da natalidade em Portugal. Uma questão social, económica e política* [The problem (s) of natality in Portugal. A social, economic and political question]. Imprensa de Ciências Sociais.

Cunha, V., Atalaia, S., & Wall, K. (2017). *Policy brief II. men and parental leaves: Legal framework, attitudes and practices*. Lisboa: ICS-ULisboa e CITE. http://cite.gov.pt/asstscite/images/papelhomens/Policy_Brief_II_Men_and_Parental_Leaves_Legal_framework.pdf.

Eichenbaum, M., Rebelo, S., & Resende, C.. (2016). *The Portuguese crisis and the IMF. The International Monetary Fund*. https://fronteirasxxi.pt/wp-content/uploads/2017/06/EAC__BP_16-02_05_The_Portuguese_Crisis_and_the_IMF-v2.pdf

EUROSTAT. (2019). "Eurostat and the European Statistical System—Statistics Explained". *Eurostat. 26 April 2019*. ISSN 2443-8219. *Retrieved 26 June 2019*.

Ferreira, V. (2016). Towards the de-feminization of care, fertility and family/work balance. In V. Cunha, D. Vilar, K. Wall, J. Lavinha, & P. T., Pereira, (Eds.), *A(s) problemática(s) da natalidade em Portugal. Uma questão social, económica e política* [The problem (s) of natality in Portugal. A social, economic and political question] (pp. 203–211). Imprensa de Ciências Sociais.

Gato, J. (2016). Beyond comparison: New trends in research with families with GLB members in Europe. *Journal of GLBT Family Studies, 12*(1), 1–4, DOI: https://doi.org/1 0.1080/1550428X.2016.1127095

Gato, J., & Leal, D. (2019). Parentalidade LGBT e contextos diferenciais de desenvolvimento [LGBT parenthood and developmental differential contexts]. In C. Andrade, C. Antunes, J. Gato, L. Faria, M. Matias, & S. Coimbra (Eds.), *Olhares sobre a psicologia diferencial* [Looks about differential psychology] (pp. 53–70). Mais Leituras.

INE—Instituto Nacional de Estatística. (2019a). *Anuário estatístico—Portugal* [Statistic yearbook—Portugal]. Instituto Nacional de Estatística.

INE. (2019b). *Retrato territorial de Portugal* [Territorial portrait of Portugal]. Instituto Nacional de Estatística. https://www.ine.pt/xportal/xmain?xpid=INE&xpgid=ine_publicacoes&PUBLICACOESpub_boui=358634995&PUBLICACOEStema=00&PUBLICACOESmodo=2

INE. (2019c). *Estatísticas demográficas 2018* [Demographic statistics 2018]. Lisboa: Instituto Nacional de Estatística https://www.ine.pt/xportal/xmain?xpid=INE&xpgid=ine_publicacoes&PUBLICACOESpub_boui=358632586&PUBLICACOESmodo=2

Instituto de Segurança Social, ISS (2020). Guia prático—Subsídio parental [Practical guide for parental subvention]. Departamento de Prestações e Contribuições. http://www.seg-social.pt/documents/10152/23362/3010_subsidio_parental/0bd0fafb-9e8d-4613-8bb4-e9bf3ac7e5f1

Kreyenfeld, M., Andersson, G., & Pailhé A., (2012). Economic uncertainty and family dynamics in Europe. *Demographic Research, 27*(28), 835–852. http://www.demographic-research.org/special/12/

Robette, N. (2010). The diversity of pathways to adulthood in France: Evidence from a holistic approach. *Advances in Life Course Research, 15,* 89–96.

Sousa, H. (1996) *Communications policy in Portugal and its links with the European union: An analysis of the telecommunications and television broadcasting sectors from the mid-1980s up until the mid-1990s.* PhD Dissertation. School of Social Sciences, City University, Londres.

Mendonça, M., & Fontaine, A. M. (2013). Late nest leaving in Portugal: Its effects on individuation and parent-child relationships. *Emerging Adulthood, 1,* 233–244. doi: 10.1177/2167696813481773

OECD. (2019a). *Economic surveys—Portugal.* Copyright Clearance Center (CCC). www.oecd.org/eco/surveys/portugal-economic-snapshot

OECD .(2019b). *Education at a glance 2019: OECD Indicators.* OECD Publishing. https://dx.doi.org/10.1787/f8d7880d-en.

Pailhé, A., Mortelmans, D., Castro, T., Trilla, C. C., Digoix, M., Festy, P., Krapf, S., Kreyenfeld, M., Lyssens-Danneboom, V., Martín-García, T., Rault, W., Thévenon, O., & Laurent Toulemon,.L. (2014). *State-of-the-art report: Changes in the life course.* Families and Societies Working Paper Series, 6. European Union's Seventh Framework.

Perista, H., Cardoso, A., Brázia, A., Abrantes, M., Perista, P., & Quintal, E. (2016). Os usos do tempo de homens e de mulheres em Portugal [The time use of men and women in Portugal]. *Policy Brief,* Lisboa, CESIS e CITE. Disponível em http://cite.gov.pt/pt/destaques/complementosDestqs2/INUT_brochura.pdf

Perista A., & Carrilho, P. (2015). *Portugal: Immigrants bear brunt of rising unemployment. European Foundation for the Improvement of Living and Working Conditions.* https://www.eurofound.europa.eu/publications/article/2015/portugal-immigrants-bear-brunt-of-rising-unemployment

PEO. (2015). Portugal economic outlook. *Focus Economics.* 17 August 2015. Retrieved 28 July 2015 from: https://www.focus-economics.com/countries/portugal

PORDATA. (2019a). *Retrato de Portugal na Europa* [Portrait of Portugal in Europe]. Edição 2019. Fundação Manuel Francisco dos Santos. https://www.pordata.pt/ebooks/PT_EU2019v20191020/mobile/index.html

PORDATA. (2019b). *Portugal statistics—Population, social protection and employment and labour market statistics.* https://www.pordata.pt/en/Europe https://www.pordata.pt/en/Portugal

Saraiva, L. M., & Matos, P. M. (2016). Becoming an adult in Portugal: Negotiating pathways between opportunities and constraints. In R. Zukauskiene (Ed.), *Emerging adulthood in a European context* (pp. 117–137). Routledge.

SEF/GEPF. (2019). *Relatório de Imigração, Fronteiras e Asilo 2018* [Immigration, Borders and Asylum Report 2018]. Serviço de Estrangeiros e Fronteiras. https://sefstat.sef.pt/Docs/Rifa2018.pdf

Vilar, D. (2016). A queda da natalidade, o controlo dos nascimentos e a saúde e os direitos sexuais e reprodutivos [Falling birth rates, birth control and sexual and reproductive health and rights and reproductive]. In V. Cunha, D. Vilar, K. Wall, J. Lavinha & P. T. Pereira (Eds.), *A(s)Problemática(s) da Natalidade em Portugal. Uma Questão*

174 • MOTA, CARVALHO, & MATOS

Social, Económica e Política [The problem (s) of natality in Portugal. A social, economic and political question] (pp. 137–142). Imprensa de Ciências Sociais.

Wall, K. (2016). Family policies in Portugal: Brief overview and recent developments. In V. Cunha, D. Vilar, K. Wall, J. Lavinha & P.T., Pereira, (orgs.) (2016). *A(s) Problemática(s) da Natalidade em Portugal. Uma Questão Social, Económica e Política* [The Problem (s) of Natality in Portugal. A Social, Economic and Political Question] (pp. 191–201). Imprensa de Ciências Sociais.

Wall, K., & Correia, S. (2014). *Changes in family policies since 2010: Country overview Portugal. Tasks 6a & 6b.* EUROFOUND PROJECT Families in the economic crisis: mapping policy responses in 5 European Member States. https://repositorio.ul.pt/bitstream/10451/22555/1/ICs_KWall_EUROFOUND_%20PortugalTask6a6b_RelatorioFinal-1.pdf.

CHAPTER 11

FAMILY FORMATION IN SERBIA BETWEEN NORMATIVE LEGACY, STRUCTURAL CONSTRAINTS, AND DESIRED PROSPECTS

Smiljka Tomanović and Dragan Stanojević
University of Belgrade

NATIONAL CONTEXT

Serbia is a Western Balkan country that shares historical, sociological, and cultural features with the Mediterranean region, but also with the ex-socialist countries of South East Europe. Social history of Serbia is usually considered through several periods: 1. from the beginning of the 9th century till the end of World War II, 2. period of socialism (1944–1991), 3. blocked post-socialist transformation (1991–2000), and 4. unblocked post-socialist transformation.

The first period refers to the establishment of an independent state (at first on its own and after World War I as part of a federation—Kingdom of Serbs, Croats and Slovenes, and the first Yugoslavia) after the five-century rule of the Ottoman Empire. The society was mostly agrarian with a very small percentage of urban

---

Family Formation Among Youth in Europe: Coping With Socio-Economic Disadvantages,
pages 175–190.
Copyright © 2022 by Information Age Publishing
www.infoagepub.com
All rights of reproduction in any form reserved.

175

176 • SMILJKA TOMANOVIĆ & DRAGAN STANOJEVIĆ

population and low industrial production. This period was dominated by the Balkan family household whose key features were patrilocality, patrilineality, and a clear gender and generational division of roles and powers (Kazer, 2002). The first half of the twentieth century brought somewhat faster modernization due to the creation of a federation and more intense external communication, but the accelerated modernization of the country came only after World War II and the socialist revolution.

In addition to the intensive urbanization and industrialization of the country, the construction of infrastructure, the development of education and the social protection system, the new political project has legally established equality between men and women. The Constitution of 1946 for the first time granted women the right to vote, the right to work (regardless of their husband's permission, as was previously the case) and the right to equal pay as men. The new legal solutions eliminated the legal subordination of the wife to the husband, divorce became easier (and made possible by mutual agreement of the spouses) and parents became equal in terms of rights and obligations towards children. The law specifically postulated the protection of women and mothers, and for the first time introduced measures for the protection of pregnant women and women in childbirth, such as maternity leave. During the 1960s and 1970s, the attitude towards abortion changed, which in 1974 was entered into the Constitution as a right of women (Gudac-Dodić, 2006). Socialism proclaimed employment of women full-time, and the project of creating a working class in a still dominant agrarian society required the development of an education system. In a few decades, illiteracy was almost eradicated, and the gap in educational attainment also narrowed, so that, by the 1980s, women were on average better educated than men (Stanojević, 2013). Significant changes were also taking place in the labor market, so that by the 1980s, about 40% of women were working (Gudac-Dodić, 2006). Although the modernization effects of socialism were unequivocal, not all patriarchal practices could change in one generation, especially given that the socialist authorities did not pay much political attention to the private sphere, which mostly remained under the influence of patriarchal norms. Equalization of men and women in the public sphere often meant putting a "double burden" on women in their work and household responsibilities and only gradually led to changes in the private sphere.

The end of socialism, in the early 1990s, was marked by the breakup of the Yugoslav federation, wars, isolation of the country, the economic crisis, rising unemployment and social inequalities, the introduction of multi-party democracy, but also a deep political crisis that lasted for a decade. This period was marked by institutional transformation and the survival of many conservative practices. Although institutions have been transformed by the introduction of political pluralism and a market economy, the role of the state in the redistribution of capital remains significant and represents a key mechanism of capital conversion appropriated by a part of the former socialist nomenklatura (Lazić, 2011). During this period, the social protection system collapsed, the population became impoverished, which, in addition to intensifying work and diversifying the working strategies of individuals and families (more often a combination of formal, additional and informal work), also resulted in greater reliance on informal forms of family support and exchange. Intergenerational solidarity also strengthened and for many people brought back certain traditional practices to the family repertoire—such as babysitting by grandparents (Babović, 2004).

The last, fourth period, began with the democratic upheaval in October 2000 and the gradual stabilization of political and economic institutions, the gradual rise in standards, the decline in unemployment and the international opening of the country. However, these processes were rather slow and were further slowed by the onset of the 2008 economic crisis. From 2008 until 2013, production growth again declined and unemployment increased by as much as 25% in 2013 (SORS, 2014).

There are certain anti-modern trends that continue through both periods of post-socialist transformation, which are also relevant for family formation. There exists widespread system corruption in various segments of society, also perceived by the citizens. According to the Corruption Perception Index of Transparency International (CPI), the most well-known ranking of countries according to perception of corruption in the public sector, Serbia is still considered a country where the level of corruption is high, as the score was under 50 out of possible 100 points (41) for 2017. Corruption is perceived as a big public issue, but also normalized by young people (Lavrič et al., 2019), who express very low level of trust in institutions, particularly political ones (Ibid.). During a period of nationalistic revival during the 1990s, but also after 2000, Serbia has witnessed strong retraditionalization of public discourse and sphere, including de-secularization: increasing influence of the Serbian Orthodox Church, religious education in primary and secondary schools (mandatory, optional with civic education), and rise of right-wing movements and organizations.

Unfinished economic and social system transformation, frequent global economic fluctuations, low trust in corrupt institutions, and retraditionalization strongly influence transitions to adulthood, including family formation.

DEMOGRAPHIC TRENDS RELEVANT TO FAMILY FORMATION

Changes in **household structure** reveal, on the one hand, the trend of an aging population, and on the other, the persistence of traditional forms of households shared between multiple generations. According to the latest census (2011), 22.3% of households are single, 18.5% of couples live without children, 36.4% of households are two-parent families, about 12% are single parents with child/children. Trends indicate an increase in the share of elderly and single households, mainly comprised of people over 65, who make up 20% of the population. Although during and after the twentieth century, we are detecting a downward trend in the share of extended family households, Serbia is characterized by a relatively high share of this family form, which in 1971 amounted to 25.9% and 18.9% in

2011 (Statistical Office of the Republic of Serbia, 2013). The reason for the continuous existence of extended families lies, on the one hand, in the cultural model of shared family life characteristic of the Balkan and Mediterranean societies and, on the other hand, to a significant extent in the lack of housing opportunities for young couples.

Family formation patterns in Serbia suggest a more traditional type with the following characteristics. High and relatively stable **marriage** rates (5.6 in 2002, 5.2 in 2018, EUROSTAT), with a very low share of cohabitation, which was 8.5% in the population over 15 (Statistical Office of the Republic of Serbia, 2013), indicate to us that the population generally opts for marriage. In a comparative framework, Serbia is one of the countries with a high marriage rate and in the region is between countries like Croatia and Slovenia which have a slightly lower rate, and Macedonia and Montenegro with slightly higher rates of nuptiality.

The average age at first marriage is increasing relatively quickly with both men and women, as this limit has shifted by two years in the last fifteen years. Thus, in 2004, the average age of first-time marriage for women was 26.2, and in 2017, it was 28.2. For men, it was 29.6 in 2012, while in 2017, it was 31.3. Although this shift is significant, Serbia still belongs to the group of European countries of relatively early marriage. The reasons for delaying marriage for later years are to a lesser extent due to global developments in value change and extended education, and to a greater extent due to the difficult post-socialist transition. That is, structural constraints (slow transitions to the labor market, inaccessible housing, and underdeveloped support for parenting) often lead to a strategy of delaying family transition for young people. Since the birth of a child is perceived as the purpose of marriage (Tomanović & Ignjatović, 2006a), marriage and birth are usually synchronized (Tomanović & Ignjatović, 2006b). The trend of delaying marriage is associated with the increasing age at first **births** which was 27.8 in 2017 (EUROSTAT). Regardless of long-term delaying childbirth trend (Figure 11.1), the low fertility rate has been stable for years and it varies from 1.45 in 2005 to 1.49 in 2018 (EUROSTAT).

Considering the high marriage rate, Serbia is characterized by a relatively low rate of extramarital births, which stood at 26.3 in 2017, but we should bear in mind that a significant number of cohabiting partners enter into marriage after having a child. Cohabitation and extramarital births are in most cases the pre-stages of married life. Early marriages are mainly related to the Roma population, so among the general population, 0.6% of women ages 15–49 were first married or in union before age 15, while among the Roma population it was 16.9%. Among women ages 20–49, 6.8% were first married or in union before age 18, while for Roma women this percentage goes to 57% (MICS, 2014).

Significant **migrations** from Serbia to the western world began after World War II and during the 1970s when SFR Yugoslavia opened its borders for the population. Since then, flows mainly of the poorer and lower educated population, have led to Germany, Austria, France, the USA, and others. A significant migra-

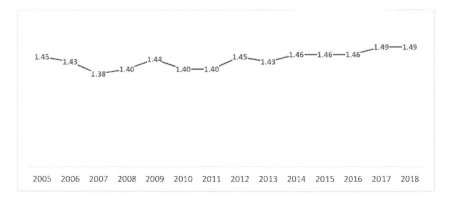

FIGURE 11.1.   Total Fertility Rates From 2005–2018. Source: EUROSTAT database

tory wave happened in the 1990s when skilled and highly educated people migrated due to the war and very bad political situation. In the last two decades, the most common reasons for migration have again become economic ones, and moving closer to the EU and opening up the European market has made it easier for people with different qualifications and educational backgrounds. Even though there is a significant discrepancy in data,[1] according to the official local statistics, there are currently over 300,000 Serbian citizens working abroad and this number is rapidly increasing. Still, the IMF Country Report indicates that between 2008 and 2016, over 400,000 people moved from Serbia to OECD countries (around 40–50,000 people a year). Projections indicate that the population of Serbia will decrease by around 5% by 2030, and around 15–20% by 2050, mostly due to migration of younger population, which will lead to a decrease and aging of the working population, increase of the old-age dependence, and pressure on healthcare and pension system (Batog et al., 2019).

SOCIO-ECONOMIC CONDITIONS

Labor Market

Structural context of transition to parenthood in Serbia is marked by: very unfavorable situation on the labor market—its irregularity, high unemployment and unregulated precarious employment of the young (Tomanović & Stanojević, 2015), as well as a gender gap in the level of employment and income.

The labor market in Serbia is characterized by a gender gap in employment, which has been slightly reducing with the increase of unemployment from 2009 (Statistical Office of the Republic of Serbia, 2014). There are also gender differ-

---

[1] For example, according to local data sources, there are currently 55,999 Serbian citizens living in Germany, and according to EUROSTAT that number is four times higher—193,144 (Bobić et al., 2016, p. 28).

ences in the level of income (Ibid, p. 76). The birth of the first child increases the employment of parents, men more than women, but the birth of each subsequent child reduces the woman's level of employment (Statistical Office of the Republic of Serbia, 2011, p. 56). The full-time employment of men and women is the legacy of the socialist ideal for the economy and for gender relations in the public sphere. Neither the working culture nor the structure of the labor market and the normative framework in post-socialist Serbia are sensitized to provide flexible work arrangements for parents.

This situation is exacerbated by labor market flexibility processes that have intensified since the economic crisis began. In Serbia, these processes are marked by, on the one hand, a significant increase in the share of temporary and occasional jobs and, on the other, an increasingly intense deregulation of work. Thus, from 2008 to 2016, the share of young people performing full-time jobs has steadily dropped 24 percentage points and the share of those with temporary contracts has more than doubled (see Figure 11.2).

The deregulation of work is reflected in the lack of regulation of new, flexible forms of work, so an increasing number of working young people cannot exercise their rights to sick leave, holidays, retirement, and health insurance, which puts them in a position of living in "extended present" and does not give the possibility of long-term planning that family life entails. Insufficient regulation of the labor market is also reflected in the important role that informal relationships play in employment and promotion so that three quarters of young people (77%) believe that it is justified to use them for these purposes (Popadić et al., 2019). Further-

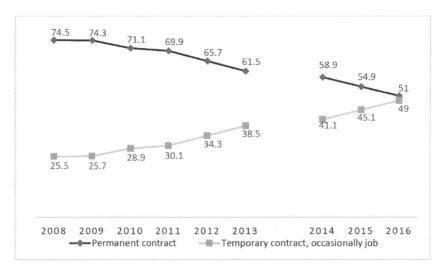

FIGURE 11.2. Types of Employment Contracts in Period 2008–2016 (age 18–29). Source: Stanojević, 2017. Labor Force Survey database

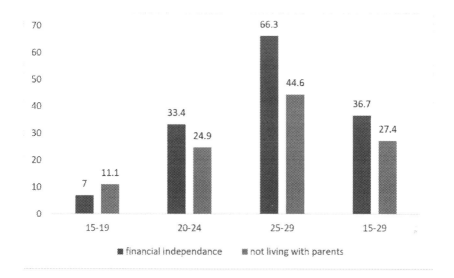

FIGURE 11.3. Financial and Housing Independence of Young People (share of young people who are fully financially independent / who do not live with parents, by age, in %). Source: Tomanović, Stanojević, 2015.

more, political clientelism is seen as legitimate instrumental channel for employment: young people use party membership as a form of bridging social capital, thereby adapting to dominant game rules (Tomanović & Stanojević, 2015). In Serbia, as well as in other SEE countries, young people "due to skills mismatches are often in a position of working in jobs that are not within their profession" (Lavrič et al., 2019, p. 29), which further complicates their transition within the work sphere. The consequence is a very low percentage of financially independent young people. The 2015 data show the share of financially independent young people indicating a very slow transition to the labor market (Figure 11.3).

Housing

Serbia belongs to the cluster of South East European countries where home-leaving occurs very late and households with extended families are common as a strategy of pooling together family resources. Around three-quarters of young people aged 15–29 lived with their parents in 2015 (Figure 11.3) and of 18–27 in 2018 (Lavrič et al., 2019). For half of them, it was a most convenient solution, while another 40% state financial dependence as the main obstacle to moving out (Ibid, p. 91). That is related to structural factors inhibiting home leaving, such as high unemployment, low wages and unaffordable housing (Iacovou, 2010). There are no social housing schemes, subsidized mortgages, state or community-

182 • SMILJKA TOMANOVIĆ & DRAGAN STANOJEVIĆ

controlled rents, or other state measures available, which would facilitate housing independence of young people in Serbia.

One of the most common strategies that the young parents apply at the beginning of their family life is to live with their parents (Tomanović et al., 2016): a quarter of young families lived in the parental household, according to a 2012 survey study (Tomanović et al., 2012).

Education

Research on education shows that its equity is still a big issue in Serbia. One of the indicators of inequality in education is school attendance: for primary school it is just 64% for Roma children compared to 96% of general population (truancy is 36% for Roma children and 4% for general population), among whom attendance of secondary school is 89%, while it is just 22% for Roma children (here, truancy is 78% for Roma and 11% for general population children. MICS, 2014).

Enrolment in tertiary education in Serbia is quite high—almost two thirds (62.5%) of young people enter higher education (World Bank, 2015). On the other hand, several recent studies point out that access to education is highly determined by socio-economic status—higher education level of parents significantly increases a young person's chances for higher education (Tomanović & Stanojević, 2015; Lavrič et al., 2019). Young people with higher SES are more educated, have higher educational aspirations, and better average grade levels (Popadić et al., 2019). Education is relying almost solely on parental family financial and other support, as indicated, among other things, by the finding from Eurostudent study that the only financial source for 88% students in Serbia is their parents, while institutional support is the main financial resource for just 7% of the students (Eurostudent, 2017).

A low level of institutional support for education and employment and an inflexible educational system do not allow young people to combine education, work and parenthood (Tomanović et al., 2012). One of the consequences is gender inequality revealed by a transition to parenthood study: young women, particularly those with lower level of education, tend to leave schooling after becoming mothers (Poleti et al., 2017; Tomanović et al., 2016).

Poverty and Social Exclusion

Serbia is one of the European countries with highly pronounced income inequalities. The Gini index for 2018 was as high as 35.6 while the EU average was 30.9 and only two European countries, Lithuania and Bulgaria, have a higher index. The (relative) poverty risk rate in Serbia in 2018 was 24.3%, which, in a comparative perspective, places Serbia as the country with the highest poverty risk in Europe.

The EU average for 2018 was 17.1% (EUROSTAT). Parenting carries a higher degree of risk since households with children are more vulnerable (26.8%), and especially those of single-parent families (36.5%) and those where parents have more than two children (53.6%). Low incomes, high unemployment rates, regional disparities in the labor market and insufficient cash transfers for families with children put them at high risk. The absolute poverty rate is 7.1% and has been constant over the last decade, with the same categories being affected as by relative poverty (SIPRU, 2019).

NORMATIVE FRAMEWORK

Normative framework of familism is dominant among young people in Serbia. It is evidenced through the high value placed on starting a family, marriage and childbirth (Popadić et al., 2019, p. 33), which are normatively equated with the acquisition of autonomy and transition to adulthood (Tomanović & Ignjatović, 2006a). This gives family transitions upmost significance within transition to adulthood (Tomanović, 2012; Tomanović & Ignjatović, 2010). The young mainly support hetero-normative model of married couple with children as the projection of their own future (Lavrič et al., 2019; Tomanović & Stanojević, 2015). Although cohabitation is normatively accepted as a legitimate life partnership, it is only practiced by between 3 and 6 per cent of the young, according to national representative surveys from 2011 to 2018 (Popadić et al., 2019; Tomanović et al., 2012; Tomanović & Stanojević, 2015).

While the 2015 study revealed that a half of young people believed abortion should be banned and expressed significant intolerance towards homosexuals (Tomanović & Stanojević, 2015, p. 85, 86), a more recent study from 2018 indicates increasing tolerance towards abortion and homosexuality among young people in Serbia (Lavrič et al., 2019, p. 55).

Gender normative regime dominated by a patriarchal pattern is apparent in young people's attitudes on appropriate age of marriage and parenthood, as well as in anticipated gender roles and identities. The timing of marriage reveals this pattern: the best perceived age was on average 28.5 for men, and 26.3 for women (Popadić et al., 2019, p. 32; Tomanović & Stanojević, 2015). One of the studies revealed that gender differences that occur in this domain are the most distinctive, compared to education and employment, but they do not reflect the detraditionalization of gender roles by young women, rather an acceptance of the traditionally defined differences between the instrumental role of men and the expressive role of women (Tomanović & Stanojević, 2015, p. 55). Young females only express contemporary attitudes in their assessment of the higher optimal age for entering into marriage, as well as their desire for a smaller number of children, which can be interpreted as "making virtue out of necessity" (Ibid., p. 55). On the other hand, a recent comparative and longitudinal study reveals that women, particularly younger ones at the age 20–24, contest the pattern by expressing less support to patriarchal value orientation than their male peers (Pešić & Stanojević, 2019).

Several studies (Blagojević, 2014; Blagojević-Hjuson, 2013; Stanojević, 2018; Tomanović et al., 2016) point at the still present self-realization of identity through gender roles of the "caring mother" for young women and a "responsible provider for the family" for young men. It has also been accepted by young parents as a part of an ethic of parental self-sacrifice for the benefit of children and their best interests (Tomanović et al., 2016). There is also trend of deconstruction of this gender norm among urban highly educated young people (Ibid.), particularly young women (Pešić & Stanojević, 2019).

INSTITUTIONAL FRAMEWORK

The country belongs to the model of institutional support to parenthood that is typical for post-socialist societies: support means a long period of parental leave, moderately developed system of pre-school institutions, but very low cash transfers and benefits for children and child care (Thevenon, 2011). Family support measures in policy practices are presented both as measures of family social protection and as measures of fertility increase, the latter being declaratively high on the government agenda in the last few years. There are currently three types of institutional family support measures: financial, organizational and advisory. Financial includes 1. parental allowance which is a one-time support measure and is granted to all parents after the birth of the child (but only up to the fourth child); 2. child allowance for parents with low income, it is received while the child is in the education system but not after the age of 21. Some of the financial support to parents is also provided by local governments, depending on the available funds. Financial support for families and cash transfers for children are very low and restricted, and are not targeting well the poor families. Family cash benefits are especially poorly targeted. One study shows that 59.4% of children eligible for child allowance are not covered with this program (Matković & Mijatović, 2012).

Paid full salary parental leave after childbirth is granted up to one year but just to employed parents. One month before childbirth, mothers must take maternity leave, three months after birth also belong to the mother as part of maternity leave, while the next eight months of parental leave may be used by either parent. Only employed parents are entitled to this measure, so only those who work are granted financial support during this period. The Law on Financial Support for Families with Children, which was adopted in 2018, changes the requirements for receiving financial compensation for the duration of parental leave. On the one hand, it made the aid available also to those without full-time employment (those with part-time jobs, and temporary contracts, which was not the case before), but it also significantly tightened the requirements, such as a minimum of 18 months of continuous work in order to be eligible for full compensation (in the amount of their earnings). Although the leave for baby-care and sick-child care has been granted for fathers by the law from 2001, they very seldom exercise this in practice, thereby reproducing patriarchal order, which is reinforced by the dominant working culture.

The infrastructure of low cost and subsidized public child care is inherited from the socialist period, but the coverage of children by day care facilities is not sufficient (38.3% of children from 3–6.5 years old in 2014), particularly of children aged under 3 (19.1%) and in rural and less developed regions of Serbia (Statistical Office of the Republic of Serbia, 2017). Therefore, parents with young children mainly rely on non-institutional resources, such as support from informal networks, particularly their parents (Tomanović, 2010). More than two-thirds of young parents (up to 35 years old) regularly (28.8%) or occasionally (37%) use their parents' support for childcare (Tomanović et al., 2012). This exchange is more common among young people from rural areas and among the employed who need this type of help mostly due to the lack of infrastructure.

Under the Constitution and the Family Law, marital and extra-marital heterosexual unions are legally equal, but most legal solutions favor marriage and do not recognize consensual unions since they are not clearly defined anywhere. Thus, when purchasing the first real estate, the right to tax deduction is exercised by both spouses, but by only one partner if it is a consensual union. Also, in case of death, the union partner does not have the right to inherit property, nor is s/he entitled to a family pension. Some of the practical policy measures in the recent past have focused solely on married couples, such as subsidized housing loans for married couples, etc.

Single-parent families are recognized in the social protection system as a particularly vulnerable category, and a specific set of measures is dedicated to protecting them. However, in public discourses, this type of family is still largely viewed as incomplete and deviant. The legislation does not recognize same-sex marriages or unions, and there are significant conservative forces in the country that oppose their recognition.

In 2018, a new Birth Incentive Strategy was adopted, which contains, in addition to direct measures to increase fertility, a range of measures to support families with children as well as young people who wish to become parents. The given strategy did not result in action plans to formulate clear practical policies, so it is expected that this strategy, much like the previous one from 2008, will remain "on paper".

The studies on young parents' experiences reveal that they were not satisfied with the support gathered from the state and its institutions, nor they counted on it in early parenthood (Tomanović, 2012, p. 140). Both quantitative (Stanković et al., 2017) and qualitative (Stanković, 2014) findings on pregnancy and child-birth point that, for some women, institutional medical treatment was an unpleasant experience, while many felt that they were objectified during the process and denied their subjectivity. Young parents, particularly mothers, complained about inadequate medical support they received while with their new-born baby (Tomanović et al., 2016). Mothers expressed dissatisfaction with almost any form of existing measures of support to parenthood: they were least satisfied with employment, financial and housing support (Sekulić, 2017, p. 27) and also with support to Work-Family balance (Poleti & Petrović Trifunović, 2017).

COUNTRY-SPECIFIC CHALLENGES TO FAMILY FORMATION

Main prerequisites for family formation stated by young people in Serbia are interrelated feelings of existential and emotional certainty and security (Tomanović et al., 2016). Therefore, country specific challenges to family formation come from the risky economic, political and social environment in general. Those have particular hazardous effects on certain categories of young people. Challenges, therefore, should be looked at cross-sectionally, considering gender, class, and ethnicity.

Economic Vulnerability of Young People

An increasingly flexible labor market within an insufficiently defined and reliable legal framework constitutes a risky economic environment, particularly for young people at the beginning of their working career. The increasing number of precarious jobs and less permanent contracts do not provide bases for economic security and long-term planning that parenthood requires.

Social Uncertainty and Low Quality of Life

The political sphere marked by clientelism and party patronage hinders issues of family formation, such as: affordable education, easy transition from education to work, fair chances in education and labor market, better support for family (affordable housing, cash transfers, infrastructure, etc.) to become public concern at the top of the political agenda. For many young parents, parenting decreases the quality of life in terms of less financial resources, living in parental household, getting an additional job (for men) or quitting the job (for women), struggling for work-family balance (particularly mothers), etc. (Tomanović et al., 2016).

Underdeveloped and Unreliable Institutional Framework

The studies provide evidence of low trust in institutions in general among young people (e.g., Popadić et al., 2019; Tomanović & Stanojević, 2015). Perception and experience of institutional framework for family formation as unreliable adds to the feeling of existential insecurity and prevents long-term planning required for parenthood among young people who do not have children. Furthermore, young parents do not have positive experiences concerning institutional support for parenthood and do not count on it (Tomanović et al., 2016).

Migrations of Young People

The above outlined the economic, political and social factors present strong "push" factors for young people in Serbia to emigrate (Lavrič et al., 2019). The so-called "pull" factors are related to the EU integration process and new immigration rules adopted by some countries (e.g., Germany) that increase chances for education and employment in Europe, Canada, the USA, etc. Emigration of

Family Formation in Serbia • **187**

the young has different consequences on family formation, depending on the host country polices, whether it is facilitating family reunification or family formation (e.g., Norway) or putting constraints on those (e.g., Malta). In any case, emigration postpones family formation in the life course of a young person. For the country of origin—Serbia, emigration of the young, which is increasingly becoming permanent, profoundly changes the demographic structure of the population, which is aging and experiencing lower fertility rates.

Gender Inequalities and Gender Related Risks

Enduring patriarchal norms and practices are evident in the labor market, such as: unequal chances for employment and more chances for becoming redundant for women, gender pay gap, etc., as well as in households through highly unequal division of domestic work. Those are specific risks that drain women's resources and result, among other things, in their leaving education and work—for lower social status women, or postponing the first child birth and giving up on having more children, for those with more education. A particular challenge for young women comes from the nationalist conservative public discourse, supported also by the ruling party, which puts pressure on them to give birth and thereby fulfil their duty to contribute to the survival of the Nation in danger.

Risks of Early Motherhood for Roma Women

The risks for young women of lower social status are particularly challenging for Roma women, with high rates of early marriages that lead to school dropouts, disadvantages in the labor market and high dependency of women.

CONCLUSION

By the features of transitions and family formation, Serbia belongs to the group of southern European countries, where young people leave the parental household at a later age in order to establish their own family household (Iacovou, 2002). Within the pattern, family transition takes center place in relation to the education-to-work transition, in both meaning and significance (Tomanović & Ignjatović, 2010). This form is supported by the institutional framework of post-socialist variation of familistic (sub-protective) transition regimes (Walther et al., 2009)—with a considerable role of the state, but with the increasing importance of family, its resources and support (Tomanović, 2012).

Country specific features of family formation are marked by a familistic normative framework that assigns a high value to starting a family, marriage and childbirth, but also with considerable structural constraints and adversities leading to the so-called "postponement culture" (Reiter, 2009)—with the postponement of the starting of a family, particularly among young people with higher education (Tomanović, 2012, p. 143).

188 • SMILJKA TOMANOVIĆ & DRAGAN STANOJEVIĆ

Bearing in mind the aforementioned, we conclude that state policies should focus on improving the labor market and legislative conditions, institutional framework and its reliability, and quality of life for population, in general, and young people, in particular, as well as on developing targeted measures of support to family formation and parenthood.

REFERENCES

Babović, M. (2004). Ekonomske strategije domaćinstava u postsocijalističkoj transformaciji Srbije [Economic strategies of households in post-socialist transformation of Serbia]. In A. Milić, (Ed.), *Društvena transformacija i strategije društvenih grupa: svakodnevica Srbije na početku trećeg milenijuma* [Social transformation and strategies of social groups: the everyday life of Serbia at the beginning of the third millennium] (pp. 239–275). Institute for Sociological Research at Faculty of Philosophy.

Batog, C., Crivelli, E., Ilyina, A., Jakab, Z., Lee, J., Musayev, A., Petrova, I., Scott, A., Shabunina, A., Tudyka, A., Xu, X. C., & Zhang, R. (2019). *Demographic Headwinds in Central and Eastern Europe, No. 19/12* International Monetary Fund.

Blagojević, M. (2014). Transnationalization and its absence: The Balkan semiperipheral perspective on masculinities. In J. Hearn, M. Blagojević, & K. Harrison (Eds.), *Rethinking transnational men: Beyond, between and within nations*. Routledge.

Blagojević-Hjuson, M. (2013). *Rodni barometar u Srbiji: Razvoj i svakodnevni život* [Gender Barometer in Serbia: Development and Everyday Life], UN Women.

Bobić, M., Vesković-Anđelković, M., & Kokotović-Kanazir, V. (2016). *Study on external and internal migration of Serbia's citizens with particular focus on youth*. International Organization for Migration.

EUROSTAT. (2020). *EUROSTAT database.* https://ec.europa.eu/eurostat/help/first-visit/database

Eurostudent. (2017). *EUROSTUDENT database.* https://database.eurostudent.eu/drm/

Gudac-Dodić, V. (2006). *Žena u socijalizmu* [Woman during socialism]. Institut za noviju istoriju Srbije.

Iacovou, M. (2002). Regional differences in the transition to adulthood. *The Annals of the American Academy of Political and Social Science, 580*(1), 40–69.

Iacovou, M. (2010). Leaving home: Independence, togetherness and income. *Advances in Life Course Research, 15*(4), 147–160.

Kazer, K. (2002). *Porodica i srodstvo na Balkanu: analiza jedne kulture koja nestaje* [Family and kinship in the Balkans: an analysis of a disappearing culture]. Udruženje za društvenu istoriju.

Lavrič, M., Tomanović, S., & Jusić, M. (2019). *Youth study southeast Europe 2018/2019,* Friedrich Ebert Stiftung

Lazić, M. (2011). *Čekajući kapitalizam* [Waiting for Capitalism]. Službeni glasnik.

Matković, G., & Mijatović, B. (2012). *Program dečijih dodataka u Srbiji* [The program of child allowances in Serbia]. UNICEF and CLD.

MICS—Serbia Multiple Indicator Cluster Survey and Serbia Roma Settlements Multiple Indicator Cluster Survey. (2014). *Final reports.* Statistical Office of the Republic of Serbia and UNICEF.

Pešić, J., & Stanojević, D. (2019). Odnos prema rodnoj podeli uloga u privatnoj i javnoj sferi u Srbiji 1989–2018 [Attitudes towards the gender division of roles in the pri-

Family Formation in Serbia • **189**

vate and public spheres in Serbia 1989–2018]. Paper presented at Feminism and the Left—Then and Now, Faculty of Philosophy Belgrade.

Poleti, D., & Petrović Trifunović, T. (2017). Institucionalna podrška usklađivanju profesionalne i porodične sfere u Srbiji [Institutional support for work-family balance in Serbia]. *Limes Plus* 2/2017: 49—74.

Popadić, D., Pavlović, Z., & Mihailović, S. (2019). *Youth study Serbia 2018/2019*. Friedrich Ebert Stiftung.

Reiter, H. (2009). Beyond the equation model of society—Postponement of motherhood in post-state socialism in an interdisciplinary life-course perspective. *Innovation: The European Journal of Social Science Research, 22*(2), 233–246.

Sekulić, N. (2017). Populaciona politika iz ugla žena—analiza iskustava i političkih opredeljenja [Population politics from women's perspective—Analysis of the experiences and political attitudes]. *Limes Plus, 2,* 15–48.

SIPRU. (2019). *Ocena apsolutnog siromaštva u Srbiji u 2018. godini* [Absolute poverty assessment in Serbia in 2018]. SIPRU. http://socijalnoukljucivanje.gov.rs/wp-content/uploads/2019/10/Ocena_apsolutnog_siromastva_u_2018_cir.pdf

SORS. (2014). *Anketa o radnoj snazi april I kvartal, Podaci pre revizije, Saopštenje* [Labor force survey April 1 Quarterly, Pre-Audit Data, Release]. Belgrade: Republički zavod za statistiku.

Stanković, B. (2014). Žena kao subjekt porođaja: telesni, tehnološki i institucionalni aspekti. [Woman as the subject of childbirth: Physical, technological and institutional aspects]. *Sociologija, 56*(4), 524–544.

Stanković, B., Skočajić, M., & Đorđević, A. (2017). Upravljanje porođajem u Srbiji: Medicinske intervencije i porođajna iskustva [Managing child birth in Serbia: Medical interventions and birth experiences]. *Limes Plus, 2,* 197–225.

Stanojević, D. (2013). Međugeneracijska obrazovna pokretljivost u Srbiji u XX veku [Intergenerational educational mobility in Serbia in the 20th century]. In M. Lazić & S. Cvejić (Eds.), *+Promene osnovnih struktura društva Srbije u periodu ubrzane transformacije* [Changes in the basic structures of Serbian society in the period of accelerated transformation] (pp. 119–139). Institute for Sociological Research at Faculty of Philosophy.

Stanojević, D. (2017). Izazovi tranzicije od obrazovanja ka tržištu rada mladih u Srbiji [Youth education to work transition challenges in Serbia]. Paper presented at the *conference Evropa i region pred izazovima promena,* Institute of Social Studies, Belgrade. 14.10. 2017.

Stanojević, D. (2018). *Novo očinstvo u Srbiji—Sociološka studija o praksama i identitetima očeva* [New fatherhood in Serbia—A sociological study of practices and identities of fathers]. Institute for Sociological Research at Faculty of Philosophy.

Statistical Office of the Republic of Serbia. (2011). *Žene i muškarci u Srbiji* [Women and men in Serbia]. Republički zavod za statistiku.

Statistical Office of the Republic of Serbia. (2013). *Popis stanovništva domaćinstava i stanova u Republici Srbiji 2011. Bračni staus podaci po opštinama i gradovima, 5.* [Census of Households and Dwellings in the Republic of Serbia 2011. Marital status by municipalities and cities]. Statistical Office of the Republic of Serbia.

Statistical Office of the Republic of Serbia. (2014). *Žene i muškarci u Srbiji* [Women and men in Serbia]. Republički zavod za statistiku.

190 • SMILJKA TOMANOVIĆ & DRAGAN STANOJEVIĆ

Statistical Office of the Republic of Serbia. (2020). *Preschool education database.* Retrieved 17 Septemebr 2020 from: http://devinfo.stat.gov.rs/Opstine/libraries/aspx/ dataview.aspx

Thevenon, O. (2011). Family Policies in OECD Countries: A Comparative Analysis. *Population and Development Review, 37*(1), 57–87.

Tomanović, S. (2010). Odlike roditeljstva [Features of parenthood]. In A. Milić, S. Tomanović, M. Ljubičić, N. Sekulić, M. Bobić, V. Miletić-Stepanović, & D. Stanojević (Eds.), *Vreme porodica. Sociološka studija o porodičnoj transformaciji u savremenoj Srbiji* [Family Times. Sociological Study on Family Transformation in Contemporary Serbia] (pp. 177–195). Institute for Sociological Research at Faculty of Philosophy.

Tomanović, S. (2012). Tranzicije u porodičnom domenu [Family transitions]. In S. Tomanović, D. Stanojević, I. Jarić, D. Mojić, S. Dragišić Labaš, & M. Ljubičić *Mladi—naša sadašnjost. Istraživanje socijalnih biografija mladih u Srbiji* [Young people are present. Study of social biographies of young people in Serbia] (pp. 127–147). Institute for Sociological Research at Faculty of Philosophy.

Tomanović, S., & Ignjatović, S. (2006a). Attitudes on transition to adulthood among young people in Serbia. *Sociologija, XLVIII* (1), 55–72.

Tomanović, S., & Ignjatović, S. (2006b). Transition of young people in a transitional society: The case of Serbia. *Journal of Youth Studies, 9*(3), 269–285.

Tomanović, S., & Ignjatović, S. (2010). The significance and meaning of family transitions for young people. The case of serbia in comparative perspective. *Annales-Annals for Istrian and Mediterranean Studies. Series Historia et Sociologia, 20*(1), 27–40.

Tomanović, S., & Stanojević, D. (2015). *Young people in Serbia 2015. Situation, perceptions, beliefs and aspirations.* Friedrich Ebert Stiftung and SeCons.

Tomanović S., Stanojević, D., Jarić, I., Mojić, D., Dragišić Labaš, S., & Ljubičić, M. (2012). *Mladi—naša sadašnjost. Istraživanje socijalnih biografija mladih u Srbiji* [Young people are present. Study of social biographies of young people in Serbia]. Institute for Sociological Research at Faculty of Philosophy.

Tomanović, S., Stanojević, D., & Ljubičić, M. (2016). *Postajanje roditeljem u Srbiji: sociološko istraživanje tranzicije u roditeljstvo* [Becoming a Parent in Serbia. Sociological study on transition to parenthood]. University of Belgrade, Faculty of Philosophy.

Walther, A., Stauber, B., & Pohl, A. (2009). *Youth: Actor of social change,* Final Report, Tubingen: IRIS.

World Bank. (2015). *Database.* http://databank.worldbank.org

CONTRIBUTORS

Dina Bite, is an Associate Professor. in Applied Sociology at Latvia University of Life Sciences and Technologies. Main scientific interests related to the development processes in rural territories, cultural and non-governmental activities as drivers for sustainable development. As a researcher, has experience in national as well as international research projects concerning youth issues, e.g., youth in Post-Soviet space, development of creative learning environment, young people as activists of non-governmental organizations.

Ms. Anna Broka is currently PhD Candidate in Social work programme at Tallinn University, Estonia and is a researcher assistant at Vidzeme University of Applied Sciences, Latvia. Originally from Latvia she got her BA degree in Political Science and continued with master's degree studies in International social welfare and health policy programme at Oslo University College (Norway). Hence, her academic career developed interdisciplinary in the fields of political science, sociology, and public health, the research focus is wellbeing of children and youth within social policy and social work discipline. Currently she is teaching undergraduate students in social work profession and is supervisor of the student's research projects in the field.

Family Formation Among Youth in Europe: Coping With Socio-Economic Disadvantages,
pages 191–195.
Copyright © 2022 by Information Age Publishing
www.infoagepub.com
All rights of reproduction in any form reserved.

192 • CONTRIBUTORS

Joanne Cassar is an associate professor at the University of Malta and is currently the head of the Department of Youth and Community Studies. Her academic publications examine the notion of young people's sexualities as social, discursive and materialist constructs and revolve around gender, sexual identities, body image and sexuality education.

Mirza Emirhafizović, PhD in Sociology, is an Associate Professor and researcher at the University of Sarajevo, Faculty of Political Sciences. His research interests encompass social demography, migration studies, as well as urban and rural sociology. He has participated in several international research projects, including COST Actions. He has been WG 2 Leader of COST Action CA17114 - *Transdisciplinary Solutions to Cross-Sectoral Disadvantage in Youth* (since 2018). Prof. Emirhafizović co-edited (together with I. Albert, C. N. Shpigelman & U. Trummer) a volume in Perspectives on Human Development titled *Families and Family Values in Society and Culture* published by Information Age Publishing (IAP) in 2021.

Liva Grinevica, PhD, is a senior expert in Latvian Council of Science and researcher in Latvian Academy of Agricultural and Forestry Sciences. For the last ten years, has been working in the research field, by coordinating the state research programs and international scientific projects. Has experience as a researcher by participating in national and international research projects on topics such as the assessment of the diffusion and effects of youth inclusion policies, economic transformation, smart growth, governance, and legal framework for sustainable development of the state and society, youth employment perspective, etc. Main research interests - youth unemployment, employment, social inclusion, regional development, business support programs.

Prof. **Tali Heiman** is a senior lecturer in the department of Education and Psychology, at the Open University of Israel. Her research interests include emotional and social coping of adolescents and young adults with and without disabilities; inclusion, teachers' coping and examining intervention programs; family coping and adjustment, and cyberbullying aspects. She is taking part in various EU research projects regarding these topics.

Dirk Hofäcker, Dr. rer. soc., is currently Professor of Quantitative Methods of Social Research at at the Faculty of Educational Sciences (Institute for Social Work and Social Policy) at the University of Duisburg-Essen. Formerly he was Research Fellow and Project Leader at the Mannheim Centre for European Social Research (MZES). He specialises in the fields of quantitative research methods and international welfare state comparison. https://orcid.org/0000-0002-2747-5765

Vera Kucharova is a researcher at the Research Institute for Labour and Social Affairs, Prague. She focuses mainly on family policy and families from a sociological point of view. She is a co-author of publications on the subjects like social and demographic issues of the family, and expert studies for the Ministry of Labour and Social Affairs of the CR. As a head of a research team for family policy 1993-2020 she was a principal investigator of a number of sectoral research projects. She received her professional education at the Faculty of Arts of Charles University in Prague and at the Institute for Philosophy and Sociology of the Czechoslovak Academy of Sciences.

Marton Medgyesi holds a PhD in Sociology from Corvinus University, Budapest and works as senior researcher at TARKI Social Research Institute and Corvinus Institute for Advanced Study. His main research interests include the analysis of income distribution in Hungary and Europe, intergenerational transfers in the family and the welfare state and attitudes (e.g. inequality tolerance, trust). He has been leader of projects such as „Dynamics of institutional trust in 21st century" (Eurofound) or "Gender inequality of intergenerational support" (Hungarian Scientific Research Fund) and has also been involved in a number of other international projects, including the GINI (EU FP7), STYLE (EU FP7), Social Situation Monitor (European Commission).

Paula Mena Matos is Associate Professor at the Faculty of Psychology and Education Sciences of the University of Porto, Portugal, teaching in the fields of clinical, health and developmental psychology. She has been coordinating several scientific research projects, and is member of the direction board of the Center for Psychology at the University of Porto, where she is responsible for the research group on *Relationships, Processes of Change and Wellbeing*. Her research interests include the topics of close relationship dynamics, attachment and emotional processes across different developmental stages and contexts (e.g., family, residential care, transition to adulthood, work-family balance, psycho-oncology, psychotherapy).

Helena Moura Carvalho holds a PhD in psychotherapy research from the Faculty of Psychology and Education Sciences at University of Porto; Portugal. Since 2006, she has been actively involved in research on human relationships and vulnerability processes, prioritizing research that could inform services effectiveness in clinical settings but also in the community. She has been lecturing in the past 10 years in mental health, psychotherapy and methods in several higher education institutions. She is currently a member of the Center for Psychology at the University of Porto.

Rosy Musumeci (PhD, sociologist) is senior researcher at the University of Turin. Her main research interests are work-life balance, working careers, job insecurity and—more recently—gender imbalances at university. She is currently

194 • CONTRIBUTORS

engaged in the 'GEA-Gendering Academia' project, funded by the Italian Ministry of Research and University, and scientific coordinator (with Manuela Naldini) of WP2's qualitative research in the H2020 project MINDtheGEPs (*Modifying Institutions by Developing Gender Equality Plans*).

Dr. **Dorit Olenik-Shemesh** is a senior lecturer at the department of Education and Psychology in the Open University of Israel. At her research work she focus on adolescents and young adults psychology, mainly in the topics of bullying, cyberbullying and Problematic Use of the Internet, in the context of social-psychological aspects. A special focus is given in her studies to the sense of well-being in young adults. She have participated in several EU research projects targeting at these topics.

Catarina Pinheiro Mota - Clinical Psychologist. Psychotherapist (Person-Centred Approach). Assistant Professor—University of Trás-os-Montes e Alto Douro —UTAD - Portugal; Integrated Researcher—Center for Psychology—University of Porto. She has been coordinating and carrying out investigations with the main research interests: Attachment in adolescence and young adulthood; Specialist on relational dynamics and attachment in residential care contexts: Implications on adolescents' resilience and mental health development.

Andrea Puhalić is associate professor at University of Banja Luka-Faculty of Political Sciences, social worker and supervisor. From June 2014 she held the position of president of Association of Supervisors in B&H. For the last decade, the main focus of her professional engagement has been strengthening the social protection system through supervision, especially in the areas of social work with children and families.

Dr. **Merav Regev-Nevo** (PhD) is a social psychologist and personal coach. As a researcher and practitioner she focused on leadership and intergroup relations. Merav is a faculty member in the department of Education & Psychology in the Open University in Israel.

Dragan Stanojević (1978) is Assistant Professor at the Faculty of Philosophy, Department of Sociology. His key qualifications are: 15 years of doing social research in Serbia and the SEE region, participation in national and international research projects. His research and policy work is focused on family relations, youth and children, education, social inequalities, social inclusion and life course patterns. Strong expertise and extensive experience in design and implementation of quantitative and qualitative surveys; familiarity with international methodologies: European social survey, LSMS, LFS, MICS, SILC, Time use surveys, World values survey, etc.

Dr. **Edita Štuopytė** is an associate professor at the Institute of Social Sciences, Arts and Humanities of the Kaunas University of Technology (Lithuania). She has prepared more than 30 scientific publications, focusing on the following research topics: family policy, activities of non-governmental organizations, social inclusion of socially vulnerable people, socio-educational work with migrants, and others. Dr. E. Štuopytė has experience in conducting research, has led a research group on social citizenship, democracy, and community development for several years, and is actively involved in COST projects.

Smiljka Tomanovic is the professor in Sociology at the Department of Sociology at Faculty of Philosophy, University of Belgrade. She is also senior researcher at the Institute for Sociological Research at the same Faculty. She participated in numerous research projects, applied projects, and also in writing of several policy papers in Serbia. She has been involved in research on and with young people in Serbia for over two decades. She has participated as a member, researcher and consultant in various meetings, seminars, and conferences etc. that are concerned with youth policies, both on national and international level. She is the author and co-author of eight books, several edited volumes, and numerous articles in international and domestic journals. She was the member of Pool of European Youth Researchers (PEYR) of Youth partnership between CoE and EC, and she is the member of ESA RN13 Families and Intimate Lives and RN30 Youth and Generation.

Dr. **Sue Vella** is currently Head of the Department of Social Policy and Social Work at the University of Malta, where she lectures in social policy. Sue also chairs the social research institute Discern. Prior to joining University, Sue led the Maltese public employment service, was a member of the EU's Employment Committee and of various boards of social agencies in Malta. Her research and publication interests include families and care; poverty, housing, employment and social security; and the voluntary sector. Sue recently co-edited a publication on Couple Relationships in a Global Context by Springer (2020).

Printed in the United States
by Baker & Taylor Publisher Services